D1161397

CRITICISM

Desmond MacCarthy

CRITICISM

Essay Index Reprint Series

 BOOKS FOR LIBRARIES PRESS
FREEPORT, NEW YORK

First Published 1932
Reprinted 1969

STANDARD BOOK NUMBER:
8369-1360-4

LIBRARY OF CONGRESS CATALOG CARD NUMBER:
78-99710

PRINTED IN THE UNITED STATES OF AMERICA

BY WAY OF A PREFACE

WHAT is the critic? That he is only one kind of reader among thousands is obvious; and that he is the most useless of writers unless his faculty reaches a rather rare degree of excellence is obvious. A critic is one who has been given a pass-key into many rooms in the House of Art on condition that he does not dwell in any one of them. His part is to open a door, examine the furniture of the room, and compare the view from its window with those to be seen from others. He must stay long enough to see what the owner of the room saw—then he had better move on. He is a creature without a spiritual home, and it is his point of honour never to seek one. And his use? His use is that, thanks to an imagination above average strength, though of course weaker than the artist's, he is better able than the ordinary reader to interpret creative experience; while his visits to other rooms enable him to know things about the work he is examining which the creator of it, who has never shifted from his own window, cannot know. The critic's first obligation is to permit himself to be absorbed in the vision of a writer, responding to it with all his emotions, and then to compare that vision with those of other writers. If asked what is the use of that, he can only reply that it is another way of doing what the artist does: his work, too, intensifies and multiplies experiences worth having.

I say he must respond with *all* his emotions, because I do not believe he should limit his response. It is true that some critics attempt to confine their comments to what they claim to be alone significant in a writer's work: its capacity for arousing " aesthetic emotion " and its technical perfection. But one of the disconcerting discoveries connected with the study of literature is that beauty to which " aesthetic emotion " is the response, resembles the shimmer upon a butterfly's wing; held to the light at a particular angle, it may dazzle and delight, but shift that angle and what before was a blaze of beauty turns dun and brown in our hands. Each generation holds the butterfly to the light at a slightly different angle. All changes in aesthetic response are caused by changes in beliefs and morals, and behind the new literature of the nineteen-twenties such changes lie. Even discoveries in technique are connected with them, for in art technique and substance can never be separated. It is because a writer wants to express something that has not been expressed before that he deviates from the methods of his predecessors; and it is because a painter wishes to draw attention to what has excited him in visible objects but has escaped the notice of his predecessors, that he alters his manner of painting. *Aesthetic taste is only further discrimination upon preferences determined by other causes.* Whatever the nature of the beautiful may be, and no man has succeeded in defining it, where and in what any particular generation will see beauty depends upon habits of mind and ways of feeling which, in their turn, are moulded by the condition of the world. The direction of our interests, whether intellectual or aesthetic, is decided by the times in which we live. And one of the main functions of the critic, when he is expounding the literature of the past, is to put the reader at the point of view from which its contemporaries saw that literature, at the same time, of course, judging it from his own; and, confronted by contemporary literature, to show its relations to the world to-day. He must therefore discourse upon current ideas and ideas once current; and the psychology of the reader of a book is almost as much a part of his subject as the book itself.

It will be clear to anyone who reads the following pages that this is the point of view from which they were written, though I did not know it at the time. They are clearly not the work of one who believes that the critic ought to turn personal impressions into general laws, but of one who holds the effort to do so is only valuable as a form of self-discipline; as a means to judging different writers with the same eyes, not as productive criteria permanently valid. Aesthetic theories appear to me valuable chiefly as a protection against the bias of mood in the critic himself. The following essays are a selection from a selection made for me from the accumulation of many years of literary journalism, and I have endeavoured to introduce some sort of unity by choosing for this volume among my articles upon past writers those dealing with authors who have affinities with contemporary literature: Richardson, Defoe, Donne, Browning— such, too, is Beckford. Many of the items are concerned with the psychology of the reader; to help him to watch himself is part of the function of criticism as I understand it. The discovery of the importance of " the subconscious " in our lives is the strongest new influence in contemporary literature. As will be seen I am still doubtful about the value of its literary results.

I must thank Mr. Logan Pearsall Smith for having helped me in selecting from my own work, and Mr. Edward Marsh for having read my proofs and removed from them also defects for which the printers were certainly not responsible.

CONTENTS

CONTENTS

CRITICISM

SAMUEL BUTLER

I

SAMUEL BUTLER played a not unimportant part in my own education (I made his acquaintance when I was ten years old), and later my work as a journalist and critic was often concerned with his books. In 1909 I edited a periodical called *The New Quarterly*, and Festing Jones gave me for it extracts from Samuel Butler's *Note Books*. Butler was not yet famous. When he died, in June 1902, the measure of his reputation was given by an article in *The Times*, regretting that so talented a man had not done more. That estimate seemed later beside and far below the mark. Samuel Butler was one of those rare, incontestable personalities in literature, who affect permanently the thought and temper of all predisposed to their influence; indeed, the first impression made on anyone reading his *Note Books*, which date from the 'sixties, may well be that many of Butler's ideas are those which are at the present moment " in the air," and by " in the air," of course, people mean in the papers or other men's books.

Later, Bernard Shaw pointed out his own debt to him in his Preface to *Major Barbara*, which was one of the earliest and most effective statements of Butler's claim to wider recognition. In this Preface, Mr. Shaw insisted that Butler " in his own department was one of the greatest writers of the nineteenth century."

As a moralist, Butler was a confirmed hedonist and Laodicean; *surtout point de zèle*, he believed was

1 B

the finest motto ever coined for humanity. He really and utterly believed that compromise was the guide to life; he saw compromise written over the face of all creation. And not only in action, but in thought, right behaviour and truth were best obtained by combining the conflicting reports of faith and reason. The blend was only perfectly satisfactory when the balance was reached unconsciously; every philosophy was nonsense when ridden home, and every moral ideal which outsoared the practice of averagely good men was suspect. Scattered up and down his books are aphorisms to the effect that a man whose mind is of the right temper must be uncertain in spite of uncertainty, and uncertain in spite of certainty, which in practice comes to something like having a sense of humour, for it is characteristic of humour to hold together, at the same moment, the profound and the superficial, the doubtful and the obvious, the serious and the indifferent aspects of things. The favourite virtue of the humorist is always toleration: it was Butler's favourite virtue, too.

The most comprehensive description of Samuel Butler as a writer is, then, that he was a humorous philosopher. The interdependence of his philosophy and his humour is, indeed, often so complete that it is puzzling to decide whether he was a philosopher who chanced upon explanations which would justify humour, or a born humorist who set out in search of a philosophy to explain the way things naturally struck him. Both processes had a share in his work. He saw jokes where no one else saw them, because, sceptical and curious, he looked at everything in his own way; and things would occur to him first as jokes which afterwards impressed him as perfectly true. Butler's sense of humour often performed the service for him that the dove did for Noah in the ark. It flew out into the unknown, bringing back to him an indication that he would soon find solid ground beneath his feet. The humorous philosopher is rare, but when he does appear his influence quickly spreads. We laugh with him, not taking him seriously, and lo! we have already caught his way of thinking.

I made Butler's acquaintance at an hotel in the valley of the Saas in Switzerland, where I was staying with my parents. Opposite us at *table d'hôte* sat an elderly man with very bushy black eyebrows, and with him, from time to time, they interchanged a few cheerful polite remarks. A day or two later I happened to feel an extreme reluctance to notice the bell which announced the midday meal, and instead of going in I continued to clamber about the valley rocks. After a short interval I saw what I knew I should see next, my mother appearing at the door of the hotel frantically waving her parasol. This was a signal which could not be ignored like the bell. She had evidently waited until lunch had well begun, and then, losing patience, come out to fetch me. I was not surprised. What did surprise me was that she was presently followed by the old gentleman with the thick eyebrows. As we all three entered the hotel together he whispered: " I thought I'd better come, with a stranger Mama couldn't be quite so angry." It was only long afterwards that I realized how it was kind of an elderly gentleman to jump up from his midday meal and hurry out into the blazing sun to protect a small boy from a scolding; but when I did, I realized also that it was thoroughly characteristic of him to suppose that *every* child was likely to be bullied by its parents. (Readers of *The Way of All Flesh* will understand.) After that, I used often to go sketching with him. No doubt while he sketched and I lay beside his easel he talked wisely, but I heeded him not. I cannot remember a scrap of our conversations.

But I do remember that on Sunday mornings at breakfast he used to say: " Do you think Mr. Selwyn would mind (Mr. Selwyn was the chaplain, and in those days every hotel haunted by the British had its chaplain), do you think Mr. Selwyn would forgive us if we did *not* go to church? " (He had been pleased to find that my favourite text was " And now to God the Father, God the Son, etc.") And off we would go together. If our acquaintance had ended there I should have little to tell, but later, when I was in London, I used sometimes to go and see him in his rooms in Clifford's Inn. I was dimly aware that he was a remarkable man—but that was not the sort of fact which interested me. I only divined it from the interest my father took in his conversation, while I ate nuts and apples and listened. Mr. Butler would sometimes give me one of his books, always with strict injunctions not to attempt to read it.

As I grew older I began to go and see him by myself. He often talked in a way which both puzzled and amused me, giving me advice of which I could make nothing at the time, advice which did not agree at all with that of my masters and pastors. For instance, he would say, looking at me gravely: " As long as you tell no lies to yourself and are kind, you may lie and lie and lie and yet not be untrue to any man." Once I remember giving up the last two hours of the Eton and Harrow match—it's true the result was a foregone conclusion—in order to go and see him. Instead of sitting and keeping the bowling averages, I went off to listen to his talk, which, I take it, is one of the greatest compliments ever paid to a philosopher in England. I must have been seventeen then, I was beginning to understand him.

In stature he was a small man, but you hardly noticed that. His slightly-built frame was dis-

guised in clothes of enviable bagginess and of a
clumsy conventional cut, and he wore prodigiously
roomy boots. But it was the hirsute, masculine
vigour of his head which prevented you from thinking him a small man. Indeed, it was a surprise to
me to hear afterwards that he had coxed at Cambridge the St. John's boat: I had remembered him,
it seemed, as even rather a heavy man. His company manner was that of a kind old gentleman, prepared to be a little shocked by any disregard of the
proprieties; the sort of old gentleman who is very
mild in reproof, but whose quiet insistence that
everybody should behave properly is most soothing
to elderly ladies of limited means. He spoke softly
and slowly, often with his head a little down, looking
gravely over his spectacles and pouting his lips, and
with a deliberate demureness so disarming that he
was able to utter the most subversive sentiments
without exciting more than a moment's astonishment. The next, his companion was completely
reassured. " No, Mr. Butler could not have meant
that. I wasn't quite quick enough. Mr. Butler is
such an *original* man." Such was the impression he
made on circumspect, humdrum people. It was
comic to anyone who knew what a bull in a china
shop he really was. And though he was a great
adept at poking gentle fun at people, he never
snubbed them or scored off them. In fact, he had
a strong abhorrence to anything of that kind. I
think he enjoyed, a little, the irony which resides in
perfect politeness, but politeness was not in the least
a pose on his part. It sprang from his dislike of
overbearingness. To take advantage of superiority
of intellect, or any other kind of superiority, moral
force, knowledge of the world, reputation, wealth,
social position, a fine manner, and to use it to brow-
beat a helpless person, was in his eyes a revolting,
unpardonable offence. I often heard him use the

5

word " caddish," and it always stigmatized that kind
of behaviour. If I were to mention the names of
those he called " cads " the list would cause great
surprise. Besides, he liked mediocre, humdrum
people; they were at any rate freer from this odious
sin than the intellectual and successful.

I asked him once if he were any relation to the
late Master of Trinity, Dr. Butler. " What! " he
exclaimed with soft and gentle emphasis, " *that*
beastly cad! " It took me a moment or two to
rearrange my ideas—on the Master, caddishness,
Samuel Butler himself! Then I guessed: Dr. Butler's
eighteenth-century suavity might easily strike his
namesake as coming suspiciously near an attempt
to play him off the social stage, though in the
Master's case it was nothing of the kind. Perhaps—
I knew they had met after Samuel Butler's *Authoress
of the Odyssey* had appeared—the Master had asked
him, accidentally and sweetly, some question about
Nausicaa equivalent in its effect to his famous
invitation at a Trinity Lodge musical party, " So
pleased you have come. Won't you take a back
seat? "

The last time I saw him was at a dinner at the
Albemarle Club, given more or less in his honour.
It was in the winter before he died, and he was
already very tired. He made, I remember, a little
fun of an intense lady who declared that Art
was more to her than Nature. He was not always
very quick to see the point when others poked fun
at him. I remember his coming back from a visit
to Lady Ritchie, who was as good a hand as he at
gentle irony, and telling me with amazement that
she had said: " Mr. Butler, I will tell you my theory
about the sonnets (Butler had just published his
Authoress of the Odyssey, and was about to publish
his book on the Sonnets): I believe they were
written to Shakespeare by Ann Hathaway." " Poor

6

lady," Butler went on, " that *was* a stupid thing to say! "

II

The importance of money as the means to a good life is a theme which Butler constantly and vehemently emphasized. The emphasis he laid on it is one of the characteristics which made him an original moralist and so acute a commentator on life. Everybody, according to Butler, must have money on the brain so long as that brain is in reasonable condition. " Though Wisdom cannot be gotten for gold, still less can it be gotten without it. Gold, or the value which is equivalent to gold, lies at the root of Wisdom." (*Note Books*, p. 172.) For the modern Simony, which " is not dealing in livings but the thinking they can buy the Holy Ghost for money, which vulgar rich people indulge in when they dabble in literature, music and painting," he felt deep contempt. But anyone who refused to admit that a *discreta posizionina* was an unmixed blessing he despised quite as much, and thought much more dangerous. He was fond of following up this idea: his handling of it is an example of his method.

The rich man to him was the hundred-handed Gyas of the poets. He alone possessed the full complement of limbs who stood at the summit of opulence. Reckoned by his horse-power, a Rockefeller is the most astonishing organism the world has ever seen; and therefore, according to Butler, the deep impression wealth makes on the imagination is reasonable, and the respect with which we so often treat those who are richer than ourselves a legitimate feeling. " It is," he characteristically added, " the same sort of affectionate reverence which a dog feels for a man, and is not infrequently manifested in a similar manner." Thus, to abuse

7

the rich, provided they are amiable, handsome, and considerate, revolted his common-sense.

" People ask complainingly what swells have done, or do for society, that they should be able to live without working. The good swell is the creature towards which all nature has been groaning and travailing together until now. He is an ideal. He shows what may be done in the way of good breeding, health, looks, temper, and fortune. He realizes men's dreams of themselves, at any rate vicariously. He preaches the gospel of grace. The world is like a spoilt child: it has this good thing given to it at great expense and then says it is useless! " (*Note Books*, pp. 35-6.)

It was, however, not the " swell " whom he himself considered the finest type. " I suppose," he wrote, " an Italian peasant or a Breton, Norman or English fisherman, is about the best thing Nature does in the way of men—the richer and the poorer being alike mistakes." Still, he would have no blaspheming against Mammon. This is one of the points at which the thought of Samuel Butler is most opposed to Christian morals. He was a thorough-going hedonist, and therefore in poverty and suffering he could see neither beauty nor any possible value. Palpable well-being, such as the sight of a fruitful orchard may suggest, and as William Morris ima- gined (too æsthetically no doubt, for Butler's taste) as the reward of pleasant companionable labour— he would recognize no ideal less homely and " objec- tive " than this. The happiness of affection be- tween gentle, strong, amorous, beautiful people, among whom there is much kindness and little grief —that was his ideal; and it is one which, translated into terms of everyday life in a complex civilization, admits of no contempt for wealth. Votaries of that earthly happiness inevitably see in the transcendental a dangerous lure, and in one who would " lose himself in a mystery and pursue his Reason to an *O Altitudo!* " a natural enemy. They distrust and dislike ideals which minimize the comfort of what is assured. This emotion underlay all Butler's literary and artistic preferences and aversions; his depreciation, for example, of Plato, Michelangelo, and Beethoven. He could never forgive the artist or poet who refused to kiss the earth; and his devotion to Shakespeare was, one suspects, due largely to the fact that Shakespeare is, after all, " the surest refuge from the saints." In Butler's mouth the theological word " grace," compared with which knowledge and other qualities were unimportant, took on a pagan meaning:

> " And grace is best, for where grace is, love is not distant. Grace! the old pagan ideal whose charm even unlovely Paul could not withstand, but, as the legend tells us, his soul fainted within him, his heart misgave him, and, standing alone on the seashore at dusk, he 'troubled deaf heaven with his bootless cries,' his thin voice pleading for grace after the flesh.
> " The waves came in one after another, the sea-gulls cried together after their kind, the wind rustled among the dried canes upon the sand banks, and there came a voice from heaven saying, ' Let My grace be sufficient for thee.' Whereupon, failing of the thing itself, he stole the word and strove to crush its meaning to the measure of his own limitations. But the true grace, with her groves and high places, and troupes of young men and maidens crowned with flowers, singing of love and youth and wine—the true grace he drove out into the wilderness—high up, it may be, into Piora, and into suchlike places. Happy they who harboured her in her ill-report."

9

Yet, at the close of the second chapter of *Life and Habit*, from which this passage is taken, he directs the reader who would have further understanding on all that is most important in life to believe in the music of Handel, the painting of Giovanni Bellini, and the thirteenth chapter of St. Paul's First Epistle to the Corinthians—counsel which he repeated in various forms again and again. So, according to Butler, St. Paul after all must have had the root of the matter in him. It was Paul the Apostle of Protestantism of whom he was thinking in the foregoing passage. The Church, according to Butler, in her less introspective ages, in her buildings, her music, her unspoken teaching, did uphold or at least sanction some kind of comely human ideal; and with the religion of the country people of Italy, who are described so delightfully in *Alps and Sanctuaries*, Butler felt at home. They at least made no attempt to be consistent and rational, and only a very moderate degree indeed of spirituality was demanded of them; above all, there was no " earnestness " among them, no forcing of people to think that they were nothing if they were not at any rate " colourable imitations of some one better than their neighbours."

Never consciously to agonize; to undertake only " that which insists upon being done and runs right up against you, hitting you in the eye until you do it "—these were precepts which he afterwards applied all round. Butler's own philosophy made him a most amiable, trustworthy, amusing man.

Among imaginative writers, some have served us by turning our troubles and pleasures into tragedies and triumphs, showing us life as a matter of momentous, immeasurable experiences, of which we are only intermittently worthy. With these, comedy is found in the inadequacy of man to

10

his destiny; and at their hands disaster and death have often taken on a beauty more desirable than happiness itself. These are the magnifiers of life. Only when it is thus transfigured by the imagination are its evils and its satisfactions tolerable: only then, they insist, do we see it truly. Their appeal is to those moments, whether of joy or grief, when common-sense has looked foolish: such moments (and nearly everybody has, or thinks he has, experienced them) are the criteria by which they would have us measure the importance of things.

The other class of writers—and it is to this class that Samuel Butler belongs—may be described as the consolers. They diminish the importance of the issues at stake. They take the long-run, everyday estimate of things as the true one. They side with common-sense. They find their comedy in the evanescence of aspirations, and in the spectacle of men protesting that they can only be nourished on ambrosial food while they are stuffing themselves with ordinary bread. If only men would not give themselves celestial airs, they say, they would be, perhaps, less amusing to contemplate, but they would have a far better chance of being happy and worthy of respect. Let a man find out what he really wants, and he will discover that it is something which exists on earth in satisfying quantities; something which the saints and the majority of the poets have unfortunately encouraged him to consider rather beneath his dignity. The magnifiers of life say, " Throw not away the hero in your soul if you would get the most out of experience "; the consolers, " Cultivez votre jardin."

Butler, as a philosopher and an imaginative writer, belongs to the tribe of Horace, Voltaire, Montaigne, Molière, and Fielding. To the idealist the tolerance of such writers towards humanity seems more insulting than the most violent misanthropy; and the quarrel between them, as Butler said of religion and science, is only to be reconciled in amiable people.

III

For the fame of Samuel Butler, Bernard Shaw did much, I did a little, and Festing Jones most of all. Fifield, the publisher, was also a great help in reprinting Butler's books, a work which has been continued by Mr. Cape. Festing Jones helped to make Butler known long before he wrote his *Life of Samuel Butler*—the best piece of modern biography in the manner of the Dutch School, in which not only the sitter but his surroundings are painted in with careful and minute precision.

It may be said that from the day these two met in January 1876 down to 1919, when the *Life* was published, their friendship circumscribed Festing Jones's life. Naturally, he had other interests, and other relations with people not directly concerned with Butler; but my impression when I first got to know Festing Jones was that even when he stepped outside the Butler sphere of influence, the spirit of "Sam" was still upon him, deciding what he should feel, what he should value, and what friends he should choose. This was not so obviously true of him during the last decade of his life, but for a good many years after Butler's death the passport to Jones's intimacy was certainly an interest in Butler. During the first few years that I knew him we talked of Butler incessantly. Fortunately it is a wide subject, with many ramifications and peppered with jokes; but I used to feel sorry for his sister, Miss Lily Jones—not that sympathy deterred me. Still, sometimes, as a great treat for her, I used to turn the conversation to other topics.

His quiet and demure precision of utterance

reminded me of Butler; also his deliberate politeness, and his black, non-committal, respectable get-
up.   Both men seemed to declare, both in dress and
behaviour, " I am determined to be quite respectable."   Neither of them was anything of the kind.
I do not wish to give the impression that Festing
Jones was a pale copy of his friend, but he was
saturated in him.   He was always aware, and later
he became more so, of a difficult and sometimes
fierce crankiness in Butler which was foreign to his
own nature, and although he half-admired this in
his friend, he never imitated it.   He did wish sometimes Sam had not been quite so crankily fierce.
He began to respond, as time went on, to the work
of musicians, poets, and writers whom Butler
had no patience with, and to understand them
without being overawed by his friend's limitations.
While Sam lived, there was only one musician for
both of them—Handel.   Those who have read
Festing Jones's two little books of travel, *Diversions
in Sicily* (Alston Rivers) and *Castellinaria* (Fifield),
will see that these quietly mischievous and affectionately observant books, though they owe much
to *Alps and Sanctuaries*, are also the expression of
an independent temperament, yet, most clearly, a
temperament with which the author of *Alps and
Sanctuaries* would be in sympathy.   Festing Jones
had a very pretty wit, and among Butler's papers,
out of which the *Note Books* were constructed, are
many acute and amusing remarks of his.   He was
a perfect friend.   One anecdote will illustrate the
closeness of their association.

A friend of mine, who was unacquainted with
Butler and had never heard of Festing Jones,
thought he recognized Butler from a photograph on
board a Dover-Calais boat.   He went up and spoke
to him.   " Yes," Butler replied, " I *am* Mr. Butler,
and Jones is down below."

After Butler's death, Festing Jones organized a yearly dinner in his honour, at which admirers of his works, and his old friends, met together, made speeches, and exchanged reminiscences. At first the attendance was small, consisting only of people genuinely interested in Butler. When the occasion became important, and the dinner crowded, Festing Jones, with characteristic discretion, stopped these celebrations. On the menu there was always printed, under Butler's photograph, a sentence from his works:

" Above all things let no unwary reader do me the injustice of believing in *me*. In that I write at all I am among the damned. If he must believe in anything, let him believe in the music of Handel, the painting of Giovanni Bellini, and the XIIIth Chapter of St. Paul's Epistle to the Corinthians."

The quotation used to remind me of the story of the Chinese rationalist sage whose coffin levitated and remained suspended, until in answer to the urgent prayers of his disciples it sank slowly to the ground.

IV

Butler's friends were much more important to him than women. Miss Savage was the only woman who meant much to him, and she only because she was witty and he fancied she was in love with him. He worried himself unnecessarily about this. Referring obviously to his over-scrupulousness in money matters, she had once written: " I wish you did not know right from wrong," and this he afterwards interpreted as a reproach for his backwardness as a lover. In 1901 he wrote two sonnets about her, excusing himself: one cruel, the other touching, both having for theme,

14

A man will yield for pity if he can,
But if the flesh rebels what can he do?

Butler was a man to whom continence was impossible. But he never fell in love with a woman;
women represented a necessity for which he paid.
This must be known if he is to be understood; and
happily nowadays such things may be mentioned.
The sex impulse was unusually strong in him from
boyhood to old age, and he canalized it in that
prosaic way which some men adopt who dread
emotional disturbance in their lives. To the woman,
who figures as " Madam " in his biography, whom
he used to visit twice a week, he did not even tell
his name until he had known her for more than ten
years; so great was his caution, so entirely had
he dissociated intimacy from such relationships.
When he was an old man he told me that now they
had become impossible, unless he had " a kindly
feeling for the woman," but that it had not been so
when he was younger. Nature took her revenge.
The divorce between flesh and feeling lead in his case
to one or two of his friendships being flushed with
an emotion he hardly understood himself, and would
have repudiated if he had—at least one gathers this
from his book on Shakespeare's Sonnets. It is
necessary to remember this in reading the strange
story of his friendship with Pauli, and, in addition,
that in Butler's eyes Pauli was " a swell." Readers
of *The Way of All Flesh* will remember the dumb
and helpless admiration that Ernest felt for Towne-
ley's easy, confident, graceful ways and appearance.
    There are only slight indications in Butler's
account of the suffering this friendship brought him,
but he has left a sonnet which I think, possibly, was
born from it. He called it " An Academic Exercise," and he wrote it to refute Sir Sidney Lee's

theory that Shakespeare's sonnets were only " academic exercises."

We were two lovers standing sadly by
While our two loves lay dead upon the ground;
Each love had striven not to be first to die,
But each was gashed with many a cruel wound.
Said I: "Your love was false while mine was true."
Aflood with tears he cried: " It was not so,
'Twas your false love my true love falsely slew—
For 'twas your love that was the first to go."
Thus did we stand and said no more for shame
Till I, seeing his cheek so wan and wet,
Sobbed thus: " So be it; my love shall bear the
    blame;
Let us inter them honourably." And yet
    I swear by all truth human and divine
    'Twas his that in its death-throes murdered
    mine.

GEORGE SANTAYANA

IT is curious: while I am reading Mr. Santayana I feel wiser than I have ever felt before, but when I try to impart that wisdom to someone else I cannot lay my hands on anything transferable. It is as though I had been tipped in fairy gold. A day or two ago, there, in the palm of my hand, lay a round, exquisitely-minted piece of wisdom, which I remember carefully putting away in my pocket; but now I dive and fumble for it in vain! I know by experience I shall not find it until I re-read one of his books. Then, and for just so long, I shall possess it again. Why is this?

The most plausible explanation is that I have not sufficiently saturated myself in Mr. Santayana's philosophy; although I have read nearly all he has written and much of it several times, this may be the true explanation. I have argued little with him as I turned his pages, and not to dispute with a philosopher as you read him is to cease to benefit by him. As a rule I quarrel and wrangle with philosophers readily enough. Why have I argued so little, Mr. Santayana?

There is (and I imagine I am expressing what many have felt) a quality in his writings which induces passivity in his readers. He is so suavely sure of himself, so elegantly and sympathetically dogmatic, so indulgent to the prejudices of others, so frank in calmly maintaining his own, that it seems crude to ask him sharply what it all comes to. He is so round a man. You have a soothing and, at the same time, a subduing impression that he understands where the difference between you and him lies better than you do yourself, and that he has allowed for such differences long, long ago. Presently he will explain your temperament from which they sprang. You may jerk and jump a little while in the net, not of his logic, but of his sympathetic sagacity, yet presently you lie passive in it, dumb as a fish drawn up from its own element into one more rarefied; and there, with ever more gently panting gills, the restless intellect at last gives up its wilful breath. It is a delicious euthanasia. When I read Mr. Santayana I find myself murmuring, with an irony I can hardly fathom, the last words of that Roman Emperor who, on his death-bed, said: " I suppose I am becoming a god." But, the book closed, I discover myself to have become no such thing. I cannot even remember how wise I lately was, or why I felt so wise.

I am not going to review his new book, *Soliloquies in England*; I am going to live with it. It has been already for some weeks about my bed and about my path, but I cannot distil a review from this new book yet. Of course I can tell you what the book is about; it is about Dickens and death and friendship, the English character and the Latin mind, religion and the Greeks, modern philosophers and Mr. Santayana himself, and his critics, and the Church of Rome, and Spanish drama and the war and youth and imagination, and skylarks and myths and English architecture, and the English Church and the Comic Spirit, and Socrates and German philosophy, and Liberalism and snobbery and culture and sanctity and mysticism and manners and solitude and Queen Mab and liberty (classic and romantic), and the subliminal self and the unconscious Censor and the poet and carnivals and—this list does not exhaust all its topics. In my opinion Mr. Santayana is the greatest of living critics. I do not trust him so much as Matthew Arnold or some other poets, to point to what is final and perfect in expression; but he is unsurpassed in measuring the minds of poets, novelists, and philosophers.

His criticism is the criticism of a philosopher, though to say that, without further explanation, will hardly recommend him. Few philosophers have been good judges in æsthetic matters, to which they have usually applied the attention of their declining minds. They usually squeeze their Æsthetics into their systems after they have been completed. Herbert Spencer, for one, is reported to have said that the difference between prose and poetry was that in prose the lines went right across the page, while in poetry they stopped at irregular distances from the margin. But Mr. Santayana is himself a poet as well as a philosopher, and this makes him a critic. He judges literature and art from a point of view which could not be securely and consistently held except by a man who was possessed by the philosopher's desire to comprehend experience, and at the same time constantly alive to the emotional values of things. Consequently the two tests that he applies to a poet are, firstly, has he succeeded in creating or suggesting a rational coherent ideal that life has revealed to him, even if he failed to attain it? secondly, what is the value of this ideal to human beings? It follows that, as critic, he is at any rate in no danger of confounding intensity with profundity of feeling, which is the commonest critical error; and that he is by no means prepared to admit to the company of great poets writers who have excelled only in the description of characters, if their relation to destiny is not also dramatized; nor those who have excelled in descriptions which only bring us nearer to the sensuous quality of things; nor those who by the use of rare, elliptic phrases excite and entertain. The last are mere

19

euphuists in his judgment, and euphuists, though they may be true poets, yet, compared with the great poets, are as goldsmiths and jewellers are to architects and sculptors.

" Poetry is not at its best when it depicts a further possible experience, but when it initiates us, by feigning something which as an experience is impossible, into the meaning of the experience which we have actually had: " that is to say, in proportion as its influence approaches to that of religion. " The highest poetry is, then, not that of the versifiers but that of the prophets, or of such poets as interpret verbally the visions which the prophets have rendered in action and sentiment rather than in adequate words."

As might be deduced from the above account of Mr. Santayana's attitude towards poetry, Dante and Lucretius are the poets who in his view have fulfilled most completely the rôle of the great poet: Lucretius with a vision of nature and the limits of human life; " Dante, with spiritual mastery of that life and a perfect knowledge of good and evil."

His first action as a critic is to measure the diameter of the world in which a poet lives. He estimates an author from the point of view of the contribution his art makes to the whole of life. What are an author's ideals? What does he instinctively love most, whether with or without the consent of his judgment? To what type of temperament and to what type of mind does he therefore belong? What is the value of his contribution to human life? How did he come by his bias, and what peculiar merits in his work do we owe to his emotional preferences? No critic answers these questions so satisfyingly as he.

He is not so much a metaphysician as a psychologist and a moral sage. Like all great critics, he has a point of view. His superiority does not lie

20

in the intensity of his sensibilities, which, though genuine, are not remarkable. We suspect him of often looking through the wrong end of the telescope at objects, which, as you may recall, gives a picture of them bright and clear but much diminished in size. He sees proportions more clearly than he feels magnitudes. He judges all things (with the exception perhaps of the charm of manly youth and the significance of Catholic ritual) from an emotional distance. Among critics he is particularly fortunate in that his own point of view enables him to keep an impartial distance from such a number of conflicting manifestations of human aspiration and intelligence, and therefore to see them in proportion. His philosophy enables him not only to regard with equanimity, but to welcome with benignity, the warring of creeds, the quarrels of the dispensers of values, the inconsistent dreams of dreamers, the chaotic preferences of practical men. Yet it is not the mere fact of death, the contemplation of which is so cheap and easy a way to the centre of indifference, that has led him to serene impartiality. The sentiment of *Vanitas Vanitatum* has for him no more universal validity than the parody of that famous saying, *Sanitas Sanitatum, omnia Sanitas*, or than the worship of vitality. He starts from the conception that nothing in the nature of things corresponds to men's preferences and ideals. Do you hate something? It is only bad because you hate it. Do you love something and desire it or admire it? There is nothing final in your preference. Whatever you find propitious to your aims you rightly call good; whatever you find hostile to them you rightly call evil; but the man who, having other aims and passions, transposes those labels, is as rational as you. This would be equivalent to having no critical point of view; but Mr. Santayana proceeds from this position:

21

" The competition between a man's passions makes up his moral history, the growth of his character, just as the competition of his ruling interests with other interests at work in society makes up his outward career. The sort of imagination that can survey all these interests at once, and can perceive how they check or support one another, is called reason; and when reason is vivid and powerful it gives courage and authority to those interests which it sees destined to success, whilst it damps or extinguishes those others which it sees are destined to failure. Reason thus establishes a sort of resigned and peaceful strength in the soul, founded on renunciation of what is impossible and co-operation with what is necessary. This resigned and peaceful strength Spinoza calls happiness; and since it rests on apprehension of the order of nature, and acceptance of it, he also calls it, in his pious language, knowledge and love of God." (Introduction to *The Ethics of Spinoza*, Everyman's Library.)

Now the co-ordination of warring ideals springing from warring human impulses, each of which has in itself an equal right to demand satisfaction, is the problem of wise living and the test of a civilization; and the test Mr. Santayana applies to writers is the degree in which they have established a comprehensive harmony between important conflicting instincts and ideals. One may have dealt with experience in the interest of one impulse or ideal, another in the interest of another. Let us see how far both have succeeded, and what sides of our nature they have cramped and left unsatisfied. His scepticism keeps him equidistant from them all.

Among poets, Coleridge was perhaps the most gifted philosopher; among philosophers, Plato was certainly the greatest poet. Poets not infrequently philosophize, but philosophers seldom drop into poetry. Had philosophers written verse more often, most of them would not have risen above the level of Erasmus Darwin. Mr. Santayana has collected his own best poems, and they are good poems.

We might have guessed that Mr. Santayana would write poetry. He resembles a sage rather than a metaphysician, and his favourite theme is an exhortation to live in the imagination; not in the bubble of our private dreams, but in a much larger bubble, which should contain as much objective truth as possible, tinged not only with the emotion of the poet himself but with the dreams of the ages. In love he is a pure Platonist. He has written a preface which, as we might expect, is very good criticism, and being the most detached of men, he has no difficulty in seeing his own work without bias. " Of impassioned tenderness or Dionysiac frenzy I have nothing," he says, " nor even of that magic and pregnancy of phrase—really the creation of a fresh idiom, which marks the highest flights of poetry. Even if my temperament had been natur- ally warmer, the fact that the English language (and I can write no other with assurance) was not my mother tongue would of itself preclude any inspired use of it on my part; its roots do not quite touch my centre. I never drank in in my childhood the homely cadences and ditties which in pure spon- taneous poetry set the essential key. I know no words redolent of the wonder-world, the fairy tale or the cradle. Moreover, I am city-bred, and that companionship with nature, those rural notes, which for English poets are almost inseparable from poetic feeling, fail me altogether. Landscape to me is only a background for fable or a symbol for fate, as it was to the ancients; and the human scene itself is but a theme for reflection. My approach to language is literary, my images are only metaphors. . . ."

" And yet," he adds, " the sincerity is absolute, not only in respect to the thought which might be abstracted from them and expressed in prose, but also in respect to the aura of literary and religious associations which envelops them." His verses, intellectual as their texture is, express a genuine inspiration. His Muse is the ghost of the Muse of a lesser Leopardi, a smaller Matthew Arnold. He notices himself her kinship with the Muse of Alfred de Musset, but I think this holds good only of an occasional mood which the philosopher disdains, though he sympathizes with it.

To Mr. Santayana philosophy is not an official occupation, a pursuit which he drops in unprofessional hours, after he has done a turn of work at solving theoretic puzzles. Philosophy is his life. His thought colours his response to all that he observes and everything that happens to him. Consequently his poetry is a part of his philosophy, like the epigrams which the Greek sages wrote. He admits that his philosophy, " especially as expressed in this more sentimental form, may not seem very robust or joyous." It is rather courageous, calm, and cold. He writes like an exile in the modern world. His poem *Avila* expresses this homesickness best, and it is one of his best poems. He sighs, but he never wails, and when in the opening of a sonnet he asks us—

What riches have you that you deem me poor,
Or what large comfort that you call me sad?

it is not very easy for most of us to reply.

DEAN INGE

DO other people, I wonder, find it as hard to get a clear conception of that eminent man, the Dean of St. Paul's, as I do? Another edition of his *Outspoken Essays* has appeared with a new preface. I have re-read some of them, and this has reminded me how incomplete my understanding of him is; and I am not used to being puzzled in this particular way. My conceptions of the personalities of authors and public men, and my sense of where each stands in relation to the points of the compass, may often be wrong, but they are usually definite.

When I was a schoolboy, I heard two sermons which impressed me; one was delivered by Bishop Gore, and one (as I took the trouble to find out afterwards from my tutor) by a man called Inge. The first preacher was passionate and moving, his gestures were restless and swift; one moment he would be rocking over the edge of the pulpit, the next his beard would be pointing towards the roof of the chapel. There was a beautiful light vehemence in his utterance, entirely different from that calculated " spell-binding " solemnity, so common, so lamentably common, which even as a boy I despised. I only remember one sentence now, but that was the keynote of the sermon; he quoted Godfrey de Bouillon's words when he was proclaimed King of Jerusalem: " I will not wear a crown of gold where my Saviour wore a crown of thorns." The second preacher was a different kind of man. He was young, shy and pale, and he looked acute; he read his sermon nervously.

25

Of it, too, I remember now only one sentence, " Do not get up from the feast of life without having paid for your share." Both sermons were on the same theme. Both preachers were addressing a congregation of rich boys, on the majority of whom the sky (though many of them have since held out their plates in vain) would probably continue to shower roasted larks. This was the first time I became aware of the future Dean of St. Paul's. When I grew up I read some of his books, *Christian Mysticism* (1899), *Studies of English Mystics* (1906), *Truth and Falsehood in Religion* (1906). Because he wrote about mysticism and wrote so well and sympathetically about it, I jumped to the conclusion that he was a mystic himself, and this supposition, perhaps, is responsible, in part, but only in part, for my difficulty in understanding him now. In an exponent of mysticism we do not of course expect the same degree of conscious and unconscious saturation with an emotion or an idea as in a mystic ; just as we do not expect it in the same degree in a critic as in an artist. Perhaps the Dean is really a critic.

The first shock I received after his appointment to the Deanery was, I remember, hearing that he had insisted upon clearing from the steps of St. Paul's the vendors of fruit, bootlaces, sweets, flowers, etc., and such of the poor who found the steps a convenient resting or lunching place. Now, if " Archdeacon Grantley " or any dictatorial worshipper of " a highly-respectable Anglican First Cause " had done this, I should not have been astonished ; but as an order coming from one who stressed the inward and contemplative side of religion, its mystical as opposed to its institutional side, and was in the course of time to reach the point of denouncing Institutionalism as a danger to religion, this was, to say the least of it, an odd proceeding. Where in the world should an old orange-woman go to lay down her heavy basket and sit, if not on the steps of a church ? If there are ragged and hopeless people about, where have they a better right to be at their ease than in the precincts of a building which continually echoes to doctrines subversive of all distinctions between human beings ?

There is a kind of daintiness about our celebrated Dean ; it is to be detected not only in his style, but in his opinions. It is not a snob's, but rather a scholar's daintiness ; nevertheless it is just as inconsistent with Christian mysticism, and is responsible for the anti-democratic twist of many of his opinions. I hope some of my readers will agree with me in finding the Dean a puzzle. " What a rational, liberal mind! " we exclaim one moment while reading him; the next, we come face to face with an angrily despondent, sceptical conservative; and no sooner have we shifted our point of view to what seems to be his, so as to look out with him, for the moment, at passing events from the same window, than suddenly a blast of positively hot radicalism blows straight in our faces.

" The Gloomy Dean " is an absurd but unforgettable nickname. One would have thought Dean Inge was the last kind of man to have a public nickname at all; but he has one, and it will stick. Even if he foretells a rosy future now, his remarks will be headed by reporters, " The Gloomy Dean sees a ray of hope." How odd it is that a man of his temperament and pre-occupations should be the begetter of so many " pars "! He does not rival Mr. Bottomley or Charlie Chaplin, of course, in this respect, but he runs Mr. Justice Darling rather close. Whenever he makes a public pronouncement, it has something in it just startling enough to make a " par." Only the other day he suggested that instead of executing criminals,

27

we should leave a loaded revolver and a draught of poison in the condemned man's cell, with directions for use. Now I do not believe that the Press searchlights go on following a man round for years and continually catching him in striking attitudes, unless (perhaps unconsciously) he hops from time to time into those rays with a certain nimbleness. He puzzles me, too, by taking, with such alacrity, to the task of commenting on current events, an alacrity surprising, at least, in one so pre-occupied with Plotinus and the inner life; and he puzzles me still more when he does speak his mind, by *not* commenting upon them like a man issuing from the recesses of meditation, but like a very gifted, tolerably fair-minded professor, with no particular spiritual commitments, though possessed of several politely-violent prejudices. His essays deserve the title " Outspoken." He defends the use of contraceptive devices, and he writes on the population question a very sensible essay. I am surprised, not by it, but by its detachment. He calculates probabilities, favours eugenics, analyses Modernism, pours a little contempt on Christian Socialism, anticipates the fate of mankind, the future course of international and national politics, defines the present difficulties of the Church of England collectedly, ably, and—beautifully; but his readers would never guess that he was a priest in any church.

His writings flush with conviction when any event has suggested the possibility of a rising of the lower classes. A revolution? Ah, that would be too silly and iniquitous! This is an odd opinion to be held so violently by a Christian who bases his religion on mysticism, for whom such happenings should have little meaning. Dean Inge once criticized Bishop Gore for being so stiff about the Creed, and yet so ready to hand over the Bible stories to critics. I find it hard, myself, to distinguish Dean Inge's own position from Modernism, which he condemns. If a brief newspaper report is to be trusted, he has now gone further than he went in his essay on *Institutionalism and Mysticism*, and has said straight out that churches are a mistake. Well, an excellent text for his next address would be, " No Dogmas, no Deans."

BOSWELL

I USED to think that when the Great Book was opened in the Valley of Jehoshaphat, it would be the entries under the head " Byron " which would contain fewest surprises for us, but apparently it is Boswell who after all has succeeded best in anticipating the Day of Judgment. These volumes [1] promise to be the complete revelation of " a man," or at any rate as complete as words can achieve. Of a normal man? Yes and no: normal in the sense that the man revealed is " human, all too human " and at the same time queer (for seen close we are all queer), but emphatically not normal in the intensity of his curiosity, his complete transparency, and his unflagging aspiration after virtues which any one day of his life might have taught him he would never attain. " My warm imagination," he once wrote when comparatively young to Temple, " looks forward with great complacency in the sobriety, the healthfulness, and worth of my future life." He continued to look forward in vain.

American scholars have made a corner in Boswell, and they are dealing with him with Germanic thoroughness. It was an American, Mr. Tinker, who edited the most complete, though still very incomplete, edition of Boswell's letters; and now comes, from America, an edition of *The Hypochondriack*—seventy essays contributed by Boswell to *The London Magazine* from November 1777 to August 1783, and reprinted for the first time in two volumes. The book is even more of a literary

[1] *The Boswell Papers*, Isham Collection.

30

curiosity than a contribution to literature, although the essays are good eighteenth-century essays and worth reprinting. Yet one tends to peep and peck about in them for information on Boswell's life and character, rather than to read them for their own sakes. One does not read, say, Boswell " On Death," though it is a laudable essay, in order to learn more about death, but more about Boswell, to see how far he will exhibit his own engaging, humble, fatuous, flighty character in treating that grave theme, and how far he will pull himself together and reflect the meditations and opinions of the great man, his friend, or of others. The editor comes to our rescue by giving us the necessary references at every point where our memories are likely to fail us.

One question she discusses is the question why Boswell wrote these essays. She concludes that the primary motive was self-discipline. She says—and it is true—that " Boswell's biographers have overlooked the fact that whatever he desired for himself —fame, distinction, success—his most constant wish was to be a good man, and that he was conscious how much his unsettled physical and mental habits contributed to his failure in that respect. In his youth he tried to acquire ' an even external tenor,' to have a ' settled serenity.' His friendships with men much older than himself, and his desire to meet great men, were largely caused by his hope of finding an inspiration to lead a sober, righteous, and godly life; his fidelity to Dr. Johnson and General Paoli came from his certainty that these were the most elevating characters he knew. He went to Europe in his early twenties with the hope that he could attain a ' serene contentment,' and ' so much taste as never to be idle for want of elegant occupation '— or, as he told Rousseau, with ' un véritable désir de me perfectionner.' Disappointed in the effect of Europe,

31

he wrote to Wilkes in 1765, ' In the course of our correspondence, you shall have the various schemes which I form for getting tolerably through this strange existence.' Of these the most important seems to have been a resort to his love of writing. Certainly it was in this year, 1765, that he formed his plan of writing *The Hypochondriack*—the idea, perhaps, occurring to him as a result of the ' *ébauche de ma vie* ' which he had sent to Rousseau at the end of 1764."

Now, from Macaulay onwards, all the robust commentators upon Boswell's character, Leslie Stephen and Carlyle for example, have interpreted his pursuit of great men as a delight in basking in reflected glory, and have treated him with smiling patronage as a comic snob. There is certainly some truth in this point of view. But it was for another and deeper reason that Boswell flew like a moth to the light towards any example of shining excellence. No man was ever more acutely conscious of himself than Boswell, and therefore more painfully aware of being a bundle of confused and contradictory impulses. His will was naturally weak (at the end of his life, after the deaths of Johnson and Mrs. Boswell, it became completely dilapidated), and he longed passionately to pull himself together. Men who had nobly succeeded had an irresistible attraction for him. With them for a while his better self was uppermost, with them his fluttering aspirations could take wing again in spite of ever-repeated falls, with them he could luxuriate in that glow of self-satisfaction which was such a relief from the torture of bewilderment and self-disgust that was his fundamentally persistent mood. Drink, frivolity and the companionship of the great and good were his means of escape from that misery. It is his great merit that he passionately preferred the last expedient, though he could not do without the others.   It is this preference which helped to make him so representative of average men; for without aspirations, however futile, no one is very interesting to his fellow-men or representative of them.   It is however a fact of great significance that he should have signed these essays " The Hypochondriack."

I do not know the medical definition of hypochondria, but it cannot be far from this: an affliction of those who are too acutely and perpetually conscious of the state of either their bodies or their minds, and in whom awareness reveals most constantly what is painful in those conditions.   It is a malady most incident to men of genius, many of whom spend their lives in watching the stream of consciousness in the hope of mastering and understanding it.   Leslie Stephen has laughed at Boswell for " emulating the profound melancholy of his hero."   " He seems," he says, " to have taken a pride in his sufferings from hypochondria; though, in truth, his melancholy diverges from Johnson's by as great a difference as that which divides any two varieties of Jacques's classification.   Boswell's was the melancholy of a man who spends too much, drinks too much, falls in love too often, and is forced to live in the country and dependence upon a stern old parent, when he is longing for a jovial life in London taverns.   Still, he was excusably vexed when Johnson refused to believe in the reality of his complaints, and showed scant sympathy to his noisy would-be fellow-sufferer."   This comment is only partly true.

When *The Boswell Papers* are given to the world, it will be seen that Boswell's sufferings were at least as genuine as those of the Sage, who in strength of mind was so vastly superior, but whose lapses from the better life were not quite so unlike Boswell's own or quite so infrequent as his moral grandeur has led the world to suppose.   All through

Johnson's life there runs a tragic tension, which found expression in sudden profound groans and beatings of the breast, a tension due to a discord between his public role of moralist and his way of living. We tend naturally to attribute this to a superior tenderness of conscience; yet the profoundly honest spirit of Johnson would contemptuously scout such a flattering interpretation. "When I say I am a miserable sinner," he would roar, " I mean it." But he did not think it good for the cause of virtue that men should know too particularly the frailties of those to whom they already look up. This was an ethical point in which Boswell was deeply interested.

I am told that in *The Boswell Papers* there is a record of a conversation between Hawkins and Boswell, in which the former says he is very sorry that he ever read Johnson's private diary, now destroyed. The implication is that it was not unlike that, let us say, of Tolstoy, which is a record of unceasing aspirations, lapses, and self-reproach. Perhaps the greatest difference of all between the two friends lay in the extent to which each allowed himself to reveal his own weaknesses. " One day," says Boswell in the *Life*, " I owned to Johnson that I was occasionally troubled with a fit of narrowness." " Why, sir," said he, " so am I, *but I do not tell it*." Boswell, and it is his supreme service to mankind, always " told."

Boswell was born with the great gift of admiration, and it was so instinctive in him that it exterminated completely that fear-of-giving-oneself-away disease to which all are prone—especially authors. That authors should be so unfortunately prone to this malady is inevitable, since one of the strongest impulses which drive men into writing is vanity. It is inevitable therefore that the author, when he is conscious of the figure he is cutting in print, should

34

trim, alter, ennoble and strengthen the thoughts and impressions he transmits, otherwise he would be defeating what is really one of his principal aims in writing—to impress others. The result of this editing is that his work is often far less intelligent and original than it might have been. We are all, not only authors, more intelligent than we appear to be. But we do not dare to risk looking like fools, and very foolish we feel when someone, who did take that risk of expressing what we knew all along ourselves (like the child in the fairy story, who cried out, "But the King is naked!"), is hailed in consequence as a genius. Boswell was a rare mixture of humility and self-complacency; his weakness and his prime virtue played up to each other, making him what every man of pen and ink should hope to be, the transparently honest man.

JOHN DONNE

I

WHOEVER wanders among the tombs of a
church where the dead of many centuries lie
together must be struck by a contrast between the
effigies of late Elizabethan or Jacobean date and
those of earlier times. About earlier monuments
there is a sentiment of finality and peace. The
pomps and passions of life are not forgotten;
crowns, spurs, chains of honour, straight cloaks—all
the insignia of power and splendour are commemor-
ated, but such things are solemnized and purged
of vanity by a recognition of the fact of death:
these are the tombs of men for whom death had a
meaning to which in life they gave assent. But the
figures on those of the late Renaissance express
rather the restlessness of existence, a desperate
clinging to those possessions which the sculptor
elaborates above the buried. There they lie, these
men and women, flounced and ruffled; puffed out
and pinched into grotesque likenesses to the creations of some pigeon-breeder's fancy; often painted
like wax-works, so that they suggest neither energy
nor repose; boasting of their wealth by extravagant
ornaments, of their fertility by graduated rows of
kneeling children, of their virtue and descent by
long inscriptions and armorial embellishments.
Everything about them evokes a distracted age,
violently envious and arrogantly acquisitive, which
could hold out little to steady a mind sensitive to

such distractions.[1] Here and there the slanting figure of a doctor of divinity or law in a long gown and soft four-cornered hat, taking a nap upon his elbow, seems to rest contented; but the majority of these monuments express little beyond an avidity for the world. If mortality is expressed in them at all, it is by a morbid insistence upon physical corruption; as in those two-storeyed tombs, where the man, decked in fine clothes, lies above, and underneath him a skeleton or a body drops into ragged decay. There are, of course, exceptional instances in which meditation upon mortality takes a more imaginative and less charnel direction. One of the most striking is to be seen in St. Paul's Cathedral. It is of older date than the building, and the only monument which survived the fire of 1666.

Niched in the wall and carved in marble of a soft mistiness, stands, almost at full height, the long figure of a man wrapped in a winding-sheet. The sheet is gathered into a frill, like a wreath upon the head, leaving the lean face bare. His eyes are closed and sunken; his beard is trimly pointed (the hair above the straight lips being brushed up from them), and his features are sharpened and smoothed in death. The folds of the drapery are flat, showing the huddled knees and drooping arms beneath. Thus swathed and narrowed, like some great white chrysalis stiffened in a winter's death, stands the effigy of John Donne, poet, preacher, satirist, courtier and " worthy," waiting for the day which called forth the most magnificent of his sonnets—

---

[1] " There were officers appointed in the Grecian games who always by public authority did pluck down the statues erected to the victors if they exceeded the true symmetry and proportion of their bodies. We need such now-a-days to order monuments to men's merits, chiefly to reform such depopulating tombs as have no fellowship with them, but engross all the room, leaving neither seats for the living nor graves for the dead."—Fuller's *Holy and Profane State* (1648).

At the round Earth's imagin'd corners, blow
Your trumpets, angels, and arise, arise
From death, you numberless infinities
Of souls, and to your scattered bodies go.

II

It may seem perverse in a critical study to begin at the grave instead of at the cradle; but with Donne the manner of his death leads us to the centre of the subject. Usually the way in which a man leaves life is of as little importance towards understanding him as his entrance into it; but Donne's " impressive and scenic departure " is characteristic both of his imagination and of his relation to his age. Just as his monument shows a taste for contemplating death curiously common to his contemporaries, and yet is distinguished from theirs, so his writings upon death and kindred subjects are marked by an imaginative intensity which raises them above the half-fascinated, half-frightened obsessions of the dying Renaissance. If he fixes his gaze upon the King of Terrors, it is to stare him out of countenance; if he dwells upon the physical humiliations of decay, it is to catch a glorious fear, transcending the cold tremors of self-stimulated disgust. In Donne's love-poetry, too, it is a singular exultation or rebound from what is physically humiliating that is most characteristic. It seems as though he must first fix these ugly facts, and utter

words, words, which would tear
The tender labyrinth of a soft maid's ear
More, more than ten Sclavonians scolding, more
Than when winds in our ruin'd abbeys roar;

and that then, as though his imagination needed to be stretched upon the rack of realism, his ethereal

38

faculty is suddenly released, and in a phrase, a line,
a verse (rarely for a longer space)—

Thinner than burnt air flies the soul.

If we grant this to be the condition of a peculiar
poetic gift, we need not be continually surprised to
find the same man at once the harshest of English
satirists (Swift not excepted) and the most spectral
of love-poets.

But before discussing Donne's lyrics, it will be
well to examine further his complex relation to his
times, by the light of this elaborate disrobing for
death—how deeply impressive to his contemporaries
we can judge from Izaak Walton's famous monograph, which, in so far as it is a biography, is but
a prelude to a requiem, a corridor, prettily deco-
rated with pictures of the author's fancy, conducting
us to that large room where the Dean lies such
" an unconscionable time a-dying." Edmund Gosse,
to whose interesting book a reader who would store
himself with further information must be referred,[1]
has shown how incomplete Walton's monograph is
as a portrait, and how untrustworthy are its statements. Fate, which is seldom more ironical than
in the coupling of hero and biographer, excelled
itself, when it bound by the tie of a dog-like and
distant admiration simple old Izaak to the Dean;
when, after landing such homely, classifiable fish
as the Judicious Hooker and Dr. Saunderson, it set
him playing at the end of his placid line so many-
tinted and fabulous a dolphin.

Gosse at the close of his biographical chapters
discusses those dramatic preparations. He comments upon the profoundly Renaissance attitude of
the principal actor thus: " It was a piece of public
tragedy, performed in solemn earnest, with an in-

[1] *John Donne*, by Edmund Gosse (Heinemann. 2 vols.).

tention half-chivalrous, half-hortatory, by a religious humanist whose temper was of the sixteenth century, and not of the realistic, busy, semi-democratic seventeenth century into which he had survived. So Sir Philip Sidney died at Arnhem, with musicians performing his own poem of " La Cuisse Cassée " at his bedside. So Bernard Palissy died in the Bastille, defying Henry III to his face in a dramatic defence of his convictions. This was the Renaissance relation to life, which was, after all, only a stage, on the boards of which a man of originality and principle must nerve himself to play *le beau rôle* to the last moment, in a final bout with veritable death, armed with scythe and hour-glass, a skeleton only just unseen, but accepted as something more than a mere convention. After Donne's day the increase of Rationalism, a decay of the fantastic and poetic conception of existence, and perhaps a certain invasion of humour into daily life, made such a death impossible." Here Gosse puts us once and for all on the right track in criticizing Donne; " even in 1631," he adds, the manner of his death " was *old-fashioned enough and unintelligible enough* to attract boundless attention."

Donne, as his death-bed proves, was in many ways a belated Elizabethan—and so far he was out of sympathy with his contemporaries; but at the same time, intellectually and in his taste, he was so much in harmony with them that his poetry peculiarly delighted those who were most representative of the new age. His sensitiveness to the influence of surroundings, his restless intellect, and his divining vanity, which formed him for a subtle sycophant and a rare companion, all combined to make a Jacobean of him, and to induce him to draw his sound gold ingot into wiry ingenuities. And this discord between his temperament and his taste— that rage for novelty, pungency and ingenuity at all

costs which he, in common with the select whose
praise he desired, caught blowing down the wind of
change--can alone account for the erratic quality of
his work.   Not only his success but his failure can
never be foreseen.   It is not safe to leave one poem
unread, however repellently unpromising it may
appear.   You cannot tell from underneath what
scrap-heap of scholastic rubbish the spring of
Helicon will not make its way, or after how many
knockings of flinty conceits together, the spark of
genius will not fly at last, bright—

> As lightning, which one scarce dares say he saw,
> 'Tis gone so soon.

The occasion of his inspiration is constantly
incongruous.   Cut from their context, who would
not have supposed these lines, for instance, part of
some grave seraphic poem by the mystical Dean?

> But if my days be long, and good enough,
> In vain this sea shall enlarge, or enrough
> Itself; for I will through the wave and foam,
> And shall, in sad lone ways a lively sprite,
> Make my dark heavy poem light, and light.
> For though through many straits and lands I
>   roam,
> *I launch at Paradise, and I sail towards home.*

But no; they are taken from a laboured and
licentious satire, which bored its author into silence
long before it reached completion, a satire in which
the descent of the vegetable soul of Eve's apple was
to have been traced through her, through her
daughter, through an ape, a sprat, a whale, a bird,
an elephant, a mouse, *via* Calvin and a few heretics,
until it should be finally lodged in the body of
Elizabeth; and that magnificent apostrophe, which
quoted might describe the spirit of Shakespeare or
of Donne himself at his brightest and best,

This soul to whom Luther and Mahomet were
Prisons of flesh,

refers literally to this very apple and its tedious
migrations.

These are but two examples of frequent inadequacy in the occasions of his splendid thoughts.
Often they are mere explosions in a void, failing to
ignite what follows, and only connected with what
precedes them by the frigid manœuvres of intellectual agility. In the first *Anniversary* lines like

She, she is dead: she's dead: when thou know'st
this,
Thou know'st how wan a ghost this our world is,

so full of the desolation of bereavement, are but a
moment of emotion in the midst of contorted and
exaggerated rant, inspired by the off-chance of
attaching a rich patron. These two *Anniversaries*,
written in commemoration of a girl Donne had
never seen, shocked by their stupendous flatteries
and hyperboles even his contemporaries, who re-
lished above all things in poetry that peculiar
mental excitement, so characteristic of him, which
strains the barely conceivable to the point of bursting into the palpably absurd. Ben Jonson remarked
that such sentiments addressed to the Virgin might
have been in keeping with the subject; but that
such adulation should be lavished on the sixteen-
year-old daughter of a pushing merchant disgusted
all, except the fond, vain old father. But it brought
Donne the thing he wanted; he was soon in possession of comfortable quarters in Drury House. The
general disapproval troubled him however; these
were his first published poems; what he had written
earlier had only circulated in manuscript. He ex-
cused himself for asserting that Death

Can find nothing after her, to kill
Except the world itself, so great as she,

and much else of the same kind, by saying that not
having known the young lady personally, he could
not tell that these assertions were untrue, and he
explained that in any case he had purposely written
about her as though she had been the ideal woman.

III

This second excuse is something more than a
quibble, and brings us back to the significant fact of
Donne's Elizabethan characteristics, and of his con-
sequent isolation in an age to which nevertheless, by
taste and habits of mind, he was so intimately
allied. In the world around him, to which he was
so sensitive, there was no reflection of his own spirit,
and consequently, except in his personal poems, he
never found a subject which suited him so well that
he did not break away from it. His numerous thren-
odies are half satires; a fact which is so glaring in
this tribute of tears (more like Prince Rupert drops
which, at a touch, shiver to dry sparkling dust), that
he must account for it by the title—" An Anatomy
of the World upon the Anniversary of the Death of
Elizabeth Drury." On the other hand, in his
satires, his Pegasus stamps the earth, impatient for
a flight in upper air. In neither case, however, is
this peculiarity always displeasing to the reader; indeed from it springs much of what is most fascinating
in Donne's work, both satire and elegy; but for the
critic it is a significant symptom. From the religious subjects, which were best suited to his genius,
he excluded himself by abandoning the religion of his
family. An examination of his devotional poems
will show that had he been true to his instincts he
would never have left the Roman faith. No trace
can be found in them of any mental characteristic

which would have stood in the way of his accepting those dogmas; but on the contrary, many traces of a disposition which would have welcomed them.

IV

What the seventeenth century called wit, and for wit Donne was held to be without rival, we should rather call fancy. " Things divorced in Nature," says his younger contemporary Fuller, " are married in fancy as in a lawless place "; and the wider the natural divorce, the more admired was the ingenuity which brought them together. Towards the time of Pope wit became more verbal and intellectual. We ourselves either require from the exercise of such mental agility some underlying congruity which the intellect can appreciate, or demand in the case of fancy that the beauty of both objects in the comparison should gain through their being set side by side. But the Jacobeans admired for its own sake the power of finding analogies, and regarded its results as poetic ends in themselves. And there is something to be said for the " conceit " as a literary method, and in our own way we too pay homage to it. Does not a great part of the attractiveness of Browning's poetry or of Meredith's prose result from a similar fertility and swiftness of mind, heaping instance upon instance and contrast upon contrast, and putting Ariel's girdle round the earth in a minute? We love a packed page. There is something gloriously exhilarating in all human approximations to the myth of the inexhaustible bottle. Poets, who are ever on the watch for fixed and stellar beauties in literature, may cry out upon us for admiring mere vitality of fancy; but I am not sure they are right. As (to borrow a metaphor) the sun rising over the fields in summer mornings, shows the blades of grass tied one to another by gossamer threads invisible before, so the rising of emotion in a writer inevitably reveals to him many unexpected connections between things; and because it is itself a symptom of emotion, this surprising agility of mind engenders an emotion in us. Let me confess, dropping the critic's mask of only liking what he thinks he should admire, that to me some of Donne's wildest conceits have transmitted his emotion, and that there have been moments when even that comparison of a flea, which has fed upon both his own and his mistress's blood, to a black temple in which they are married, has seemed —well, not as bad as the discriminating would have it.

V

The literal description of Donne's qualities as a lyric poet runs into the suspected formula of combined and contradictory attributes. We must say of him that he is at once spontaneous and intricate, sophisticated and direct, one of the most fanciful and one of the most realistic of love poets. Much that is temperamentally characteristic in these poems can be suggested by saying that they are those of a man of action, or rather of a man whose spirit could only rest either in extremes of thought and feeling—or in actions. In leading a life of action Donne was continually frustrated; indeed the greater part of his biography consists in the story of vain efforts to get his hands upon the gear of the world. First he prepared himself for a diplomatic career, subsequently for the law; and after many vicissitudes, as an attendant upon Essex during the expedition to Cadiz, as secretary to the Chancellor Lord Ellesmere, as devil for controversial divines, he ended at last in a somewhat reluctant acceptance of a living in the Church. All active careers failed him, and poverty continually compelled him to make what practical use he could of his poetry in order to attract patrons. His personal charm, his vigorous and varied conversation, his turn for delicate flattery, his quick wits, well worth the picking on any subject and in any emergency, secured him constant relays of powerful friends along the road. But one thing stands out from his story: he never wanted to be either a priest or a man of letters. In the year during which Walton represents him as searching his soul in preparation for a calling which he felt to be sacred, his letters show him endeavouring to become Ambassador at Venice (a wild hope indeed), or at least secretary to the Virginia Company. And it is also clear from his reluctance to publish, his apparently contemptuous aloofness, and his exclusive association with the rich and powerful, that he had no strong wish to excel primarily among men of letters. Ben Jonson already occupied the only place he could have borne to hold among poets, and Ben Jonson (with the exception of that fantastic buffoon, Coryat) is the one man of letters with whom there is a trace of his having associated on friendly terms. Between these two it was not unlikely that such an understanding should arise. Donne would have served that curmudgeonly old critic as an excellent stick with which to beat his rivals, and by praising Donne, who was not a printed poet, he could avoid the charge of never praising a living author. Besides, they both belonged to the aristocracy of learning, and in their mutual independence each must have seen something worth conciliating. But however that may be, it is impossible to resist the evidence that Donne wished to wear his genius after the manner of Raleigh, and a quality in the poems themselves corroborates the impression that the writer felt that literature should be " a ring upon the finger," and not the aim of a life's devotion. To explain what this quality is requires a short digression.

VI

Among poets Robert Browning has been Donne's most enthusiastic admirer. He was attracted, no doubt, by a vivacity and vigour resembling his own; but also probably by something in Donne more subtly akin to his own nature. *Pauline*, Browning's first poem, which in the rush of its energetic rapture equals the triumphs of his later eloquence, is the outpouring of a very young man, who would *be himself* all the different kinds of men he admires—lover, philosopher, musician, prophet—and is by no means content to be only a poet. It is an extremely characteristic first work of one of the least contemplative of great writers. In Browning's poems the will is nearly always excited, the emotion conveyed being seldom one of detached admiration. The degree to which a subject stimulates his will is one of the most important measures of its fitness for his hand. Hence the presence in nearly all his finest poems of details, which, not strictly beautiful in themselves, recall actual or realistically probable circumstances; for nothing is so potent to excite the will as an actual reminiscence. Now Donne resembles him in this; he loves the rough touch of actual fact. Just as some poets describe what they have imagined, like Keats, while others like Byron describe what they have seen, so some find in reverie and thought the starting-point of their inspiration, while others, like Browning and Donne, find it in the vivid recollection of some instant of emotion with all its conditions. In common with all imaginative writers, given an inch they may take an ell, but that inch must be something they have lived

47

through, not dreamt through. Such poets may
not unfairly be described as poets of action, because this temperament implies an equal, if not a
greater, love of experience for its own sake than of
beauty itself; and beauty, when they do attain it,
has a peculiar quality akin to the spontaneity and
force which in action makes the moment great.
Much that Donne has written is struck straight from
the impact of experience. His lyrics seldom seem
the fruit of meditation; and their first lines, unrivalled for the depth to which they plunge into the
theme, read like thoughts which might have flashed
across his mind, or have been spoken, at the very
moment of feeling—

> I wonder by my troth, what thou, and I
> Did, till we loved? Were we not wean'd till
>   then?

> If yet I have not all thy love,
> Dear, I shall never have it all.

> For God's sake hold your tongue, and let me love.

> He is stark mad, whoever says
> That he hath been in love an hour.

In other passages, which have not the impul-
siveness of speech, we still hear the voice, though
now it is the voice of some solitary lover raving and
gesticulating under a night sky:

> Oh more than moon,
> Draw not up seas to drown me in thy sphere!

> I long to talk with some old lover's ghost,
> Who died before the god of love was born.

I have already drawn attention to the impulse
which drove Donne, in contemplating either death
or passion, to emphasize their most opposite aspects.
Like the mediaeval religious painters he goes to

48

both extremes, at once exalting the altitude and
marking the limits of spiritual emotion. He observes himself in the half-romantic, quasi-scientific
manner of Burton's *Anatomy of Melancholy*. Indeed, there is not a little Burton in the composition
of his genius. Donne himself was what would be
now called a " neurotic "; that is to say, when his
interest was not strongly excited from without, his
restless observation was turned upon those faint,
varying physical sensations which accompany every
vacillation of spirits, and in consequence he was
never conscious of enjoying stable health:

And can there be worse sickness than to know
That we are never well, nor can be so?

This ceaseless scrutiny of the machinery of
human nature made him watchful of the subtle in-
teraction of sense and spirit in himself as a lover,
and the results of his observation made him impatient of idyllic poetry. The roughness of his own
literary methods (" this sullen wit, which just so
much courts thee, as thou doest it ") was not only
an innovator's protest against insipidity, but an
emotional revolt against the unreality of romantic
chivalry. Who can imagine Spenser complaining
with humorous tartness of having to replace a lost
bracelet, or writing—

A naked thinking heart that makes no show
Is to a woman but a kind of ghost?

But where among those " treasures of fluidity
and sweet ease " can we find such living sentiments
of devotion as in Donne?

I will not look upon the quick'ning sun,
But straight her beauty to my sense shall run;
The air shall note her soft, the fire most pure;
Water suggest her clear, and the earth sure.

Time shall not lose our passages; the spring,
How fresh our love was in the beginning;
The summer how it ripen'd in the ear;
And autumn, what our golden harvests were.
The winter I'll not think on. . . .

. . . . .

Take therefore all in this: I love so true,
As I will never look for less in you.

Or compare this cry of joy in torment with
the " pains " of conventional love poetry—

Filled with her love, may I be rather grown
Mad with much heart than idiot with none.

Self-analysis and his impulse to reach the quick
of every emotion, coupled with his own intimate
experience that fidelity to fact was the liberating
condition of his own ecstasy, made the typical
Elizabethan love-lyric seem to him tame and untrue.
The hearts of such writers, he thought, " lived ten
regions from their tongues."

Methinks I lied all winter, when I swore,
My love was infinite, if spring make it more.
But if this medicine, love, *which cures all sorrow*
With more,[1] not only be no quintessence,
But mixt of all stuffs, paining soul, or sense,
And of the sun his working vigour borrow,
Love's not so pure, and abstract, as they use
To say, which have no mistress but their Muse.

The azure loves of nymphs and shepherds
corresponded to nothing in his own experience.

Search every sphere
And firmament, our Cupid is not there:
He's an infernal god and underground
With Pluto dwells, where gold and fire abound.

[1] This paradoxical compression of much experience into a single
phrase, which reveals more and more significance under the pressure of
attention, is extremely characteristic.

To this combination of curiosity and intensity in Donne's temperament must be attributed the exceptional range and variety of the emotions comprised in so small a book. He has written unquotable poems, in which lust roars upwards, like a blazing fire, and in others he has touched the bright extremity of pointed flame where it just quivers into air. Elegy XVIII, " On his mistress going to bed," is one of the few fine lust-poems in English literature. The following quotations will suggest at least four further different kinds of passion; and what mingling of desire and reaction, harsh joy and covetous passion, bitter tenderness and tenderness without alloy, and, lastly, what moments of ethereal delight, have found in Donne their exaltation—

1

Whoever loves, if he do not propose
The right true end of love, he's one that goes
To sea for nothing but to make him sick.
Love is a bear-whelp born; if we o're lick
Our love, and force it new strange shapes to take,
We err, and of a lump a monster make.
Were not a calf a monster that were grown
Faced like a man, though better than his own?
Perfection is in unity; prefer
One woman first, and then one thing in her.

What before pleas'd them all, takes but one
    sense
    And that so lamely, as it leaves behind
A kind of sorrowing dullness in the mind.
    Ah, cannot we
As well as cocks and lions jocund be
    After such pleasures?

2

First let our eyes be riveted quite through
Our turning brain, and both our lips grow to;
Let our arms clasp like ivy, and our fear
Freeze us together (that we may stick there).

3

On man heaven's influence works not so,
   But that it first imprints the air;
So soul into the soul may flow
   Though it to body first repair.
As our blood labours to beget
   Spirits, as like souls as it can;
Because such fingers need to knit
   That subtle knot, which makes us man;
So must pure lovers' souls descend
   T' affections, and to faculties,
Which sense may reach and apprehend,
   Else a great prince in prison lies.
T' our bodies turn we then, that so
   Weak men on love reveal'd may look;
Love's mysteries in souls do grow,
   But yet the body is his book.

4

I never stoop'd so low, as they
Which on an eye, cheek, lip can prey;
    Seldom, to them which soar no higher
    Than virtue, or the mind to admire;
For sense and understanding may
    Know what gives fuel to their fire;
My love, though silly, is more brave;
For may I miss, whate'er I crave
If I know yet, what I would have.

Finally, two examples, one of bitter tenderness
and one of a gentleness rare in Donne's poems, may
be added—

52

When my grave is broke up again
Some second guest to entertain—
For graves have learn'd that woman-head
To be to more than one a bed—
    And he that digs it, spies
A bracelet of bright hair about the bone,
    Will he not let us alone
And think that there a loving couple lies,
Who thought that this device might be some way,
To make their souls at the last busy day,
Meet at this grave and make a little stay.

    Sweetest love, I do not go,
      For weariness of thee,
    Nor in hope the world can show
      A fitter love for me;
    But since that I
    Must die at last, 'tis best
    To use myself in jest,
      Thus by fain'd deaths to die.
    .   .   .   .   .

    Let not thy divining heart
      Forethink me any ill,
    Destiny may take thy part
      And thy fears fulfil;
    But think that we
    Are but turn'd aside to sleep;
    They, who one another keep
      Alive, ne'er parted be.

    In despair of interpreting the nature of things
" extreme and scattering bright," or of analysing
that imaginative subtlety of which *The Dream* [1]

---

[1] As lightning or a taper's light,
Thine eyes and not thy noise wak'd me;
    Yet I thought thee
(For thou lov'st truth) an angel at first sight.
But when I saw thou saw'st my heart
And knew'st my thoughts beyond an angel's art,
When thou knew'st what I dreamt, when thou knew'st when
Excess of joy would wake me—and cam'st then;
I must confess, it could not choose but be
Profane to think thee any thing but thee.

is but one example, the critic who would attempt to define Donne by antitheses can only point, on the one hand, to such feasts of execration as *The Apparition* or *The Comparison*, and on the other, to such passages as—

> Twice or thrice had I loved thee,
>   Before I knew thy face or name;
>   So in a voice, so in a shapeless flame
> Angels affect us oft, and worshipp'd be.
>   Still when, to where thou wert, I came,
> Some lovely glorious nothing I did see!

VII

When we turn to the religious poems the first thing that strikes us is the monotony of the experience expressed. In this respect they are a contrast to the love poems; no such complexity of intimate personal experience is to be found in them. Donne as a religious poet neither penetrates, like Vaughan, the " dazzling darkness " of the mystic, nor, like Herbert, can he describe those tender movements of the soul towards a greater piety. Though the temperament which shows in his life and in his writings is that of a man who, in spite of distractions, might have sought constantly " to fix the focal point of experience beyond the horizon," he cannot be counted among those who, " drawing all things to one, enjoy true peace of mind and rest of spirit." Though his theme is often doctrinal, he never dressed the dogma in " the glorious madness of a muse whose feet have trod the milky way." Crashaw upon the articles of faith far outstrips him; Donne could never thus express the wonders of his religion—

> That the great angel-blinding Light should shrink
> His blaze to shine in a poor shepherd's eye:

That the unmeasured God so low should sink,
    As pris'ner in a few poor rays to lie;
That from His mother's breast He milk should
    drink,
Who feeds with nectar Heaven's fair family;
That a vile manger His low bed should prove,
Who in a throne of stars thunders above:

That He Whom the sun serves should faintly peep
    Through clouds of infant flesh: that He, the old
Eternal Word, should be a child, and weep:
    That He Who made the fire should fear the cold:
That Heaven's high Majesty His court should keep
In a clay cottage, by each blast controll'd:
That Glory's self should serve our griefs and fears:
And free Eternity submit to years.

    After that—

Eternal God, (for whom whoever dare
Seek new expressions, do the circle square,
And thrust into strait corners of poor wit
Thee, who art cornerless and infinite)

sounds over-ingenious and thin. He only catches
fire when remorse is his theme, and even then it
cannot be said that in his poetry tears

            take comfort and turn gems
    And wrongs repent to diadems.

For it is not so much even repentance as the *desire*
to repent, the *effort* to feel more deeply, that really
moves him.

    Batter my heart, three-person'd God; for you
    As yet but knock; breathe, shine, and seek to
        mend;
    That I may rise and stand—o'erthrow me, and
        bend

Your force to break, blow, burn, and make me new.
. . . .

Yet dearly, I love you, and would be loved fain,
But am betroth'd unto your enemie:
Divorce me, untie, or break that knot again,
Take me to you, imprison me, for I,
Except you enthrall me, never shall be free,
Nor ever chaste, except you ravish me.

He speaks of his " devout fits," which come and
go away

Like a fantastic ague, save that here
These are my best days when I shake with fear.

VIII

In the sermons, his wailing rhetoric, which rises
and swoons like the wind and trembles at its height,
works continually upon two passions: fear and the
desire to feel the mysteries it expounds. He terrifies
his listeners with annihilation; he forces them to
follow the gradual changes of the body, from corruption to corruption and death to death; he conjures
up before them the ghost of their blank ignorance in
the setting of darkness and solitude—" I respite thee
not till the day of judgment, when thou wilt call
upon the hills to cover thee; nor till the day of
thine own death, when thou shalt have evidence
enough of thy Maker by feeling hell. I respite thee
but a few hours, but six hours, but till midnight.
Wake then; and then, dark and alone, hear God ask
thee then, and remember that I ask thee now, Is
there a God! And if thou darest, say No! " [1] It is
difficult to convey an idea of this eloquence of gloom
and star without long quotations. There are
scattered imaginative sentences in the midst of

[1] Quoted by Sir Leslie Stephen in *Studies of a Biographer*.

crabbed disquisitions of interminable length: " That world, which finds itself truly in an autumn, finds itself a spring in our imaginations "; epigrams such as " He who sets too high a price upon his body will sell his soul cheap "; and magnificent conceits such as that with which the following passage closes.

" The Holy Ghost calls it joy (' for the joy which was set before Him He endured the cross '), which was not a joy of his reward after his passion, but a joy that filled him even in the midst of his torments, and arose from them; when Christ calls his *calicem* a cup and no worse (' Can ye drink of My cup '), he speaks not odiously, not with detestation of it. It was indeed a cup, *salus mundo*, a health to all the world."

As a preacher he shared the characteristics of his contemporary divines. " Whatever could be read into a text,"[1] says Dr. Jessopp, " or whatever could be drawn out of it was regarded as perfectly legitimate. . . . Granted that every syllable and every letter in the printed pages of the Old Testament and of the New found its place there by divine inspiration, and carries with it a divine authority, and what a tremendous power the preacher had at his disposal "—and, we may add, what an opportunity for a mind like Donne's! Avoiding, on the one hand, examples of comic ingenuity in this direction, as when logic leads him to conclude that to ravish a reluctant cardinal must be the worst of all sins; and, on the other, leaving Donne's meditations upon putrefaction and vermiculation to be imagined, the two following extracts will show the quality of his rhetoric, the first at its best, the second at the height of his most characteristic ecstasy.

" The ashes of an oak in the chimney are no

---

[1] *John Donne* (The Leaders of Religion series, Methuen & Co.), by Augustus Jessopp, D.D.

epitaph of that oak, to tell me how high or how large it was. It tells me not what flocks it sheltered while it stood, nor what men it hurt when it fell. The dust of great persons' graves is speechless too, it says nothing, it distinguishes nothing. As soon the dust of a wretch whom thou would'st not, as of a prince whom thou could'st not look upon, will trouble thine eyes, if the wind blow it thither; and when a whirlwind hath blown the dust of the churchyard unto the church, and the man sweeps out the dust of the church into the churchyard, who will undertake to sift those dusts again, and to pronounce:—this is patrician, this is noble, flour, and this yeomanly, this the plebeian, bran." [1]

Now hear Donne when his enthusiasm is upon him and he grasps whatever words first come to hand, as if all words must be inadequate to the meaning. He is attempting to describe heaven—

" But as it is said of old cosmographers, that when they had said all that they knew of a country, and yet much more was to be said, they said the rest of those countries were possessed with giants, or witches, or spirits, or wild beasts, so that they could pierce no further into that country; so when we have travelled as far as we can with safety, that is, as far as ancient or modern expositors lead us, in the discovery of these new heavens and new earth, yet we must say at last, that it is a country inhabited with angels and archangels, with cherubim and seraphim, and that we can look no farther into it with these eyes. Where it is locally, we inquire not; we rest in this, that it is the inhabitation prepared for the blessed saints of God; heavens, where the moon is more glorious than our sun, and the sun as glorious as

[1] Sermon XV.

He that made it; for it is He Himself, the Son of God, the sun of glory. A new earth, where all their waters are milk and all their milk honey; where all their grass is corn, and all their corn manna; where all their glebe, and all their clods of earth, are gold; and all their gold of innumerable carats; where all their minutes are ages, and all their ages eternity; where everything is every minute in the highest exaltation, as good as it can be, and yet superexalted and infinitely multiplied by every minute's addition; every minute infinitely better than ever it was before." [1]

Such passages give some idea of the energy which lay behind his lyric flights of rapture. This is oratory indeed. And if we picture the graceful and spectral appearance of the orator, the beautiful, eager vehemence of his gestures, we shall not be surprised that men listened spellbound or broke into groans and exclamations; and at the close of such impressive exhibitions of scornful or ecstatic zeal, withdrew, hushed or whispering, to find themselves, owls in daylight, in the streets once more.

It is not easy to read Donne's sermons. It is not easy to read any sermons, unless you feel they are doing you good—and oddly enough, that satisfaction, though it is one of the most pleasant which can be derived from reading, is seldom prolonged. The book which supplies it is soon ungratefully laid down, and though the reader is firmly persuaded that he will return to it, yet months, often years, pass without his opening that book again. Now Donne's sermons do not even offer to any great degree this exalted, but quickly exhausted satisfaction. Few modern readers ever rose from their perusal feeling sure they were going to lead better lives. To the theological historian they are of course

---

[1] Sermon on Lady Danvers.

of exceptional interest; but the interests of the theologian are strange and unshared by the general reader, who opens Donne's sermons with almost exclusively aesthetic and inquisitive purposes, and is baffled for many pages together by a fantastic and ardent exegesis. We require, therefore, special encouragement to persevere. So having dressed with unusual care, preferably in a garb of sombre richness, put on your skull-cap, light two tall candles, draw your high-backed chair towards the rubies and ashes of a declining fire, and then open one of the old folios of Donne's sermons. Unless interrupted too soon by dinner, or by too keen a desire for it, you may succeed in finishing one of them; nor are these ancillary aids to concentration to be despised.

WILLIAM COLLINS

MOST reading people are familiar with Collins's *Ode to Evening* and with the famous twelve-line poem written in the beginning of the year 1746—

How sleep the Brave who sink to Rest
By all their Country's Wishes blest,

but little else that he has written is so well-known.

Mr. Edmund Blunden's edition has made me do what I had not done before—read all the poems which have been preserved. These are few in number, and most were written before his sensibility had attained its best expression. His life was short; his writing-life still shorter. He was a precocious poet; but his own leaven had barely begun to work within the tradition he inherited, before a morbid misery obliterated his mind. Collins was a lesser Coleridge, born too soon to develop all his originality completely. There is a kinship between Collins's poetry and those early poems of Coleridge in which fervid wonder and high-strung feeling contend with the composure of eighteenth-century diction or with conventional vatic gesture. The two poets resembled each other in tastes, in their love of fairy-lore, old ballads, and erudition, though in Collins there was no subtle, ardent, speculative curiosity. In temperament, too, they were not unlike. Both were affectionately sociable, and delicately, ecstatically humble when in love (see Collins's verses on *A Piece of Bride-Cake*); both were addicted to dreaming of enormous undertakings, both irresolute; both were con-

61

scious of possessing powers, which, alas! any distress
of mind suspended; both were poor hands at hack-
work and " doing their duty "; both were acquainted with strange mental terrors (see Collins's
Ode to Fear, with its fine opening:

> Thou to whom the world unknown,
> With all its shadowy shapes, is shown)

and both preserved, through lives chequered with
shame and disappointment, youthful tenderness of
conscience and humility of aspiration.

In Collins's case we must generally infer these
qualities, though the scant records of his career
confirm them, and so does Johnson's brief memoir,
in which his stately severity of diction does not conceal understanding and respect. Indeed, his sympathy with the man was far greater than his admiration for his work. In Johnson's eyes Collins was a
literary heretic who went in search of questionable
and absurd beauties. The homage which his verse
paid to his latinizing predecessors was, as Johnson
and other contemporaries perceived, never whole-
hearted; it was disturbed by a devotion to a " new "
spirit, nearer itself to that of an older English
poetry. Collins in his literary admirations went
farther back than Cowley. He was infected, critical
contemporaries thought, by that literary Pre-
Raphaelitism which Johnson satirized in Warton:

> All is strange, yet nothing new,
> Endless labour all along,
> Endless labour to be wrong.
> Phrase that time has flung away,
> Uncouth words in disarray,
> Tricked in antique ruff and bonnet,
> Ode and elegy and sonnet.

He was considered obscure. And yet, to us, how
slight that infection seems! How seldom, after all,

did he use phrases " that time had flung away."
He strikes us rather as a writer of his own age. He
will refer constantly to the poet's instrument as his
" Shell "; the " Turtles," either of Peace or Love,
appear and reappear in his verses; fields are
" Meads " or " Lawns," rivers " Tides." Classical deities abound; every abstract noun is liable to
personification; spells usually are " potent," ears
" partial," and smiles " transient." Well may we
wonder that this poet should have been suspect as
an innovator; yet the ears and eyes of contemporaries are sharper than those of posterity in such
matters; they were not deceived.

The next generation too perceived the peculiar
quality of Collins, only with delighted recognition.
Coleridge recognized in him his spiritual forebear;
and among his many unattempted literary projects
was an edition of Collins. He wrote to Thelwall in
1796: " Collins's ' Ode on the Poetical Character '—
that part of it, I should say, beginning with ' The
Band (as faëry legends say) was wove on that
creating day '—has inspired and whirled *me* along
with greater agitations of enthusiasm than any
most *impassioned* scene in Schiller or Shakespeare."
(By the way, let me warn the reader who looks that
poem up that it is not likely to whirl *him* away.)
Its appeal, doubtless, to Coleridge was due to its
bringing into clearer consciousness his own conception of a poet's mind, which later, as critic and
poet, he made clearer still. Collins's diction (as Mr.
Livingston Lowes has shown in his admirable *The
Road to Xanadu*) left in some instances a direct
imprint on Coleridge's own verse. In Collins's ode
The Passions these charming lines on melancholy
occur:

In notes by distance made more sweet,
Pour'd thro' the mellow horn her pensive soul:

63

And, dashing soft from rocks around,
Bubbling runnels join'd the sound;
Thro' glades and glooms *the mingled measure* stole;
Or o'er some *haunted* stream, with fond delay,
Round an *holy* calm diffusing,
Love of peace and lonely musing,
In hollow murmurs died away.

And in *Kubla Khan* one remembers:

. . . was heard *the mingled measure*
From the fountains and the caves.

" The ceaseless tumult of the sacred river,"
says Mr. Lowes, " recalled the mellower tumult of
the bubbling runnels ' dashing soft from rocks
around,' as Coleridge's ' Through wood and dale,'
but eight lines earlier, had echoed Collins's ' Thro'
glades and glooms,' and ' haunted ' and ' holy,' still
in successive lines, had already stolen into the
measures of the dream:

A savage place! as *holy* and enchanted
As e'er beneath a waning moon was *haunted*. . . . "

I make use of Mr. Livingston Lowes' researches
because they illustrate the central fact about
Collins's reputation: that from Coleridge to his
latest editor, Mr. Edmund Blunden, his poems have
been very highly valued by poets; while to critics,
who delight in tracing literary rivers of poetry to
their sources, he is particularly interesting. Nevertheless, the reader who is neither poet nor critic
may well find himself at first wondering at the
enthusiasm, say, of Swinburne, and even be disappointed when he turns from the *Ode to Evening*
or from judiciously selected quotations to the
complete text. But despite that Palladian diction
and those " Pindaric raptures," which went out
with the art of oratory, he too will be aware in

Collins's verse, if he listens attentively, not only of a gentle austerity and tender gravity in phrasing and a " simple-seeming subtlety," but also of that harmonious movement which is characteristic of the verse of a born poet. Mr. Blunden's preface may help him to perceive these qualities; and if he turns to a little book by the same writer, recently published by the Hogarth Press, *Nature in Literature*, he is likely to find other serviceable hints. Mr. Blunden, in the chapter called " The Spirit Wooed " (the Spirit he means is Nature, whom he himself has courted in verses surprisingly delicate and observant), says that the *Ode to Evening* has " for more than twenty years amazed and sustained " him: " Collins, copiously brilliant in the various effects of verses, could not rest content with the usual sound of rhyme in the presence of his ' nymph reserved '; and by a stroke of genius he chose the unrhymed form which Milton, whose artistry he fed upon with the appetite of sufficing originality, had somewhat stiffly practised. . . . Rhymeless, we call it; but, as evening is haunted by rumours and echoes of the quietened day, so the idyll of Collins is musical with a series of subdued and sometimes remotely-set rhymes and assonances ":

> Whose numbers, stealing through the darkened
>   *vale*,
> May not unseemly with its stillness suit,
>   As, musing slow, I *hail*
>   Thy genial loved return!

And that concluding word is, he adds, " a quiet consummation of a concluding note, the ' small but sullen horn.' "

The lines from which the last phrase is taken run as follows:

> Or where the Beetle winds
> His small but sullen Horn,

As oft he rises 'midst the twilight Path,
Against the Pilgrim borne in heedless Hum. . . .

which will recall Gray's beetle which " wheels its
droning flight "—a phrase still happier and more
compact.   I cannot agree with those who would set
Collins beside Gray. Swinburne contrasts the elegiac
excellence of Gray with the superior lyric power
of Collins; but Swinburne, at the time he wrote,
was anxious, if possible, to disagree with Matthew
Arnold on every occasion, and Arnold had already
placed the poetry of Collins on a lower level; while
Swinburne's response to movement in verse—a
quality in which the odes of Collins excel—was
always instantaneous and enthusiastic.   But even
Collins's best poems are not without small imperfec-
tions which Gray, the impeccable, would not have
passed.   Take even the almost perfect stanzas in his
finest poem:

> Then lead, calm Vot'ress, where some sheety Lake
> Cheers the lone Heath, or some time-hallow'd Pile,
>   Or up-land Fallows grey
>   Reflect its last cool Gleam.
>
> But when chill blust'ring Winds, or driving Rain,
> Forbid my willing Feet, be mine the Hut,
>   That from the Mountain's Side,
>   Views Wilds, and swelling Floods,
>
> And Hamlets brown, and dim-discover'd Spires,
> And hears their simple Bell, and marks o'er all
>   Thy dewy Fingers draw
>   The gradual dusky Veil.

Fallows do not reflect a lake, but are reflected
in it.   If the words pass into the mind unanalysed
the picture is perfect, but that later test reveals a
flaw.

" Collins," says Johnson, " who while he studied *to live* felt no evil but poverty, no sooner *lived to study* than his life was assailed by more dreadful calamities—disease and insanity." This sad sentence almost sums up his life. He was born on Christmas Day, 1721. His father was a prosperous hatter in Chichester who was three times mayor. William Collins was admitted as a scholar of Winchester in 1733, and a year later his father died a ruined man. In the natural course of events he would have proceeded to New College and have ultimately become a fellow. " Unhappily, there was no vacancy. This was the original misfortune of his life." Such a niche as the one Gray found would have been safest for him. He appears to have left Oxford because there was no prospect of his becoming a fellow, since, though an excellent scholar, he was neither a clergyman, lawyer, nor physician. Mr. Blunden is probably right, however, in surmising it was the lights of London that lured him away from the easy path. Collins had plenty of confidence in his own abilities, but he did not understand that the merits which the world rewards are not the same as those which are most respected in a university. As a poet " upon the town," he had not the energy to support himself easily. What he endured is best suggested by Mr. Belloc's definition of poverty: " It is that state in which a man is perpetually anxious for the future of himself and his dependants, unable to pursue life upon a standard to which he was brought up, tempted both to subservience and a sour revolt, and tending inexorably towards despair." He was relieved by a legacy of £2,000 left him by an uncle, Colonel Martin, in 1748, but unfortunately it was also then that he became aware of the approaches of a debility and depression which deepened to insanity as the years went by. He died in 1759.

ROBERT BROWNING

BROWNING in early days owed more than most poets to the aggressive championship of youth. It is curious to look back upon contemporary reviews of Browning's poems, and thanks to the pious industry of the Browning Society this requires no arduous research. These reviews and essays are generally marked by two characteristics: an almost truculent championship as if the writers were in possession of an æsthetic revelation, and a regretful, though by no means uncomplacent, avowal that their poet-prophet is at once too deep a thinker and too obscure a writer to win general recognition. Give the world fifty, a hundred years, and it will recognize and understand; but we few, we band of brothers, must be content to know we are right without hope of popular corroboration: that is the prevailing note of these heralds, who as a matter of fact immediately preceded the poet's triumph.

To their surprise Browning became popular. His early champions had under-estimated the attractiveness of his pre-occupation with religious and moral questions, and overrated the drawback of his " difficulty." They did not allow either for the allurement which lies in the suggestion that each new admirer will find himself among the few, and anticipate the verdict of posterity; nor did they realize that a poet who vigorously, subtly and picturesquely discusses the problems of life, and carries himself resolutely in the face of doubts which perplex his contemporaries, is sure soon to meet with thousands of readers eager to understand him.

Moreover, Browning's conceptions of man and the universe were not, in themselves, hard to understand. They were not strangely profound or even very interesting. They were simple, cheering, robust and summary, but the processes of his thought, his darting flashes of imaginative intuition, his instantaneous dexterity in snatching here a clue and there a clue, his enormous power of accumulating arguments, hints, illustrations, facts, metaphors, and of welding them all into some sort of manageable mass, to be finally sent bowling down the hill like a great snowball growing larger and more formidable as it gathers impetus—these qualities in him were amazing, and they made him more impressive than many clearer and more penetrative thinkers.

It is admitted that Browning is an intellectual poet; that is to say, a poet whose imagination is most often stimulated by subjects and aspects of things to which he is directed by an intellectual interest. He seldom attempts to express anything so vague as a mood, and consequently he is seldom at his best as a lyric poet. He is rather a master of the arresting, complicated situation, or the critical moment in the story of a man's heart or his faith. In his power of evoking scenes from past stages of civilization, with their passions, manners, and modes of thought, he has had only one equal among historians, Carlyle. Then, too (and here was the main source of his sweeping popularity), he was the modern poet *par excellence* of passion as it exists between men and women. Passion is the right word for the emotion which he expresses best; for on the one hand, that emotion is always imaginative and never degenerates into lust, while on the other, it never passes beyond the actual into a contemplation of beauty itself. He has also written poems of devoted human affec-

tion; but these, fine as they are, though they also do
him honour as a man, do not rank as artistic achievement with his poems of passion.

Returning to the accepted definition of Browning as an essentially intellectual poet, what, then,
was the ruling characteristic of his intellect? Was
it for philosophic power his mind was most remarkable, as many admirers have thought? His mind
was keenly speculative, but in the temper of it was
something positively antagonistic to that passion
for order, certainty and reason which makes the
thinker. Browning loved a world lit by broken,
vivid lights, a landscape seen beneath cloud and
gleam, better than a clear world. He was, without
restriction or regret, a romanticist. To him the
mere spectacle of the ceaseless activity of man's will
was itself an abundant satisfaction, while to the
science of ends he was comparatively indifferent.
Indeed, of *all* great poets, he was perhaps the least
contemplative. He might write " on earth, the
broken arc, in heaven the perfect round "; but it
was not the idea of perfection which stimulated his
poetic power, only the effort and struggle towards it;
nor was that idea ever so present to him as to make
him rejoice one whit less whole-heartedly in the
big, blooming, buzzing confusion of the world,
where the irrational human will chases one object
after another without questioning its value. Naturally he felt most at home in the Italian Renaissance,
or in his own times, both ages of multifarious,
thrilling cross-purposes.

Sometimes in his poems the object pursued is a
woman, sometimes political power, sometimes the
truth about enclitic δε, sometimes fame, sometimes worldly position, sometimes mystical illu-
mination. But mark the poet's attitude towards
the characters whose passions he interprets: it is
the brave, unmeasured, impetuous pursuit, the

70

blind, uncritical, determination to have and to hold, which rouses his inmost sympathy and makes him write his best. What does it matter, he seems to say, if the object be of little worth; it is the thoroughness of man's striving that is his glory. This life is not his only chance; there are " brave adventures new " before him still—" leave Now for dogs and apes, Man has Forever! " This shout of high encouragement to keep hotfoot on the chase of promiscuous quarry is also a defiant challenge to reason; to the religious reason as well as the philosophic, for both insist upon the primary importance of determining what is most worth pursuing. In Browning faith was rather an emotion of exultant conviction that " all's right with the world " than a key to the relative values of things in it.

If we examine his mind we shall discover its bent to be (in spite of his religious and speculative curiosity) not that of the philosopher, but of a very different type, the advocate. Browning had the instincts, the faculties, and the zest of an incomparable special pleader. The statement and defence of a *case* was the task which roused his mind to its keenest activity. Sometimes the case was one which he wanted with all his heart to prove, more often one taken up because its defence and statement put his master-faculty to the hardest tests. Advocacy was his ruling intellectual passion, and into its service he pressed one of the most vivid and alert imaginations in literature. Consider his work: apart from love poems (though many of these are statements of cases, speeches for the prosecution or defence), apart from historic scenes in verse, the mass of it is composed of magnificent special pleadings, matchless for agility and verve, amazing for the tactical skill with which advantage is taken of every stray and scrap of evidence, every weakness, every doubt upon the opposite side, to secure a favourable verdict for his client or to mitigate a hostile one. Like the born advocate, the poet is never so formidable, ubiquitous, and alive, as when he stands for the weaker side. He reminds one of a fighting engineer like Gordon, never so happy as when defending a position that seems hopelessly weak, by means of impromptu trenches, blankets, bales, and packing-cases, keeping the enemy at bay with the slenderest resources deftly and daringly employed. He is attracted to subjects in proportion as they offer such opportunities. *The Ring and The Book* is a prodigious *tour-de-force* in stating with incredible fullness and intricacy the case for each actor in the story.

Mr. Sludge the Medium, Aristophanes' Apology, Bishop Blougram's Apology, were "subjects made to his hand," because they were cases in which the defence was by no means easy. *Paracelsus* is the defence of a *raté* mystic, and *Sordello* the apology for a man who has failed to answer the call of his spirit. What is *The Grammarian's Funeral* but the justification of an apparently useless dry-as-dust, or *Ivan Ivanovitch* but a difficult murder trial, or *The Statue and the Bust* but an unexpected indictment of a couple who in pleading innocence might well have hoped to have the Court with them? And if the poet is grappling with the arguments of Strauss or confuting Renan through the mouth of St. John, is it not still emphatically a case he is stating? The dramatic soliloquy (Browning's speciality) is the form which lends itself most readily to intimate justification. His very style is that of an advocate. He does not, like other poets, bring you into the presence of the subject and leave you there; but he remains at your elbow, to see that not one point, no, not the minutest, escapes you. You feel the pressure and ardour of his mind as of a man arguing with you personally. He watches and interprets your thoughts, anticipating objections, forestalling in parentheses the possible trend of your thoughts, carefully netting you in a complexity of suggestion before he drives home his strongest point. Like an orator, he never shrinks from repeating himself; like an orator, he knows that once he has staggered you, adumbrations, hints, faint corroborations, will carry weight; like an orator, he would sooner forget his subject than his auditor. And all these processes are carried through with a top-speed rush. His obscurity is not obscurity, but swiftness of thought; on the surface of his page lies not darkness, but rather the quick dazzle of too much light. Lastly, in this master-faculty of his mind we discover also the secret of his failure as a dramatist. He puts himself in the place of his characters, lending them his quickness of thought and imagination. He sees their motives and actions through their own eyes; he has to a supreme degree the gift of dramatic sympathy. But dramatic sympathy, though it is necessary to the dramatist, is not sufficient by itself. The dramatist must also have the power of contemplating characters from outside, of seeing them not only as they appear to themselves, but externally in relation to other characters. Browning's characters derive their dramatic vividness rather from their relation to his own mind than from their relations to each other. Consequently when he wrote drama, a form which compels the commentator to withdraw, the life and energy which his men and women possessed as long as he could explain them, faded away.

COVENTRY PATMORE[1]

COVENTRY PATMORE is a more magnificent poet and a more interesting " prophet " than even the literary seem as yet able to believe. He was a prophet-poet: " My Call," he wrote in a private notebook, " is that I have seen the truth and can speak the living words which are born of having seen it "; and, again, " My love not only dares the most searching light of philosophy, but requires it." He might have written here " my poetry "; for his love inspired it, and, to Patmore, poetry was indeed *splendor veritatis*, " truth in the glory of its shining."

I am not forgetting that many critics have enthusiastically praised him, Gosse, Quiller-Couch, Lionel Johnson, Arthur Symons are among them, but their praise has, as yet, hardly raised his status in English literature. He is only considered one of the remarkable poets of the Victorian era. In *The Cambridge History of English Literature* he figures among " the lesser poets " of his time, that is to say, with Ebenezer Jones, Keble, Sydney Dobell, Hake, Trench, etc., not one of whom reaches even to his knees; while Clough, FitzGerald, Mrs. Browning are accorded there the treatment due to major poets. Mr. Saintsbury writes of him that " accidental coterie admiration has sometimes exalted him too high "; and he adds the usual commendation, " He was a very remarkable poet in more ways than one." " Very remarkable " might pass as a fair estimate in a comparison with the few

[1] *Selected Poems of Coventry Patmore*, edited by Derek Patmore (Chatto and Windus, 3s. 6d.), who has written a good introduction.

greatest poets of all tongues and ages; but in any
other relation it is too low.

Patmore is, after all, the greatest religious poet
in English literature since the seventeenth century,
not excepting Christina Rossetti, and perhaps
greater than Crashaw, with whom, of all other
English religious poets, he has most affinity. Doctrinal poets are rare. It is, by the by, curious that,
in proportion to their importance in life, patriotism
and doctrinal religion should have inspired so little
poetry of the first order during the last three
hundred years. Patriotism is an emotion which,
when strong enough to prompt a poet, is seldom
without dubious alloys—and perhaps that is the
explanation; while Protestantism has certainly discouraged in sacred poets the devout audacity which
extracts emotion from the distinctities of faith.

There is something, too, in the spirit of Protestantism itself inimical to celestial passion; it is
in the expression of awe and submission rather than
of love that its poets have excelled. It is even
shocking to the Protestant religious sense that
anyone should assert that the goal of life is not to
love God, but to be " in love with " Him, and that
such passion is reciprocal. Yet to Patmore that
was a fact. It was the key to the mysteries of his
religion; it was the burning core of the Universe,
and in the light which it shed he interpreted the love
between man and woman; thus he became both a
mystical-religious and a mystical-amorous poet.

Eternal peace and tempests of delight tax
language to the uttermost, and Patmore knew that
" views of the unveiled heavens " have seldom inspired poets; he noticed also that " the most
ardent love is rather epigrammatic than lyric," and
that the saints abound in epigrams. But the
supreme merit of his most splendid Odes is that he
did blend in them lyric impetus and passionate

concentration. The Odes are filled with a " great rejoicing wind," yet every phrase in them clings to a thought. The verse-form he chose, with its un-even lines and dramatic pauses, had no independent form apart from emotion. It was such a means of direct communication as some modern poets are now seeking. How finely he used his freedom cannot be well shown except by quoting a whole poem; so perfectly and invariably do alternate pause and rush lead to a final climax or *diminuendo*. But perhaps the following fragment may suggest his skill:

She, as a little breeze
Following still Night,
Ripples the spirit's cold, deep seas
Into delight;
But, in a while
The immeasurable smile
Is broke by fresher airs to flashes blent
With darkling discontent:
And all the subtle zephyr hurries gay,
And all the heaving ocean heaves one way,
T'ward the void sky-line and an unguess'd weal.
Until the vanward billows feel
The agitating shallows, and divine the goal,
And to foam roll.
And spread and stray
And traverse wildly, like delighted hands,
The fair and fleckless sands;
And so the whole
Unfathomable and immense
Triumphing tide comes at the last to reach
And burst in wind-kiss'd splendours on the
    deaf'ning beach,
Where forms of children in first innocence
Laugh and fling pebbles on the rainbow'd crest
Of its untired unrest.

The loveliness of the metrical change at:

> She, as a little breeze
> Following still night

can only be fully felt when the opening of the poem is also before one; but no ear is likely to miss the skill with which, from that point onwards, these irregular lines are conducted to their climax, nor I hope, that sense of *effort*, so subtly audible in the slow, difficult lines which precede and prepare the relief of the explosion :

> And so the whole
> Unfathomable and immense
> *Triumphing tide comes at the last to reach,*
> And burst in wind-kiss'd splendours on the deaf'ning beach.

The poem is, of course, an allegory of natural love, which an omitted prelude has linked to Patmore's philosophy of divine love.

It matters little in expounding Coventry Patmore's poetry whether we approach him as a love-poet or a religious poet. He was a Catholic. He accepted the dogmas of his religion, but he interpreted some of them in a mystical sense based on intense personal experience. I am not aware that he was ever charged with heresy, though his interpretations as a poet and seer were the kind which the Church (I think I am right in saying this) watches with an apprehensive eye: there is a risk of their tipping over into heresy, and, in any case, they are apt to be dangerous, and they are sure to be misunderstood by the world. The book in which Patmore explained them most carefully he burnt at the suggestion of the poet Gerard Hopkins, who declared he was " telling secrets," but afterwards regretted his advice.

However, from what Coventry Patmore wrote,

both in prose and verse, there is no doubt what those spiritual experiences were. The like of them is to be found in the records of not a few saints, in the Spanish Catholic mystics, and in particular (I am told) in the works of St. John of the Cross. Their nature can be suggested by saying that the ultimate goal of spiritual life, the union of God and the Soul, differs only in intensity and completeness, not in kind, from the most perfect imaginable union between lovers. It follows that the vocabulary of human passion is the one approximation to a language fit to express the extreme experience. To speak of it in other terms is, to these mystics, a faithless base timidity; and yet unless their minds are, when they speak of it, white as a furnace in a thorough blast, their most precious things may " become a post the passing dog defiles ". Because Coventry Patmore in *The Unknown Eros* and other odes has attained to that incandescent austerity, he must be ranked in his proper place, not, please, among the interesting but lesser of the Victorians, but among the religious poets of the world. Of course, there are other kinds of religious poetry in which poets have reached an equal or greater excellence, but in his own tongue and on his own spiritual ground who is his match?

That religious ecstasy should instinctively use the language of amorous passion therefore never disturbed Coventry Patmore. He would have been pleased at discovering that Rochester's most deeply passionate poem beginning:

Why doest thou shade thy lovely face? O why
Does that eclipsing hand so long deny
The sun-shine of thy soul-enliv'ning eye,

had been lifted straight from Quarles, and turned by Rochester from an address to God into a love-poem, by the simple device of substituting " dear "

for " Lord " in such lines as " Speak, art Thou
angry, Lord, or only try'st me? " He would have
seen in this proceeding an unconscious testimony to
a profound truth. Nor would our modern psychological books on Sex and Religion have shocked him,
though their authors, as blind " truth-criers who
know not what they cry," might have roused his
angry contempt. There could be nothing shocking
to him in the idea of the two sacred sources of emotion being inter-connected. Quite the reverse. Like
many mystics he was exceedingly hard-headed.

In the English Prayer Book it is written that
" marriage signifies unto us the mystical union of
Christ with His Church," words which to most
couples who stand before the altar are only solemn
abracadabra. To this love-poet they had a meaning
which he never ceased to explore. There were only
two profoundly interesting things in life for him,
religion and love. He revelled in getting angry
over democratic politics, bad manners, and worse
literature; but religion and love alone were important to him. Before he formulated his mysticism, he studied love. The result was that exceedingly odd poem *The Angel in the House* and its
continuations which made his name. They are
richer in genuine love - lore than any Victorian
poem, and at the same time stuffed with rosy, cosy,
prosy domestic details. These enraptured contemporary sentimentalists, but the poet was not fundamentally one of them: he was already writing:

> How long shall men deny the flower
> Because its roots are in the earth?

But he was not yet the Uranian singer of the
Odes, though such a one is foreshadowed by many
delicate passages of pathos and delight in this queer
hybrid work—half domestic novelette, half passionate exact psychology; he was not yet the worshipper

of the Unknown Eros, whose rites could only be
conveyed in enigmas:

There lies the crown
Which all thy longing cures.
Refuse it, Mortal, that it may be yours!
It is a Spirit, though it seems red gold;
And such may no man, but by shunning hold.
Refuse it, till refusing be despair;
And thou shalt feel the phantom in thy hair.

YEATS

MR. YEATS' collected poems have been my
companion lately. For me this is the only way
to arrive at a judgment, since I find my matter in
a poet's less successful or unsuccessful poems as well
as in his masterpieces. Above all I must discover
first if he can raise me to a contemplative mood when
at different times I am different men; or if only
certain states of mind, and those perhaps not the
most imaginatively active, are propitious to him.
It is difficult also to make sure whether it is only
parts of a poem which delight us, or the whole;
whether a line or a phrase thrills only while it surprises us, or whether there is something inexhaustibly
satisfying in a poet's words.

The uncertainty of our judgments on poetry is
unfortunately as much due to our moods of sensibility as to our dullness. We read a poem at the
right moment and we are exalted, we read a better
one at another moment and we feel little. We do
not remember very clearly the nature of that exaltation, we only remember it was intense; and we
not only forget its quality, but fail to note the associations, personal and passing perhaps, which induced us to admire. And yet it seems weakly dis-
loyal to distrust, at the suggestion of others, that
experience afterwards, and indeed it is idiotic to
deny what we have felt. But it is nearly as idiotic
to interpret that recollected emotion as a final test
before we have compared it with the emotions which
other poems have given us. For this reason
Matthew Arnold's advice to carry in our memories

examples of the finest poetry is excellent. But he should have added that these should never be used as prophylactics against immediate response. We respond on the whole so feebly to beauty, that in aesthetic experience to let *le mieux* be *l'ennemi du bien* is folly. Only when we proceed to criticism is this check beneficial. Enjoy, understand to the uttermost, but keep judgment in reserve. Let us take advantage of every accident and private disposition which makes it easy to feel what the poet felt, to see what he saw; read him as though he were the only poet, the inventor of poetry (for only by being impressionable can discoveries be made), and then, only then, remember what other poets have done. Judgment! Most of us get tired of suspending it. We want to cry out, " I will be true to my own taste; this is the best "; for the superlative, which implies comparison, is the easiest way of articulating admiration, while the faculty of judgment, like the delta of a river, forms slowly, accumulating often to be washed away again, the silt of experience ever shifting now to this side, now to that. But it is fed by the river of spontaneous emotion, and across that no dam should be built.

If anyone asked me if the sum of pleasure I had derived from the best poetry was not far greater than that which poetry of an inferior quality had given me, I should not know what to reply. Poems of modest merit have often given me delight as intense as the best, nor have I felt the difference till I could once more compare the quality of the emotion created in me. I have felt neither faults nor failures till I could respond once more to the faultless.

The following criticism does not pretend to thoroughness. My remarks here are intended to be like those of a man who, walking up and down a friend's room and suddenly seeing on the table a book he is familiar with ("Oh! you have been reading Yeats "), begins at once to turn its pages.

If you read Yeats' poems in the order in which they were written, you will notice a marked change in their character. He began as a poet of the Celtic Twilight. I am not sure that that phrase was not invented to describe the quality in his poetry which first impressed the imaginations of his readers — the wistful, tender dreaminess of such poems as "I will arise and go now, and go to Innisfree." The ancient myths of Ireland, the mysteries of the Rosicrucians, poetic necromancy, these were his themes, and he clothed these themes so remote from actual life in ornate literary language. There is no doubt that some of the most beautiful things he has written belong to this period, but as time went on a change came over his manner. It was partly due, perhaps, to the influence of Synge, but also to some change in the tone of the poet's own mind. He remained the exquisite craftsman he had been, but a craftsman of a different kind. There is a short poem which expresses very well this new direction. It is called *A Coat*, and it runs thus:

> I made my song a coat
> Covered with embroideries
> Out of old Mythologies
> From heel to throat;
> But the fools caught it,
> Wore it in the world's eyes
> As though they'd wrought it.
> Song, let them take it,
> For there's more enterprise
> In walking naked.

We do not at once think of Mr. Yeats as a love poet when his name is mentioned, nor would it be at all a central description of him, yet it is true that his contribution to that exalted and multifarious kind of poetry has been rare and exquisite. Delicate, cold and grand, extreme yet truthful, his love poetry is (and how rarely this happens!) peculiarly his own. No one would describe him as passionate in the usual sense of the word, and his love poetry is singularly free from the harshness of desire; nor is he among those

> Impulsive men that look for happiness
> And sing when they have found it;

nor has he written on

> Pretty things that may
> Please a fantastic head.

Nor would it quite do to call him a Platonist, for he has sung too often that monstrous thing " returned but unrequited love." Let us compare his variation upon Ronsard's famous sonnet with the original:

> *Quand vous serez bien vieille, au soir, à la chandelle,*
> *Assise auprès du feu, dévidant et filant,*
> *Direz chantant mes vers, en vous esmerveillant:*
> *Ronsard me célébroit du temps que j'estois belle.*
> *Lors vous n'aurez servante oyant telle nouvelle,*
> *Desja sous le labeur à demy sommeillant,*
> *Qui au bruit de mon nom ne s'aille resveillant,*
> *Bénissant vostre nom de louange immortelle.*
> *Je seray sous la terre, et, fantosme sans os,*
> *Par les ombres myrteux je prendray mon repos:*
> *Vous serez au fouyer une vieille accroupie,*
> *Regrettant mon amour et vostre fier desdain.*
> *Vivez, si m'en croyez, n'attendez à demain:*
> *Cueillez dès aujourd'huy les roses de la vie.*

Mr. Yeats' version has less vigorous and masculine beauty; it is by no means so simple and central.

> When you are old and grey and full of sleep,
> And nodding by the fire, take down this book,
> And slowly read, and dream of the soft look

Your eyes had once, and of their shadows deep;
How many loved your moments of glad grace,
And loved your beauty with love false or true;
But one man loved the pilgrim soul in you,
And loved the sorrows of your changing face.
And bending down beside the glowing bars,
Murmur a little sadly, how love fled,
And paced upon the mountains overhead
And hid his face amid a crowd of stars.

There is no passionate threat or exhortation to
love in this, and a new idea has crept into it, pity
for old age and for the passing of woman's beauty.
The last two lines are significant. The poet is expressing an exaltation beyond physical love, but
springing from it, and it is precisely this which inspires Mr. Yeats' best love poetry. His love poetry
is very seldom a confession; and although there is
a visionary strain in it, that is not the strongest.
His love poetry is that of one who dominates passion
by another passion: the artist's desire to attain
perfect purity of form. All emotion is omitted
which might cross that purpose, even if the elements
left out might in themselves add force to the expression. Consequently there is, perhaps, more
pure poetry in Mr. Yeats' work at its very best than
in that of any other living poet. A poet's best is
always a small part of his work, yet it is proper to
judge him by it. And the peculiarity of Mr. Yeats'
best is that there is no alloy in it. It can be set
against poetry more magnificent than his own, the
finest in the world, without stirring the misgiving
that it is, so to speak, made out of inferior stuff;
though it has of course been outshone, it is not
outclassed.

Reflection in his love poetry is indirect; how
much, for instance, lies latent in this short dialogue
called *The Mask*. The woman speaks first:

" Put off that mask of burning gold
With emerald eyes."
" O no my dear, you make too bold
To find if hearts be wild and wise,
And yet not cold."

" I would but find what's there to find,
Love or deceit."
" It was the mask engaged your mind,
And after set your heart to beat,
Not what's behind."

" But lest you are my enemy,
I must enquire."
" O no, my dear, let all that be,
What matter, so there is but fire
In you, in me? "

Rossetti once called a sonnet " a moment's monument." Few moments, however exciting, are worth
so grandiose a commemoration. Mr. Yeats, when
he chooses a form, is careful to see that it is com-
mensurate with the emotion expressed. In their
slight way how excellent are these two little love
poems:

A DEEP-SWORN VOW

Others because you did not keep
That deep-sworn vow have been friends of mine;
Yet always when I look death in the face,
When I clamber to the heights of sleep,
Or when I grow excited with wine,
Suddenly I meet your face.

MEMORY

One had a lovely face,
And two or three had charm,
But charm and face were in vain
Because the mountain grass

Cannot but keep the form
Where the mountain hare has lain.

How surely, and yet with what delicate indirectness,
strong feeling is conveyed!

Let me quote one more poem:

THE DAWN

I would be ignorant as the dawn
That has looked down
On that old queen measuring a town
With the pin of a brooch,
Or on the withered men that saw
From their pedantic Babylon
The careless planets in their courses,
The stars fade out where the moon comes,
And took their tablets and did sums;
I would be ignorant as the dawn,
That merely stood, rocking the glittering coach
Above the cloudy shoulders of the horses;
I would be—for no knowledge is worth a straw—
Ignorant and wanton as the dawn.

Mouth this poem to yourself. How magnificent it
is! " From their pedantic Babylon. . . . And took
their tablets and did sums." . . . It is a perfect
expression of poetic arrogance, which is the mood
of the poem itself. Observe how the lines—

I would be ignorant as the dawn
That merely stood, rocking the glittering coach
Above the cloudy shoulders of the horses—

though they scorn direct description, by the magic
of words give us the sense of seeing, or rather allow
us to believe that we *see*; so perfectly do they convey the emotion we should experience *if* we saw.

That is the triumph of poetic diction, to make
us feel that we have been in visual, auditory, tactile
communication with objects; that we have grasped

a vision through our senses as well as through the mind, yet without direct appeal having been made either to our ears or eyes.

That merely stood, rocking the glittering coach.

Is it a coach we see or the dawn? We do not know, we do not care.

Above the cloudy shoulders of the horses.

The adjective " cloudy " is not an adjective of description applied to the horses in particular, but part of a whole in which we do not know whether it is the evocation of Apollo's chariot or of the dawn itself which contributes most to our emotion. Shakespeare often accomplishes this feat:

But look, the morn in russet mantle clad,
Walks o'er the dew of yon high eastern hill.

That, too, is not a picture; it is a sensation which forms itself at will into different pictures in different minds.

It is because Yeats so constantly achieves this miracle that his readers know him to be a true poet.

Suddenly I saw the cold and rook-delighting Heaven
That seemed as though ice burned and was but the more ice.

But it is not in separate lines alone they find it, but in whole poems, which, grave with thought, saturated with the influences of time and place and natural beauty, are nevertheless as intangible and complete as a sigh. Like nearly all poets, he is most a poet when it is feeling rather than meditation that directs the sequence of his imagery; but he has also excelled in that poetry in which a thought is the controlling impulse, and a poem thus becomes beautiful clothing for a thought.

T. S. ELIOT (1921)

WHEN two people are discussing modern poetry together, the name of T. S. Eliot is sure to crop up. If one of them is old-fashioned, and refuses to see merit in the young poets who attempt to do more than retail " the ancient divinations of the Muse," the other is sure to say sooner or later: " But what about Eliot? You may dislike *vers libre* (I admit it is easy to write it badly) and dislike attempts to manipulate modern experience in verse; still, what do you think of Eliot? You cannot dismiss him." And the other will reply: " Well . . . yes . . . Eliot . . . I grant you there seems to be something in him." I wish to try to find out here what that " something " is which recommends the poems of Mr. Eliot, if not to the taste, at least to the literary judgment of even those who think the young poets are, for the most part, on the wrong path.

Mr. Eliot's verse is the best expression, hitherto, of those contemporary tendencies and sensibilities which have elsewhere sought and failed to find satisfactory form. What distinguishes him first from other innovators in verse to-day is his knowledge, and his respect for literary tradition. His poetry is not, like much " modern " verse, an impulsive revolt, but rather, in so far as it is something new, a cautious deviation. He is a poet who constantly looks over his shoulder to see how far he has travelled, and he is always searching the path before him for the footprints of predecessors. He is a writer who is uneasy when he feels himself alone. A painful and constant effort to orientate himself, not only as a poet, but as a thinker, is a notable characteristic in one who is considered a leader of literary revolutionaries. His caution indeed sometimes amounts to pedantry; nor is this in him surprising; for pedantry, implying as it does postponement of vital issues, is a rest to sensitively conscientious minds.

Mr. Eliot, like Mr. Ezra Pound, is an American. This is not a very important fact about him, still it has its importance. When either of them publishes a book, they proclaim at the same time that they are scholars who have at least five languages at command, and considerable out-of-the-way erudition. The allusions in their poems are learned, oblique, and obscure; the mottoes they choose are polyglot, the names that occur to them as symbolic of this or that are known only to book-minded people. In short, they both share the American love of bric-a-brac. A half-forgotten name, an echo from a totally forgotten author, a mossy scrap of old philosophy, exercises on their imaginations the charm that the patina of time upon a warming-pan or piece of worm-eaten furniture does upon their more frivolous compatriots. Both poets are indirectly descended from the poet Browning, in whom the instinct of the collector was equally strong. Both share with Browning a passion for adapting the vivid colloquialism of contemporary speech to poetic purposes. It has not been grasped so far as I know by critics, that linguistically Browning stands in the same relation to Victorian poets as Wordsworth *thought* he did himself to the poets of the eighteenth century.

Collector of bric-a-brac, mystificator, mandarin, loving to exclude his readers as well as to touch them intimately, Mr. Eliot would be lost as a poet were it not for his cautious and very remarkable sincerity. A reader who seizes an obscure reference is flattered; it gives him a little thrill. But though this thrill may seal him one of the poet's admirers, it is not an aesthetic thrill. In the same way even the verbal obscurity of a poet may tell in his favour, once he has convinced us that his meaning is worth finding; in the effort to get at his sense we may actually get his phrases by heart, and the phrase which sticks always acquires merit in our eyes. I do not say that Mr. Eliot's reputation owes much to these causes, but that they have helped it in some quarters I do believe. Certainly he is a poet whom to admire at all fervently marks one down as among those who are not a prey to the obvious.

FitzGerald did not like Browning (partly perhaps because he knew Tennyson very well), and in one of his letters he throws out a phrase about "that old Jew's curiosity-shop." Now Browning's curiosity-shop is a huge, rambling place, cobwebby, crammed, Rembrandtesque; while Mr. Eliot's reminds one rather of those modern curio-shops in which a few choice objects, a white Chinese rhinoceros, a pair of Queen Anne candlesticks, an enamelled box, a Renaissance trinket or two, a small ebony idol, are set out at carefully calculated distances on a neat cloth in the window. One sees at a glance they are very expensive—no bargains here; but there is behind no vast limbo of armour, cabinets, costumes, death-masks, sword-sticks, elephants' tusks, dusty folios, gigantic cracked old mirrors, sedan chairs, wigs, spinets, and boxes that contain pell-mell watch-keys, miniatures, lockets, snuffers and tongue-scrapers. The man who keeps the shop is not a creature with a Rabelaisian gusto for acquisition, whose hand shakes with excitement as he holds up the candle, expatiating volubly; he is a sedate, slightly quizzical, aloof individual—a selector, rather than one of those collectors to whose maw the most indigestible treasures are delicious nutriment. Such is the difference between Browning's and Mr. Eliot's attitude towards the harvest of erudition.

I have compared them so far only to differentiate them; moreover, Mr. Eliot's subject always consists of the ingredients of the modern mind, and never, as Browning's often did, of the minds and souls of men and women who lived long ago. But it is instructive to compare them also at points in which they resemble each other, always remembering that the temperament of the elder poet is hot, responsive, ebullient and simple, while that of the younger is subtle, tender, disillusioned, complicated and cool. Both are possessed by the passion of curiosity to a greater degree than is common with poets; in both the analytical interest is extremely strong. Consequently Mr. Eliot, as well as Browning, loves to exploit that borderland between prose and poetry which yields as much delight to the intellect as to the emotions. Most of his work is done in that region; and the most obvious thing to say about it as a whole is that even when it is not the best poetry it is always good literature. Re-read *The Love-Song of J. Alfred Prufrock* or *Portrait of a Lady*: it will be obvious not only that he owes much to the diction and rhythm of Browning, but that he is doing the same thing as Browning for a more queasy, uneasy, diffident, complex generation.

" The latest Pole transmit the Preludes, through his hair and finger-tips "—is not that pure Browning? Moreover, Mr. Eliot's favourite form is a soliloquy of the spirit, or monologue. Many of his poems thus fall between the lyrical and the dramatic form; they are little mental monodramas, broken now and then after the manner of Browning by a line or two of dialogue, or by exclamations such as are common in Browning's poems (" Here comes my

92

husband from his whist "), or by asides to the reader. But these asides never have the argumentative, button-holing quality of Browning's. There is nothing in Mr. Eliot of the impassioned advocate. He is rather a scrupulous, cool analyst of extremely personal and elusive moods, and his method is to convey a transient shade of feeling, or a curious, and usually languid, drift of emotion, by means of the rapid evocation of vivid objects and scenes. He does not care whether or not there is a logical or even a usual association between the objects he presents to us one after the other. He is like a dumb man who tries to explain to us what he feels by holding up one object after another and showing it to us, not intending that we should infer that each in turn is the subject of his thoughts, but that we should feel a particular emotion appropriate to it. This makes his poems hard, even when they are not, as they often are, too obscure. The reader is always liable to dwell too long on the scenes or objects which he evokes so skilfully, instead of swiftly skimming off them, as it were, the emotion they suggest, and then passing on to the next. A poet who thinks in pictures and allusions, and expects us to understand his mood and thought by catching one after the other the gleams of light flashed off by his phrases, must often be obscure, because compact phrases (Mr. Eliot's are extraordinarily compact) are apt to scatter refracted gleams which point in different directions. Indeed, we are often expected to catch not one of these flashes but several at a time.

First, however, let me give an example of his method of thinking in pictures or symbols. Take *Gerontion*. The whole poem is a description at once of an old man's mind, and also of a mood characteristic of one to whom life seems largely a process of being stifled, slowly hemmed in and confused; to whom experience, truthfully apprehended, gives only tantalisingly rare excuses for the exercise of the lyrical faculty of joy within him. Mr. Eliot's poetic problem is the problem of the adjustment of his sense of beauty to these sorry facts. His weakness is that he seems rather to have felt the glory of life through literature, while all that contrasts with this glory has for him the exciting precision of direct apprehension. " The contemplation of the horrid or sordid by the artist," he says in one of his criticisms, " is the necessary and negative aspect of the impulse towards beauty." In him this impulse in the negative direction is far the stronger of the two.

> Here I am, an old man in a dry month
> Being read to by a boy, waiting for rain.
> I was neither at the hot gates
> Nor fought in the warm rain
> Nor knee deep in the salt marsh, heaving a cutlass,
> Bitten by flies, fought.
> My house is a decayed house
> And the jew squats on the window sill, the owner,
> Spawned in some estaminet of Antwerp,
> Blistered in Brussels, patched and peeled in
>   London.
> The goat coughs at night in the field overhead;
> Rocks, moss, stonecrop, iron, merds.
> The woman keeps the kitchen, makes tea,
> Sneezes at evening, poking the peevish gutter.
>
>   I an old man,
> A dull head among windy spaces.

Now, in the first verse of what proves later a dark intricate poem, the symbolism is obvious; yet it is an example of the characteristics which make Mr. Eliot obscure. When the old man says he has not fought in the salt marshes, etc., we infer that he

means that he has not tasted the violent romance of
life. We must not dwell too literally on the phrases
by which he builds up the impression of sinister
dilapidation and decay—" Blistered in Brussels,
patched and peeled in London," etc. In reading
Mr. Eliot an undue literalness must at all costs be
avoided.

> I that was near your heart was removed therefrom
> To lose beauty in terror, terror in inquisition.
> I have lost my passion: why should I want to keep
>   it
> Since what is kept must be adulterated?

These lines, which occur in the same poem, are
perhaps the most personal he has published. Mr.
Eliot has something of the self-protective pride, reserve and sensibility of the dandy—like Laforgue.
His impulse is not to express himself in poetry, but
to express some mood, some aspect of life which
needs expression. He sets about it coolly, like a
man making up a prescription, taking down now
this bottle, now that, from the shelf, adding an acid
from one and a glowing tincture from another. He
belongs to that class of poets whose interest is in
creating a work of art, not in expressing themselves;
and the fact that his subject-matter, on the other
hand, is psychological and intimate, makes the
result particularly piquant. But even the works of
the most detached poet, if he is not imitating old
poems, have an affinity to each other which has its
roots in temperament. The temperament, as in
Laforgue's work, which shows itself in Mr. Eliot's is
that of the ironic sentimentalist.

> But where is the penny world I bought
> To eat with Pipit behind the screen?

he asks, after concluding that he will not want
Pipit in Heaven.

Where are the eagles and the trumpets?

Buried beneath some snow-deep Alps.
Over buttered scones and crumpets
Weeping, weeping multitudes
Droop in a hundred A.B.C.'s.

The contrast between peeps into glory and the
sordidness of life is never far from his mind. It is in
literature that he himself has seen the eagles and
heard the trumpets—not in life.

His style has two other marked characteristics.
His phrases are frequently echoes, yet he is the reverse of an imitative poet. They are echoes tuned to
a new context which subtly changes them. He does
not steal phrases; he borrows them for their aroma.

Defunctive music under sea
    Passed seaward with the passing bell
Slowly: the God Hercules
    Had left him, that had loved him well.

The horses, under the axletree
    Beat up the dawn from Istria
With even feet. Her shuttered barge
    Burned on the water all the day.

Just as " weeping, weeping multitudes " in the other
poem quoted above, is an echo from Blake, so
" Defunctive music " comes from *The Phoenix and
the Turtle*, and " Her barge burned on the water "
and " the God Hercules had left him " of course,
from *Antony and Cleopatra*. But the point is
that the poet means to draw a subtle whiff of
Cleopatra and poetic passion across our minds, in
order that we may feel a peculiar emotion towards
the sordid little siren in the poem itself, just as he
also uses later a broken phrase or two from *The
Merchant of Venice* for the sake of reminding us of
Shakespeare's Jew, compared with the " Bleistein "

of the poem. His other characteristic is the poetic one of intensity; it is the exciting concision of his phrasing which appeals especially to his contemporaries:

> I should have been a pair of ragged claws
> Scuttling across the floors of silent seas.

Or again,

> . . . the smoke that rises from the pipes
> Of lonely men in shirt sleeves, leaning out of
>   windows.

He is master of the witty phrase too: "My smile falls heavily among the bric-a-brac."
He is the most interesting of "the new poets."

VERSE PLAYS

OUR conversation—it presently turned into a competition of suggestions—was about unsaleable books. Suppose for a wager you undertook to write a book which would have the smallest sale, what subject and title would you choose? It was agreed that a little book entitled *How to Ride a Tricycle* would not do badly from this point of view; but, in my opinion, a five-act tragedy in verse, entitled *The Venerable Bede*, would run it close.

It has always been a matter of astonishment to me that all poets, sooner or later, should write plays in verse. Sometimes, indeed, they will devote many years to this occupation. Why do they do it? A glance at the complete works of famous poets ought to show them that such works are bales booked for oblivion. Invariably, the volumes labelled " Plays " are those which remain unopened—though there is of course " The Cenci " in Shelley's works. But who reads *Otho the Great*? Surely very few of those who constantly read Keats' poems. Which of the many volumes of Browning are most seldom opened? His plays. Do those who wish to remind themselves how fine a poet Tennyson was take down *The Falcon* or *Becket*? You are perhaps a Wordsworthian, but have you read *The Borderers*? Are admirers of Swinburne often seen absorbed in *The Sisters* or *Bothwell*, though the latter does contain many magnificent passages? Among the faithful readers of Robert Bridges, how many ever glance at his *Nero* or *Achilles in Scyros*? How

many even know that he has written a play called
Palicio? No doubt there are distinguished and
lovely things in them, but we are daunted by the
prospect of having to hunt for them. They are
buried. Lamb has his million readers; his *John
Woodvil* only here and there a student. Do you
admire Matthew Arnold? What, then, do you think
of *Merope*? Not read it? I thought so. I have a
wide literary acquaintance, but I doubt if there is
one among them who has ever read Coleridge's
Osorio or his *Zapolya*. The only portion of Landor's
work which is never read is his dramatic work.
Which of the years of Byron's fiery life, without loss
to the profit, excitement and amusement of mankind, might have been spent in silence and sleep?
Surely the year which produced *Marino Faliero,
Sardanapalus* and *The Two Foscari*. Who, except
men whose profession it is to know such things, can
even tell you the author of the poetic plays, *Halidon
Hill* and *The Doom of Devorgoil*? Yet he is not an
obscure writer; his name is Walter Scott.

The evidence is conclusive. Yet of living
poets, how many either have spent, are spending,
or hope to spend their time, gifts and emotions, on
this thankless form? I am not urging poets to aim
at popularity; nothing so foolish. All I wish to do
is to ask the question: " Why choose as the re-
pository of your ideas and fine emotions a form for
which the great majority of literary people, and *all*
unliterary people, many of whom are, as we know,
capable of being moved by poetry, have an almost
invincible distaste? "

Of course, verse plays find some readers, but an
alarmingly large proportion of these are engaged
themselves in either writing or in meditating plays
in verse. The poet-dramatists certainly read each
other, but even they are not very enterprising in the
range of their dramatic reading. This is usually

confined to the works of their friends, with occasionally the play of a friend of a friend thrown in; one
by a friend of a friend of a friend is practically never
included. No doubt a poet-dramatist will often
spend a whole morning in writing to another poet-
dramatist about his play. And this is something to
the good—unless, as sometimes happens, he also
reviews it. Then the contrast between the warmth
of the letter and the guarded nature of the public
utterance has been known to lead to the next play
by each poet losing one reader respectively. Rather
a serious matter.

How familiar to me is this conversation:

POET-DRAMATIST: I have been reading P.'s
Tragedy of Hereward the Wake.

AFFABLE HAWK: Oh?

POET-DRAMATIST: I think it's about the finest
thing he's done.

AFFABLE HAWK: Really! Don't you think
his . . .

POET-DRAMATIST (*hurriedly*): At least, it has
got some magnificent things in it . . . I don't know
if it would be effective on the stage. Probably not.
Of course, he didn't write it for the stage. The stage
is hopeless.

AFFABLE HAWK (*meekly*): Yes.

POET-DRAMATIST: You haven't read it? Of
course, the *beginning* hangs fire, but the sixth scene
of the fourth act—or is it the second?—in the marsh,
you know—is magnificent. (*A pause.*) Someone
read bits of it to Mrs. Pat . . . I believe she said if
she had a theatre she would love to put it on . . .
No, I'm mixing things up—Miss—oh, what's her
name?—liked the part of Esmeralda. I don't know
if the Stage Society is going to do it. I don't say it
hasn't faults. It has *tremendous* faults; but I see
what he's after; it is *interesting.*

The " Affable Hawk," who after all has the gumption to know that P. is a real poet, mentally translates this into: The play has some lovely lines and phrases in it, and perhaps some passages which, if the characters had ever come to life, would be admirably expressive of passion; but it is absurdly ambitious, absolutely unactable and parchingly boring to read.

If by some rather fluky contingency—the chance, say, that Lord Beaverbrook happens himself to be at work on a play about St. Francis of Assisi, and therefore feels an unwonted sense of the importance of literature, and something almost approaching brotherhood towards P.—*The Tragedy of Hereward the Wake* does, after all, get staged, what follows? Abuse of the production. It is universally declared that no living actor or actress can speak verse. Although the hand of the clock may be at 4.30, and there are still two more acts to come, the cuts are said to have ruined the play. The actor or actress who put a little well-meant energy into his or her part is voted particularly execrable by the fastidious. The roving-space behind the dress-circle is full of poet-dramatists. I can see my colleague, Mr. Desmond MacCarthy, moving, an embarrassed phantom, among them. (His reputation as a critic, poor fellow, varies much; for he cannot be relied on to support any particular line of dramatic effort through thick and thin, and so is continually swopping enemies for friends and friends for enemies without acquiring a faithful bodyguard of readers. Still, it may be worth dropping a word or two or a comment into his sieve-like ears.) I see him nodding a brightly wan assent to praise and blame, and receiving with docility the injunction that he must not judge the play from the production, but *read it*. The Press next day is very stupid about it. That does not matter. What does matter is that the

101

poet-dramatist, having learnt something—but oh!
not nearly enough—begins another play. By the
time it is finished perhaps his lordship has been
advised to abandon his own, or has other plans for
saving souls, and P.'s work merely goes to increase
the size or number of those volumes which in the
collected edition of his works will bear the title
" Drama." His lyrics may live upon the lips of
men; his narrative or meditative verse may provide
a means of exalted communion with the world; but
into *those* volumes only the anthologist will dive,
bringing up perhaps some ringing speech of Quintus
Curtius before he jumps, or a four-line description of
an apple-tree beneath the window of Lady Jane
Grey. What waste! Shakespeare? Yes, I have
heard of Shakespeare; but in his day verse-drama
was a living form. If he were reborn to-day, are
you sure he would use it?

BECKFORD AND BECKFORDISM

I

THIS is the first complete edition of *Vathek*,[1] as Beckford planned it and in the language in which he wrote it. It was written in French in his twenty-second year. Beckford came of age in 1781. The celebrations at Fonthill were of an appropriate lavishness. One hundred guests sat down to breakfast and 300 dined at five; music, dancing, fireworks from Friday to Monday; then, to the enormous relief of the heir, he was left alone with a few intimates. Not only was this young man the richest commoner in England, but for the eighteenth century his wealth was fabulous. His mother was a Hamilton, a granddaughter of the sixth Earl of Abercorn. She felt that the education of such a child must be out of the ordinary, and my Lords Chatham and Camden agreed. So the boy was brought up by tutors. In the matter of languages and general culture he was very well educated indeed. He took music lessons from Mozart; he studied architecture under Sir William Chambers, who was then building Somerset House; and the Great ex-Commoner himself gave him hints in declamation. He was also fortunate in his principal bear-leader, the Rev. John Lettice. His mastery of French was remarkable, as *Vathek* proves, and he acquired no mean knowledge of the classics, of Arabic and Persian, and of painting and archæology. But such upbringing inevitably sequestered him

[1] *Vathek*. By Beckford. Edited by Guy Chapman. (Constable, two vols. 31s. 6d.)

103

from his own generation. It was as weak in teaching the art of getting on with others as it was strong in culture. The key to Beckford's career is that he possessed enough wealth to gratify an exorbitant imagination, and that his imagination was hungry.

Granted a temperament of exceptional suscepti-bility, it was inevitable that such a boy should develop into an eccentric. His eccentricity, how-ever, was much exaggerated by contemporaries. His love of magnificence and ostentation was equalled by his craving for privacy and intimate emotions; wealth enabled him to indulge both im-pulses. In early youth scandal connected his name with that of William Courtenay, his junior by several years, and afterwards Earl of Devon, and his inclination to withdraw into arrogant privacy was encouraged by offensive rumours.

The sensuous extravagance, too, of his imagina-tion (*Vathek* was in their hands) led gossips to infer that the mystery into which he retired concealed enormous orgies. As a matter of fact, he was a rather exceptionally temperate man, but his county neighbours were as completely unable to understand him as he them. When he encircled eight miles of his estate with a twelve-foot wall to keep out their hounds and huntsmen, resentment at such un-neighbourly behaviour transmuted itself into the suspicion that behind that wall things happened unfit to bear the scrutiny of decent eyes. And when he pulled down an already sufficiently exotic and gorgeous mansion to build a stranger and more monstrous Gothic pile, the Abbey of Fonthill, with a tower 300 feet high, upon which 500 men worked day and night, and to which, when complete, only a few unaccountable guests were admitted, it is easy to imagine how busy tongues would be about the life of its owner. Beckford in the popular imagina-tion was identified with his hero the Caliph Vathek, who " did not think that it was necessary to make a Hell of this world to enjoy Paradise in the next," and after unheard of excesses and indulgence in infatuate pride, was damned " to grief without end and remorse without mitigation."

This legend persisted. It even distorted the image of the aloof, crotchety, handsome old connoisseur who retired to Lansdowne Crescent in Bath, after losing nearly all his colossal fortune. But it has not been bad for Beckford's posthumous fame. He has become one of those authors whose work, remarkable in itself, has been rendered more interesting by the life of its author. *Vathek* is one of those books which appeal only to a limited number, but to them it appeals strongly. It mingles in an original manner the grotesque with the sublime, the frivolous with the tragic. It is marked by the lucidity and moral scepticism of the eighteenth century, and yet filled with that romantic grandiose melancholy which was to find more complete expression in the writings of Chateaubriand and Byron. It has had the honour of attracting the tenuous and fastidious genius of Mallarmé, who edited the French version (without the Episodes) in '76; and in the opinion of Richard Garnett, whose judgment was liberal and sound, *Vathek* is a story which, judged as a story, " might appear without disadvantage in the *Arabian Nights*, with Aladdin on its right hand and Ali Baba on its left." The episodes, or subsidiary stories, which in this edition are introduced for the first time (the best is unfinished), are admirable in a less original way. Though more emotional than the Oriental stories of Hamilton, whom he claimed as his ancestor, and better told than *Vathek* itself, they lack the phantasmagoric extravagance and lurid intensity of the main story.

Vathek had its origin in a hint from one of

Beckford's many tutors, the Rev. Samuel Henley, assistant-master at Harrow, who subsequently behaved very shabbily by printing his own translation of it without Beckford's leave, and without mentioning his name; but its inspiration rose out of one week of fantastic happiness to which Beckford's memory afterwards constantly returned. Never again did Beckford succeed so completely in creating a fragment of actual experience so completely in harmony with his imagination as that which he enjoyed soon after coming of age. Mr. Guy Chapman has discovered among the Hamilton papers (Beckford's daughter married the 10th Duke of Hamilton) a document in Beckford's handwriting recalling, fifty years later, that magical week which he spent with Louisa (Mrs. Beckford Peter), her brother George Pitt, the lovely Sophia Musters, and William Courtenay, who was on his holidays from Westminster School.

" Our *société* was extremely youthful and lovely to look upon, for not only Louisa, in all her gracefulness, but her intimate friend—the Sophia often mentioned in some of these letters—and perhaps the most beautiful woman in England, threw over it a fascinating charm. Throughout the arched halls and vast apartments we ranged in, prevailed a soft and tempered radiance—distributed with much skill under the direction of Loutherbourg—himself a mystagogue. The great mansion at Fonthill which I demolished to rear up a still more extraordinary edifice was admirably calculated for the celebration of the mysteries. The solid Egyptian hall looked as if hewn out of a living rock. . . . Through all these suites— through all these galleries—did we roam and wander—too often hand in hand. . . . Delightful, indeed, were these romantic wanderings—delight-

ful the straying about this little interior world of
exclusive happiness surrounded by lovely beings,
in all the freshness of their early bloom, so fitted
to enjoy it. Here nothing was dull or vapid—
here nothing resembled in the least the common
forms and usages, the ' *train-train*,' and routine of
fashionable existence—all was essence—the slightest approach to sameness was here untolerated—
monotony of every kind was banished. . . . The
delirium of delight into which our young and
fervid bosoms were cast by such a combination
of seductive influences may be conceived but too
easily. Even at this long sad distance from these
days and nights of exquisite refinements chilled
by age, still more by the coarse, unpoetic tenor
of the present disenchanting period—I still feel
warmed and irradiated by the recollections of that
strange, necromantic light which Loutherbourg
had thrown over what absolutely appeared a
realm of Fairy or, rather, perhaps, a Daemon
Temple deep beneath the earth set apart for tremendous mysteries—and yet how soft, how
genial was this quiet light. . . . It was, in short,
the realization of romance in its most extravagant
intensity. No wonder such scenery inspired the
descriptions of the Hall of Eblis. I composed
Vathek immediately upon my return to town
thoroughly imbued with all that passed at Fonthill during this voluptuous festival."

I have quoted this passage at length because it
serves the purpose of criticism better than criticism:
it initiates. After reading it one understands the
flavour and trend of Beckford's romanticism, and
measures the violence of his revolt against the commonplace, which his wealth enabled him to indulge,
and of his desire to realize romance in life " in
its most extravagant intensity." As time went by,

107

that desire dwindled into building houses which only
faintly resembled the architecture of his dreams;
planning gardens which, though they astonished,
were unworthy of the *Arabian Nights*; collecting
pictures and books, and travelling sumptuously.
He might rub his Aladdin's lamp, but Wyatt was
hardly a djinn; and, as far as his biography by Mr.
Lewis Melville informs us, he found no fresh peris of
any importance to inhabit his paradise. He married
an acquiescent wife, free, as he said, of " wifeish-
ism," a lady of distinguished birth, who bore him
two daughters and died young; when malicious
rumour dared to assert that hers was no natural
death.

With the passing years his luxurious yearning
for romance changed its character. Still obeying
the cry of his spirit, " anywhere, anywhere out of
the world," he found a Gothic rather than an
Oriental dwelling for his imagination. With the
approach of middle-age ancestor-worship set in.
He became absorbed in heraldry and pedigrees, and
in the architecture of the Middle Ages, thus contributing to the Gothic Revival. Of distinguished
descent on his mother's side, his pride attributed
noble if not royal antiquity also to the modest and
mercantile Beckfords. From being in his own eyes
a sort of Oriental Mage with a tremendously sensitive
heart, he diminished to an eighteenth-century aristocrat, full of scorn for his contemporaries, finding in
pride of birth (partly ill-founded) and superiority of
taste the grounds for distinguishing himself from the
rabble of mankind.

His magic wand of sugar-cane was no longer
potent to conjure up halls of splendour and cathedral
towers, but it was still mighty when he visited auction rooms and when he travelled. The necessity
to regard himself, and be regarded, as an exceptional
being swayed him to the last. His connoisseurship

was made at once more interesting and less reliable by the susceptibility of his imagination. Certainly, when the treasures of Fonthill were revealed at its sale, the contents proved disappointing to the judicious, and Hazlitt ran them down in a violent article. But Hazlitt, who was full of anti-aristocratic pride, and can hardly be counted among the judicious, did not even know that Beckford had removed the things he cared for most, and that the auctioneer had inserted others to obtain the cachet of Beckford's name. Beckford's library was perhaps the finest private library ever collected.

That, however, is a mere adjunct to his fame, which rests upon these Oriental Tales and upon his admirable books of travel. His place in the sky of literature has been compared to that of the star which is at once the star of evening and of morning; the influences of the setting eighteenth century and the dawning nineteenth met and mingled in his work. But it is above all thanks to his orchidaceous personality that he still attracts the more ardent of his admirers, who, perhaps, envy him too much to see him with detachment. He *did* make an heroic attempt to live in an actual Palace of Art— that palace which the cussedness of things somehow always turns into a toyshop.

II

Beckford and Beckfordism, by Mr. Sacheverell Sitwell, is an essay originally intended as an introduction to a proposed, and now postponed, edition of Beckford's works. It is written in a mazy, murmuring style which is as pleasantly audible to the listening ear as a stream, a gently-flowing, glinting stream which takes many bends and carries along with it much curious detail and information. " Beckford," says Mr. Sacheverell Sit-well, " is the most soothing subject for a nostalgic mind to contemplate, and we may feel certain that the more Baudelaire or Mallarmé knew of Beckford the more they would delight in his aloofness and in that great talent so rarely exercised."

This is illuminating evidence of the fascina-tion which Beckford continues to exercise over cer-tain natures in each generation—the " nostalgic minds ": that is to say, over those who are con-stantly home-sick for the days of a picturesque and privileged past, and at moments even repeat Poe's cry, " Anywhere, anywhere out of the world." Baudelaire in that curious and moving notebook, " *Mon Coeur Mis à Nu*," published after his death, reveals that he regarded Edgar Allan Poe as a sort of patron saint, and even turned to him in prayer; a fantastic impulse which is saved from being ludicrous by our sense of the tragedy of the poet's tormented predicament. Now, though it is highly improbable that Beckford is ever invoked in this manner by his admirers, there is no doubt that he is a patron and hero of some " nostalgic " and imagina-tive minds in each generation.

Imagine that you are a young man whose day-dreams readily turn in the direction of palaces and lonely splendours, the possession of treasures and a despotic dignity; imagine that you are wealthy enough, in some poor stinted way, to have sur-rounded yourself with objects of virtu, and have been so placed in life that you have observed with disgust the prosaic and philistine existence of con-temporaries who live in far greater splendour and lavishness than yourself; imagine, too, that you are by temperament a poet, painter, or musician, but one with greater powers of appreciation than execu-tion, and then, inevitably, Beckford will appear to you an extraordinarily sympathetic and interesting figure. He too loved the Palace of Art; and he is remembered, not only as an instructed collector of rare beautiful things or as the author of *Vathek*. But, when best remembered, he becomes the patron in spirit of the imaginative who are not content to live in the imagination.

This is " Beckfordism " in the deeper sense. The permanent interest of Beckford's career lies in its reflecting the failure, folly, and exhilaration of such foredoomed aspirations; of a *diminuendo* from a sinister mage, at the waving of whose wand a Gothic Abbey rose behind high secret walls, within which every sort of extravagant orgy was supposed to take place, into an aloof, rosy, old, aristocratical connoisseur, enjoying to the last a battle in the auction rooms, and living in considerable comfort at Bath. Beckford began with £80,000 a year, and ended with a capital of £80,000: a well-spent life.

Mr. Sacheverell Sitwell is far from being Beckfordized himself. Indeed, his dealing with Beckford's acquisitive instincts is at moments satirical. His essay is a study of imaginative impulse finding expression in architecture and literature; of Beckford as a symptom rather than as a man, and not so much a forerunner of a fashionable literary Orientalism as an enchanted curiosity-hunter ransacking an older world for objects of virtu and for distinctive social " notes," vestiges of a " golden past." Where for us, and where for Beckford, a golden past ended is the theme of an ingenious opening disquisition. For us Beckford himself is, of course, part of it, but does not its glow linger for us, Mr. Sacheverell Sitwell asks, till 1870? Is not that the last date up to which we are able to persuade ourselves that never were such men and women, such proud societies, such figures and such dash? For Beckford the dividing line behind which Fancy could magnify and arrange facts to please herself was the French Revolution.

Mr. Sitwell's essay contains a literary judgment well worth consideration: that Beckford is more remarkable as a traveller and observer than as a creator of fantasies. He draws attention to the merits and interest of Beckford's *Travels in Portugal and Spain*, and to the superb merits, in especial, of Beckford's account of his visits to the monasteries of Alcobaça and Batalha. He surmises that Portugal furnished him, as a young man, with many precedents for extravagance. And here Mr. Sitwell helps our imaginations by sketching himself the historical background to the places, scenes, and manners which Beckford describes, and stimulates us by supplying curious criss-cross references both to a remoter past and even to times amusingly near us now.

It is this skill in catching symptoms of the same phenomena, though separated in place and time, that entertains us in these pages, so that we link up in imagination to the traditions of the lavish Court of the Braganzas, founded upon the diamond mines of Brazil, the spectacle (noted by the author himself) of Don Carlos, the nephew of the originator of the first and himself the excuse of the second Carlist war, " a gigantic old gentleman, with full white beard and great black sombrero," stepping out of his Venetian palace into his gondola with attendant negroes, and finally the portly form " closely dressed with inevitable top-hat " and large button-hole, of the Marquis de Soveral, so familiar ten years ago in Piccadilly.

He points out that Beckford drew from those Portuguese abbeys and from Mafra, the palace-monastery of the Portuguese kings, with its gloomy portals and deserted halls, the ideas which his wealth enabled him to put into execution at Fonthill; also that it is a mistake to suppose that Font-hill was a work unique in its extravagance and spirit. " In several other places in England, out of the wide and sweeping park-lands, allowed in the taste of that day to roll nearly up to the house, towers and spires almost identical with those of Fonthill began to rise up above the oldest limes or elms. Belvoir, with its enormous terrace; Eastnor, with its skyscraping hall; and Ashridge, the most fanciful of all these, were now finished or remodelled." He surmises that Beckford must have lived at this period of his life under his " perilous tower " (by the by, it fell like an umbrella twice), knowing well that the " presumption and psychological daring of rich men were drawing towards their end."

The Gothic architecture, of which Beckford was a pioneer, spread all over Europe, and Mr. Sitwell draws our attention to Eisgrub, in Moravia, the property of Prince Liechtenstein, " with its English-Gothic castle, Oriental tower, Chinese pavilion, and its park of 100 square miles, containing lakes and forests, many villages, and two towns "; and to the half-Moorish, half-Gothic castle built in the Crimea by the English architect Blore for Prince Woronzoff.

Then there is the last and most grandiose of all examples of " Beckfordism," both in the psychological meaning given to that word by a restless analyst like myself and in Mr. Sitwell's archæological sense; those " most undisciplined monuments," as he calls them, of that impulse towards lonely self-centred splendour, the strange palaces of Ludwig II of Bavaria, Neu-Schwanstein and Hohen-schwangau. These are built high among the mountains and above the lakes that divide Bavaria from Switzerland. Pinnacled on crags, crammed and covered inside with symbols and scenes from Wagner's operas, Neu-Schwanstein is a mausoleum of that hopeless hope that dreams can become facts—

I

and remain beautiful. His third palace, the castle of Herrenchiemsee, is not architecturally an example of " Beckfordism "; it is a rival Versailles, built under the spell of the most ego-intoxicating music. Dilapidated, desolate now, it still raves in gilt and glass, in blue velvet and pink marble, of unreal splendours; but what it brought to its creator in happiness he might have got as well by sitting, like Hogarth's madman, naked upon straw and in a paper crown.

Now, through its empty rooms and galleries— empty from the beginning because designed for one alone—stolid tourists stray and stop, wondering whether everything is, after all, so wonderful. Perhaps those are most enviable who can feel a magnanimous pity for the ghost which haunts them, that of a handsome heavy man in the prime of life, with thick black hair and magnificent enthusiastic eyes, but, alas! also an ominous puffiness of jowl. At any rate, it is to him they owe Bayreuth.

What does mankind owe to these decidedly expensive Beckfordian dreamers? Something—something for the imagination, it seems to me, which the mountain peasants, who to the end were loyal to Ludwig, became aware of when, at the sound of bells on winter nights, they peeped from their hovel-windows, to see flash by the golden sledge of their mad king.

PROPHETS, PRIESTS, AND PURVEYORS

A FRIEND of mine once said, talking with me of
Art and artists, that all great writers could be
divided into three classes—Prophets, Priests, and
Purveyors. Tolstoy obviously belonged to the
prophet class. He was one of those writers who
value their art because it conveys, and only in so
far as it conveys, " a message." Among eminent
English writers to-day Bernard Shaw also belongs
to this class; his motive in writing is to impart
criticism upon life which he believes to be important
to society. The Priests are those who dedicate
themselves, not primarily to the service of mankind,
but to the service of Art. They are mostly poets;
Milton (though there was a strong dash of the prophet in him) is a high-priest among them, who from
boyhood trained for and strove after perfection.
Priests among prose writers are rarer. We may
include, perhaps, Sir Thomas Browne among them,
and Gibbon; but they are mostly products of
modern self-consciousness; such were Landor, Flaubert, Anatole France, Pater, Henry James.

To both the Prophets and the Priests of Art the
world owes many masterpieces, and far the larger
part, but not all, of its poetry. Yet it is among the
Purveyors, among writers who have regarded themselves, not as prophets revealing truth, nor as beings
dedicated to producing something perfect, but as
men supplying a need of the moment, that some of
the greatest names of all are found: Shakespeare,
Molière, Balzac, Dickens. Tolstoy's and Plato's
aggressive attitude of contempt towards so much

115

that is beautiful is disconcerting in them—not in
the common philistine, Heavens no! It is disconcerting, too, to find even a comparative indifference to the function of Art in authors who have so
excelled in the production of it. And yet it is in a
way also rather a comforting and satisfactory discovery.

In the case of the Prophets the matter is easily
explained. To criticize works of art on moral and
religious grounds is for them to pay Art the highest
compliment they know. If works of art were not
subject to criticism from that point of view they
would be, in their eyes, merely trivial inconsequent
manifestations. They are conscious of so many and
terrible maladjustments between man and the Universe that the temporary peace and satisfaction
obtainable from a little bit of experience as interpreted by an artist, seem to them a small matter,
unless it obviously also helps towards some fundamental adjustment; and if such satisfactions hinder
that, it is better they should cease: men cannot
" feed upon the shadow of perfection."

The Priestly type of writer, on the other hand,
feels that those moments of aesthetic contemplation
and satisfaction are themselves fragments of the
ideal life. They may be sporadic and help towards
nothing, but they are supremely worth while. It is
his business to transmit them, however irrelevant to
the rest of life they seem; and it is his point of honour as a votary of Art to see that whatever he writes,
however unimportant the content, conveys at least
a sense of something perfectly done, bringing contentment to the mind. It is natural that most of
the finest poets should have belonged to the class of
Priests, since in poetry perfection is essential.

The giant Purveyors are a different race. They
have neither the urgent desire to change the lives of
others which possesses the Prophets, nor the loyalty

to perfection characteristic of the Priests. They are not vexed and tortured by a new interpretation of life which must out of them, like the former; nor have they the clean-cut integrity and patience of the latter. They do not always write for money, though they are usually unabashed in getting as much as they can; and not for the reason which actuates the Priest of the Art of Letters—to pursue their art undisturbed, but to live more variously, like the fortunate among ordinary men. The giant Purveyors write for the joy of writing, and because to exercise their astounding powers is to double and redouble the intensity of their own experience. As a rule they love to hear the noise of their fame. The Prophets, when they turn critics, despise them for being content with current ideas, and for building with untested bricks; and often call the beauty of their work frivolous, empty display. The Priests are filled with despairing admiration for that royal and careless power which carries the work with a rush up to the triumphant heights to which they themselves slowly climb; never therefore achieving just that effect of effortless ease—perhaps one as miraculous, but not just that. At the same time they feel a profound regret and disapproval at the Purveyor's lack of respect for Art. How often he stuffs rubbish into his masterpieces! " Is there not sad stuff in Shakespeare, what, what? "

The characteristic of the Purveyors is that while the Prophets write for the World, the Priests for their most secret selves, they write for the public. It is absurd to set one writer who is great above or below another, because he belongs to one of these three classes and not another; or to wish that all were either Prophets or Priests or Purveyors. Each class produces masterpieces. But what about the little writers who also can be thus classified? the Minor Prophets who exhibit " the contortions of the sybil without her inspiration," who show the acridity of the censor of morals without his insight, and whose thunder is unaccompanied by lightning —the sort of writer of whom one says, " There *may* be something in him, but, oh dear! but, but, *but.*" Or the small dapper Priest, the neat little Abbé of letters, who sniffs at Tolstoy's *Resurrection* and exhibits his small enamelled snuff-box, expecting us to be happy for ever gazing upon *that*—he is riling too in a world bursting with splendours and misery— almost as exasperating as the robust Purveyor of no talent at all, who thinks he knows all about Art: that it is a straightforward job and a matter of keeping in touch with the times and sitting down regularly at a desk. But I see I am attributing pretension to each, which is not fair. In the first place there are many sizes in between the great and the small; and then even the small, when they take their own measure accurately, cease to be either ignominious or even negligible. Nevertheless, on the whole, the history of literature shows that it is safest to be a Priest.

THE ARTISTIC TEMPERAMENT

THERE is a saying that everybody has one book in him worth reading, which looks like an encouragement to memoirists and autobiographers. It is only an indirect way of saying that truth, however humble, is always interesting. It suppresses the fact that it is difficult to tell, cannot be told indeed, unless a writer has avoided telling lies to himself long before he ever thought of writing down his memories. With the best will in the world you can no more sit down and tell the truth than you can suddenly write a poem. Memoirists and autobiographers therefore are prudent to rely upon the general interest of their facts and avoid self-revelation. The candour which can make that worth attempting is either a gift of the gods or the reward of a life-time. Some achieve candour; others have candour thrust upon them— with what worthless results!—by their publishers; a few are born candid.

To achieve self-portraiture a man must be both self-complacent and detached. Unmitigated self-complacency has produced some amusingly transparent autobiographies, but those who have written best about themselves are, as a rule, men who have taken their work, or something in themselves, so seriously, and are so self-satisfied in consequence, that they have ceased to care a rap what impression they make in other respects.

In Mr. Gerhardi self-complacency and detachment are fortunately balanced, and his *Memoirs of a Polyglot* is consequently a real piece of self-revelation. It is also an entertaining book, full of wit, malice, vivid impressions of people who are talked about, pathos, literary criticism, and acute spontaneous comment upon character and life. It is the book of a man who has found his way through the world by the light of his own lamp.

Like Mr. George Moore he was born candid, and his subtlety springs from a kind of childishness. Like the author of *Ave atque Vale*, he values one thing in himself so highly that he can do without our respect on all other accounts. He makes an impression of social irresponsibility, and of loyalty to the artist in himself. No doubt you could bribe Mr. Gerhardi into writing a rotten book (indeed, he has had a shot at it), but nothing could make him think that book worth writing, and he would despise you more for thinking so or bribing him, than himself for writing it for money. Valuing himself for having preserved—without the smallest effort, by the by—his integrity of vision through life, he naturally takes a detached view of his general behaviour, and can record his faults, follies and failures with amusement or unblushing curiosity.

The literary artistic temperament is apt to strike others as a queer mixture of conceit and humility, heartlessness and sympathy. His fellow human-beings meet with a deeper response in such a man than in others, yet he can do without them. He appropriates their joys and lets their sufferings prey on his mind and devour his nerves, and yet he may feel no obligation towards them. If he dissects them as though they were nothing to him, he is also prepared to destroy his joy in his own most precious emotions for the sake of a little clearer knowledge of life. If he cannot spare others, at any rate he cannot spare himself. This is perhaps why mankind tolerate in their midst this uncomfortable creature, who will not join one of the conspiracies or loyalties which tend to make things easier: though he may take bribes, he is unbribable. Even if you frighten him for a time, the truth may any day come snivelling out of him. This is not moral courage, in which he may be lamentably deficient, but he is so made that he cannot be interested in life, or do his work, on any other terms. He may be the most selfish of men, but willy-nilly he is compelled to be selfless in his work. In this book you will find the reflection of this temperament.

It is no surprise to learn that Mr. Gerhardi, who was born of British parents in Russia, where he remained till the Revolution ruined his father, was considered the dunce of his family. Naturally, he would not take notice of the same things as other people; he could not help attending instead to what did not matter. And it was the same when he became a Derby recruit:

" In the army, however, individuality is not encouraged. ' Jeerady,' the drill sergeant would shout, ' You innerve me.' Or, with reference to my equivocal movements, the hesitant figure I cut on the parade ground, he called me ' that Chinese puzzle.' My inefficiency was not cunningly planned, but was pure lack of interest in my surroundings. As in childhood I was unable to devote attention to that which others considered important, but unconsciously stored away trifles which illustrated particular aspects of the general, so here also I would note individual aspects which illustrated the tragic comedy of mankind at war. So interested was I in the expression of the drill sergeant's face that he said: ' I've got a picture of meself in me pocket. I'll show it to ye afterwards.' In a thundering voice: ' And *now* will you look to yer front! ' "

It is clear that he has been dodging " the wrath

121

of the collective spirit " all his life; in the family, in the Army, in official employment, at Oxford, in society. And, under cover of a mild propitiatory helplessness, he has escaped uncaught: no surrender, but no painful consequences. He has saved himself by appearing " hopeless," thus preserving his faculties for their proper end. He has even escaped from the jaws of overwhelming patronage. A newspaper magnate took him up and carried him about in yachts and *trains de luxe*, told him he was a genius, attempted to make the fortune of " Futility," dumped him down like a bag, took him up again, and left him, so to speak, in the cloak-room. Has all this made any difference to him? No: receptive but unalterable, he has been equally interested in the rise of his hopes and the flatness of his disappointment, while remaining as impartially observant of his patron as though he had never been either kind or indifferent.

When he flew to India with the Maharanee of Cooch Behar, and the flying-boat smashed on the rocks and the water gushed in, his feeling was: " So this can happen to oneself also. Good God, how strange! " and he was inclined to remonstrate with Fate, " This airplane trip was only a lark, you know; you really can't think of killing me for that." And when someone shouted, " Ladies first! " it became clear to him that it was most important *he* should not perish.

" But sheer good manners kept me in check: I stood still and deferred to several passengers, through no love of my fellow-creatures, but dislike of panic and the fear of showing fear. . . . Nobody praised me; they were preoccupied with themselves. But I had merited my own approbation for behaving with composure. At the slightest encouragement I might have sacrificed my life,

122

for of such emotion heroes are made. Or my nerves might have betrayed me. I don't know. Clearly, it would have been touch and go. It is fitting, therefore, that the deeds of heroes be immortalized in the memory of men, for their own exaltation lasts but a moment at the price of a lifetime."

The last comment is characteristic. Perhaps now, even without reading the book, you may begin to have an inkling of the author's detachment, which sometimes expresses itself as sharp irony, sometimes as delicate sympathy. It enables him also to sum up the situation in India better than most people who have studied it. What struck Mr. Gerhardi was a feeling abroad in the country not unlike that which he had sensed in Russia on the eve of the revolution: " Inarticulate, unfocussed dissatisfaction with the present state of things, and no very workable alternative to take its place." He noticed the morbid feeling of inferiority in the educated Indians towards the ruling English race; the divided feelings of the princes in attempting to reconcile their hurt pride with their interests which are protected by British rule; and he observed that " the intellectual lucidity (though I should hesitate to call it vigour) of the Indians is insulted by the incurable hypocrisy of a certain English type (ridiculed by Bernard Shaw) who must needs identify his own interests with the supposed good of others."

" India's attitude towards England is like that of an adolescent daughter who can live neither with nor without her mother. And the position of the Viceroy is not unlike that of a mother of a young girl on board my homeward boat who complained to me that, whenever she corrected her daughter, the daughter did not answer back, but withdrew into herself or walked away—the attitude, I suppose, which old Tolstoy termed ' non-resistance to evil.' What, asked the conscientious mother, could she do with a daughter who met well-intentioned criticism with ' no co-operation ' tactics? ' Give her a good hiding,' advised a passenger. ' What! For no apparent cause! The whole ship looking on! Never! Besides, don't forget, she is now 17. And if I hurt her she would dislike me more than ever.' . . . One thing emerges clearly: There is nothing to be done—and we are the very men to do it. That is, to ' hang on ' to India, tentatively, complaisantly, almost absent-mindedly, while the Indians, a nation of barristers, exhaust themselves in garrulousness—hang on to India till the time comes when England will feel, without undue sentimental regret, that it is just as well, all things considered, to be rid of India. Since one day, ' in the fullness of time,' there will be neither gratitude nor material advantage to be got from staying there any longer. . . . But we who believe in the recuperative, adaptive, improvising genius of the British race view the future with—yes, equanimity. To face realities, to deaden the shock, to bridge precipices is, after all, the essence of statecraft."

This is surely good sense, as good as any that has been written about the Indian situation. It shows, too, the value of detachment in practical affairs. But I am anxious about the future effects of such detachment upon Mr. Gerhardi's creative power. A literary artist, besides being in a sense immune from experience, must also be at the mercy of it, so that he cannot tell afterwards whether he has owed more to the naive impulses which drove him to meet life, or to the aloofness which softly and inevitably disentangled him again. In Mr. Gerhardi artistic

detachment has been reinforced by cultural rootless-
ness. There is therefore a danger that he may not
care enough about anything except his work, to save
that from becoming thin and fantastic. It seems
to me rather ominous that he should already see in
Proust's attitude towards experience a reflection of
his own. Spontaneous response to life alone can
nourish creation: he is too young to put up the
Proustian shutters and regard the outside world as
existing only for the sake of its reflection in his
private *camera obscura*. The problem of every
" poet " (Mr. Gerhardi prefers this word in the
Greek sense to " artist ") is to strike a balance
between devotion to his art and love for their own
sakes of the things which feed it. Where that
balance lies, depends upon the nature of his talents.
If he loves life too much, he will never assimilate it
properly; if he lives for his art alone, he will have
next to nothing to write about.

LITERARY BOOMS

THE other day I was walking down the Strand with a friend. He has written many books and some are very good indeed. Even those which died a natural death in infancy contained pages which showed what he could do, and an individuality of phrase which makes those who love his best books like even his worst. In short, he has a solid reputation.

We passed a poster; his name was on it in large black letters. He made a grimace. " Angels and ministers of grace defend us! " he exclaimed, " I hope I am not going to have a Boom."

" What! don't you want to make money? " I said. " Why, only half an hour ago, while we were sitting over lunch, didn't you say that you wished that a little man, bent double under a sack of gold would come in and dump it at your feet? And there is," I said, pointing to the vendor of papers, who was holding the poster like an apron in front of him, " There is the little old man, and you won't look at him! "

" A Boom," he replied, " is fatal to a man like me. Only the greatest can survive a Boom. When Goethe wrote *The Sorrows of Werther* all Europe wept and went into ecstasies, and Napoleon took it with him on campaigns. Goethe survived his Boom, I admit. *Pickwick* had a prodigious Boom, and Dickens towered till he died. But they were men of the first magnitude, and notice this, they were young, very young, when it happened. Goethe was twenty-one; Dickens twenty-three. Byron was

a youth when *Childe Harold* made him a popular
idol—' O the ivy and myrtle of sweet two and
twenty!' The richest mines in them were un-
worked; they had immense surprises in them still,
and how rich those treasure were!

" But a Boom for a middle-aged man like me, who
has already expressed himself, is simply fatal. It
may mean a year or so of big cheques and gratifying
fuss, but afterwards heart-breaking, draggle-tailed
disappointment. ᵃIt means people will soon be sick
of me; that they will take up my newest book with
an unconscious prejudice against it. Everything
that can be said in praise of my work having been
said again and again, the intelligent will set to work
to interest the public in their own cleverness by
displaying my faults. I shall become a mark for
detraction. If I repeat myself (and we are all
musical boxes with a set of tunes), even with improvement, the public will still be told that my latest
book is not a patch on my early ones. And the
young (one minds this) will begin to hate the very
sight of my name. They will chuck me with joy
into the limbo of overrated reputations. No, thank
you, no Boom, please, for me. It wouldn't, in the
long run, even pay me in money. A hit to the
boundary is all very well, but a Boom is ' lost ball,'
six and out—I believe that's how the little boys
score in Battersea Park cricket."

I was impressed by the energy of his protest,
and when we parted I reflected on literary Booms.
How brief they were! That was the first thing that
struck me; next, that they were getting briefer and
briefer as the *machine à la gloire* became more re-
sonant and effective. I had already seen the reputations of many novelists and poets, splendid spreading
growths like Jonah's gourd, wither away. How
unnecessarily cruel it was! I remembered how
Stephen Phillips had once been hailed as the greatest

of modern poets. The elderly pundits, whom the
quality of his verse had reminded of the poetry
which had thrilled them in their youth (it is horribly
true, we only really understand the poetry we loved
before we were twenty-five), had acclaimed him.
I recalled, too, the silence which followed their
fanfaronnades upon Fame's trumpet, and the contempt of the young generation for poor Phillips. I
thought of X and Y and Z, of A and B. There was
a whole alphabet of them! I remembered how hard
it had been to get the generation which followed
that which adulated Tennyson to recognize even his
most indubitable beauties. I marked in myself a
tendency to curl my mind into a prickly ball like a
hedgehog when a work of some incessantly-belauded
contemporary came into my hands.

Then I thought of Martin Tupper. Byron said
he awoke one morning to find himself famous;
Martin Tupper awoke one morning to find himself a
laughing-stock. And what a Boom he had had! He
had sold many more thousands of the *Proverbial
Philosophy* than ever Byron sold of *Childe Harold*.
The Spectator, in reviewing it, said: " Martin Tupper
has won for himself the vacant throne waiting for
him amidst the immortals, and, after a long and
glorious term of popularity among those who know
when their hearts are touched, has been adopted by
the suffrage of mankind and the final decree of publishers into the same rank with Wordsworth, and
Tennyson, and Browning." The *Court Journal*
declared it to be " a book as full of sweetness as a
honeycomb, of gentleness as a woman's heart; in its
wisdom worthy of the disciple of Solomon, in its
genius the child of Milton."

" If men delight to read Tupper both in
England and America, why," asked *The Saturday
Review*, " should they not study him both in the
nineteenth and twentieth centuries? " *The Daily*

News wrote: " The imagination staggers in attempting to realize the number of copies of his works which have been published abroad . . . he may now disregard criticism."

Alas, in his later years, this must have been hard to do. Lord Melbourne had made him an F.R.S.; the Court had patronized him; Society had idolized him; the Press had eulogized him; wherever he went he had received what he calls himself " palatial welcomes." " I have experienced almost annually," he writes in his Autobiography, " the splendid hospitalities of the Mansion House and most of the City Companies." The Prince Consort invited him to Buckingham Palace. " Ladies," he tells us, " claimed him as an unseen friend." He was so nearly being made a peer that with prudent foresight he had coronets painted on his dinner service.

Suddenly the bubble of reputation burst. Obscurity descended on him like an extinguisher. Years afterwards, writing in 1886 (he lived to be nearly as old as Queen Victoria), he mentions as a curious fact that " it is taken for granted that the author of *Proverbial Philosophy* has been dead for generations." He tells us how he and his daughter were at a party where someone, on hearing her name, had asked her if she were descended from the famous Martin Tupper, and how, on her pointing to her father, the inquirer had started as though he had seen a ghost. He had seen a ghost. For years Tupper had been leading a posthumous existence, and a posthumous existence of the most unpleasant kind. He had become an emblem of the fatuous-sublime, of early-Victorian absurdity; he was referred to as unconsciously, cruelly, and cursorily as if he had been a character in a book. Poor old man! Boom! There is something ominous in the very word. Boom! Boom! Boom! Listen, it is the sound of a cannon shattering reputations!

LITERARY SNOBS

DEAR Literary Snobs (how many of my readers will, I wonder, consider themselves as personally addressed? I think about fifteen hundred ought to do so—and among those will be many whose literary enthusiasms are most intense), if it were not for you, writers would receive less thrilling encouragement. You have introduced into the life of letters something of the excitement of politics or the Stock Exchange; those violent vicissitudes of fortune which, if they depress, also exhilarate and console, though they embitter. If after years of moderate renown an excellent author suddenly finds himself extremely famous, it is chiefly your doing. Your enthusiastic imaginations are the workshops where haloes, pedestals, animated busts, and ample, though not perhaps immensely lavish, royalties are manufactured. Only, the initiative is never yours. The diffidence of your separate judgments is as obvious as the genuine fervour of your collective admiration—fickle indeed but ardent, when once a suitable recipient has been recommended. Like Wordsworth's cloud, you " move all together if you move at all." But though it may safely be said that you never choose the recipient yourselves, the glow, the glory of the sunburst which sometimes surrounds the cloaked figure of the lone literary traveller (usually toward the end of his journey) is nearly always your work. Sometimes indeed those rays are positively scorching, so that the traveller's reputation begins to wither even while it ripens; and the very critics who most rejoiced to see fame thus following the pointing of their fingers, turn churlish and uneasy at the sight of such—of so much —docility. If they do not start blowing cold themselves, they will at any rate probably begin to remind you that your beneficent rays might be a little more evenly distributed. This is one of your great faults, that you ever exalt your chosen one to a pitch past bearing by those who compare and remember. A critical reaction inevitably results, and with it, round again you veer. How depressing it is, how disturbing to the judgment,

> When among the world's loud gods
> Our god is noised and sung!

I do not blame you; you can't help it. Still, it is hard on the traveller who has discarded his cloak to bask in adulation, that while he is perhaps actually mopping a grateful brow and murmuring, " Too kind, too kind," the sun should suddenly go in, and a chill from a quickly-blackening east should strike him. Small wonder if he then grows suspicious and mutters darkly of conspiracies against him; no one can stand his reputation being blown out and burst like a paper bag, unless he knows you for the flibbertigibbets that you are.

Your enthusiasms, your salaams, your acrobatic prostrations, your chops and changes have made me feel very old, older than my years. It is not natural that I should have seen quite so many literary reputations flourish and fade: I am not approaching my ninetieth year. And yet it is not a series of hasty blunders, which you have had, as hastily, to retrieve. No; your enthusiasms (thanks to a few good guides) have been, though sometimes excessive, nearly always admirably directed. Tennyson, Browning, Carlyle, Swinburne, Meredith, Henry James, and now Thomas Hardy— these writers are worthy of admiration. You are

131

not to be blamed for falling in love with them one after the other. It is the glory of the amateur to be susceptible. If there has been sin in you, it has been rather the sin of Amnon, who, after having eaten of the cakes that Tamar made, and having loved her, threw her away. You remember the passage? It is one of the most impressively moral passages in the Old Testament (2 Samuel xiii): "Then Amnon hated her exceedingly; so that the hatred wherewith he hated her was greater than the love wherewith he had loved her. And Amnon said unto her, Arise, be gone."

You know how those words are ever on your lips; how you cannot admire Dickens without abusing Thackeray, nor Dostoievsky, without directing destructive sniffs at Flaubert or Turgenev. To hear you talk about Tennyson at the present moment, one would think he never wrote a better line than,

> The little town
> Had seldom seen a costlier funeral.

Meredith, whose heightened reflection of the beauty and courage of life seemed to you, not so long since, to eclipse older novelists, you made, before he died, the Grand Old Man of English Letters. But now—" Arise, be gone!" Ruskin and his magnificent prose?—" Arise, be gone!" Carlyle (a writer born to the use of words if there ever was one)? Swinburne, who once made your judgment reel with his winding, surging melodies? "Arise, be gone!" Those of you who are fascinated by recent attempts to compress poetry into hard, bleak conversational speech, invariably assert, I notice, that Milton was no poet—apparently without suspecting that this is a silly thing to say. Some of you have been arrested lately by the queer intensity of negroid art. Well, you have enlarged your aesthetic experience, and that is always worth doing. But you cannot express the satisfaction that a little dark pot-bellied squat-legged image gives you, without declaring that Phidias is a duffer. " Arise, be gone! "

You have met in life emotionally poor natures who have only a sufficient stock of amity for one friend at a time; who, in order to make a new friend, must drop an old one. They are never sane judges of human nature. You resemble them aesthetically. Your minds are like little buckets which must be emptied of enthusiasm before they can be filled again, and you spend your lives running backwards and forwards from the well to the sink.

I should like, however, to end this letter on a more friendly note. It is true that your literary judgments are not interesting, but you get a great deal of fun out of your rapid revulsions and temporary admirations—and fun is human. Moreover, if you are always ludicrously unfair, you are at any rate unstinting in praise while giving it, which is, in a way, amiable. Well, now, I will give you a few tips after your hearts. You know how exhilarating it is to be among the first to scramble into the train of the latest literary fashion, and how depressing it is to find you have only got in at the last moment and will have to bundle out at the next stop. You know your fatal love of making G.O.M.'s. You were right to glorify the delicate art of Henry James; but you didn't sit long in the Jacobean train, did you? You are right to admire Hardy; but get out before the smash comes, before the aesthetic *sauve qui peut* begins. The smash will come, because no author can sustain the reputation of being " the one and only." Critics will point out that, though Hardy has a profound tragic sense, he often tries to express it through crudest melodrama; that though he writes with lovely originality, his books are full of inept sentences, such as, " There

133

was not a point in the Milk-maid that was not deep rose-colour "; and that though he has written five or six perfect poems, most are only quaint lamenting tunes drawn from an old snoring 'cello. And then . . . well, you know how easily you are stampeded. Now, the Tennyson train and the Walter Pater train are, on the other hand, practically empty; get your corner seats now, and you will have a nice long run.

OPEN LETTER TO A YOUNG WRITER

DEAR W.X.Y.Z.—You ask me, " Ought I to make writing my profession? " It is a question which men of letters have been asked before, and they have sometimes (Stevenson, for example) replied at considerable length in print. I, too, shall write you " An Open Letter," for, if what I have to say is of use to you, it is as likely to be of use to others.

In youth the impulse to choose the career of letters has commonly two roots: reluctance to do anything else, and admiration for the works of others. If the impulse occurs later in life, it is more likely to spring from either consciousness of some degree of talent or from disappointment in other directions. This is not your case. You are in the hopeful, not the discouraged or the practical, period of life.

It is, perhaps, hardly necessary to point out that a distaste for other professions and an admiration however discriminating for masterpieces, are not guarantees that one possesses any talent oneself. I say " perhaps," because at your age it is not very easy to distinguish in oneself between a gift for writing and a gift for reading. Though obviously different occupations, they both employ the imagination and the intellect. You cannot yet have tried to write persistently enough to measure the chasm which divides them. Probably all you know for certain is that you enjoy your own rare mind and other people's work. When you have found you were turning with relief from composition to appre-

135

ciation, you have probably concluded that you were merely " not in the mood for writing." That may have been the right explanation, or it may have been a sign that you were born to enjoy and understand, but not to create. Only this is certain: that there is nothing more delightful than enjoying the masterpieces of literature with a dream at the back of one's mind that one is destined to produce one. It is so delightful to spend early manhood in this manner, that, means permitting, no honest hedonist can find it in his heart to deny to youth the mingled pleasures of unbounded admiration and vague ambition. But should you be in a position to go on smoking for years what Balzac calls " enchanted cigarettes," hazily sketching masterpieces in your head, remember that it is as well to start weaning yourself early from great expectations. If you do not, there is probably a bad period ahead of you, during which you will compare yourself most unfavourably with your friends—even too unfavourably; will despise yourself, and be compelled to have recourse to rest-cures, psycho-analysis or some other equally humiliating expedient—perhaps to joyless love-affairs, in the hope that they may flatter you into a more tolerable opinion of yourself.

Now the way to avoid going about in this miserable hang-dog fashion, somewhere between the ages, say, of twenty-five and thirty, is to start moderating at once the immensity of your secret ambitions; and the most effective way of doing that is to publish. Publish early, publish quickly. Let the cat out of the bag! As long as it is in the bag, you will hardly be able to keep yourself from caressing it as though it were the most magnificent of tigers; but when it is scampering about, that will be no longer possible. Your disappointment with yourself, your shame even, may be at moments acute; but it is quite on the cards that, at other moments, you will conclude it is not, after all, such a bad little cat. Self-love will direct your attention to its good points; while the knowledge that its patchy coat and weak back are subjects of general comment will prove, believe me, a more effective inducement to produce better offspring, than all your private aspirations. And when you suspect that probably none are more down on the creature than those you would fain please most, your friends, self-love may also help you towards a discovery important to your future career and to the development of your originality—the discovery that they are not the only people in the world who know what's what. The dread of disappointing friends is one of the miseries of youth to which justice has never been done. Every young man who is worth anything, and has been at all fortunate, finds himself surrounded by those whom he inevitably supposes to be the pick of the world; whomsoever he meets afterwards, he will never look upon their like again. The misery of disappointing them can amount almost to anguish. But it must be faced; and it will be as well, when that time comes, to remind yourself that *one* reason why you think your friends so wonderful is that it reflects great credit on yourself that they should be. " We few, we band of brothers "—you see the implication. And that reminds me—if you do take to writing, never write for a clique. " Whom, then, shall I write for? " you ask perhaps; " for myself—for posterity? " No; the one injunction is an encouragement to every sort of feeble egotism; the other to becoming imitative and priggish. One of the cleverest of living women, Vernon Lee, has put it best. Write, she says, for an imaginary reader who is an enormously improved reflection of yourself. Such a reader will see, even more clearly than those who dislike you, all your little affectations, propitiatory mannerisms,

137

bluff but hollow tricks of confidence and frankness; and you, knowing that they are seen, will endeavour to correct them. At the same time, though such a reader will count every one of your pilferings, your genuine originality and your subtlest intention will not escape him. He will hear the song even within the egg; that is very encouraging. He does not exist, of course, that reader, but you must write as though he did.

Most men of letters do not choose writing as a career; they slip into it. This is true of many of the best writers. They are at a loose end; they think they will try their hands at an essay or a story. They get £2 7s. 6d. and some praise for the one, or more praise and more money for the other, and say to themselves: " Hullo, here is a pleasant way of earning a living." Of course, it does not turn out as pleasant as all that; but they have slipped into being authors. Not a few men of genius have begun like that. Of course, there have been self-dedicated spirits among them; but if Milton trained himself from the beginning to be a great poet, Cervantes wrote *Don Quixote* as an after-thought, and *Robinson Crusoe* was the by-blow of an elderly journalist who, tired of embellishing facts for public consumption, thought that for a change he would write a tale that would carry conviction, like a news pamphlet.

Before you decide this important question (I mean, of course, important to yourself) I should examine what it is that attracts you to the life of letters. If it is ambition, what is the extent of that ambition? Suppose I were a prophet and could tell you: " Yes, you will achieve something. You will succeed in writing as well as old Smalltrash, or (I mean to test you hard) myself." Would you be very depressed? Would that rob the career of letters of nearly all its charm? The curious thing about literary aspirants is that they allow themselves a latitude of ambition which they would see was quite foolish in any other profession. However ambitious, a young man would know himself to be a fool if he said: " I am not going to the Bar unless I am going to be Lord Chief Justice or Lord Chancellor," or a young politician, if he said to himself: " I won't stand unless I am to become Prime Minister." Yet the chances are more in favour of a gifted but not extraordinary man rising to the greatest eminence in any other walk of life than literature. Circumstance may play into the hands of decent mediocrity; a man is not really remarkable, but there is no one else about, and so he becomes the general of his country's armies, or a party leader. While in literature true eminence (I don't mean of course notoriety and big sales, but the kind of eminence which you honour in writers) can only be won by genuine superiority and achievement. You cannot possibly tell if you are gifted in this exceptional way; therefore, if it is only the hope that you may be, which is drawing you towards writing, you ought to consider first very carefully the brighter aspects of other careers. But if—in so far as it is possible to enjoy hard work—you enjoy writing, and are content to aim at doing things well, then, if you don't marry and become a bread-winner, you may some day deserve a little bit of that homage you delight to pay.

It is an odd impulse, this common one, to address our fellow-men at large. That it is generally a worthy one I do not believe. On the whole, I rather suspect that the mainspring of the initial literary impulse is vanity. Of course, when you are committed to letters as a trade, you pursue them partly from the same motive as a man or woman pursues any other means of livelihood. But why are particular people so strongly attracted to it from the start? I refuse to believe that, in most cases, it is an urgent sense of the importance of what they have to say. They wish to assert themselves and impress others; and if they believe otherwise, they deceive themselves. Everyone who longs to write, or, having begun to write, has still a chance of earning a living in any other way, ought to be aware that the gratifications of authorship are exceedingly precarious and rather ignoble. Suppose you are engaged upon a piece of work for which you are un-fitted (this is a very common predicament), if you then realize that your motive is not the work itself, but only the prestige which you imagine may accrue to you from it, you will hardly be able to stand the grind. You will throw it up, especially if it is borne in on you at the same time that this prestige in the eyes of others, instead of being flawless, is freaked with contempt and humbug. For one admirer you win, you may be sure another reader is exclaiming as he reads, " The fool, the jackass." You will turn to something else, realizing that to mankind it does not matter a pin whether your book gets written or not, and to yourself only a little, provided you can find other safer, more modest ways of asserting your self-importance. Of course, if you have acquired a love of writing, or have been born with such an aptitude for it that it is a delight to exercise the faculty, you will persevere; and in that case your book may be worth reading.

MODERN FRENCH LITERATURE

I

M. BERNARD FAŸ'S *Panorama de la Littérature
Contemporaine* is a little book which I recommend to those who want to see contemporary
French literature in perspective. It is an essay
rather than a book, yet the subject is, of course, a
large one. I admire M. Faÿ's work, its lively con-
densation, its conclusive directness, its shrewdness;
although his point of view is not the same as mine.
He trusts tendencies which I distrust, tolerates
literary qualities which irritate me, while he considers
others commonplace which I hold to be important.
Obscurity seems to me a literary defect; mysticism
nearly always pretentious and insincere; Catholic-
ism a capitulation. When I add that the literature
of the private dream nearly always strikes me as
trivial and childish though it may achieve moments
of beauty, M. Faÿ will have no difficulty in placing
his present critic; and my readers will feel no surprise that I have not often been able to give a
cordial welcome to young post-war writers. Yet
M. Faÿ's book is one of the few books of criticism I
have read recently which I shall read again.

Although the above confession is as candid as I
can make it in a few words, I am not entirely easy in
my mind regarding my attitude towards the new
French literature. I know I do not understand the
young thoroughly enough to justify concluding
positively that they have discovered and are discovering nothing of much value. I only have a
strong " feeling " that they are wrong, and a similar

strong " feeling " in my seniors I found quite easy, in my own youth, to discount. M. Faÿ has helped me to understand *les jeunes,* who are first cousins to our young, by showing how they got where they are. He has sketched their pedigree.

French prose by tradition is an admirable instrument for making a man understood by his fellows; it is eminently social, utilitarian, and intellectual. Each generation of French writers has helped to make it more exact and logical. French prose, says M. Faÿ, formed itself while France was centralized; romantic prose was born out of the Revolution. " France," he adds, " accepted Romanticism because it gave the individual a new means *de jouir de soi-même* and of defending himself against the outside world. . . . Romanticism made discoveries of inestimable value. After two centuries of analytical and logical poetry it introduced into France religious poetry." The poet now became a magician, prophet, seer, in his own and others' eyes. Hugo at first was a grandiloquent, sonorous, social poet. He lacked spiritual culture and inner life, but later he developed a kind of mysticism of the word: " *Hugo prêcha l'unité du monde, dont le poète est le centre vibrant.*" Poetry was a mass of words; words were realities; God was a word:

Car le mot c'est le Verbe et le Verbe c'est Dieu.

The Parnassians, who followed, M. Faÿ passes over as unimportant. There was emptiness to fill and they did not fill it. It was left for Baudelaire to deepen the spiritual life which found expression in French poetry of the period, without, however, changing its forms and diction.

I am condensing what is already condensed in the book. That is inevitable, though it makes it more difficult to recognize M. Faÿ's brief definitions

of writers and tendencies. I want, however, to call
a halt here and draw attention to the fact that
though the romanticism of Hugo may be repulsive
and contemptible to the exponents of the modern
movement, and to M. Faÿ himself, the debt of *les
jeunes* to Hugo is here admitted. It is larger even,
in my opinion, than M. Faÿ thinks, and certainly
larger than they would like to admit. Their own
rhetoric is revolutionary and different from Hugo's,
but their extravagant wordiness combined with
prophetic arrogance, is precisely what strikes an
unsympathetic critic like myself. It does not make
any difference that their images may be brutal, their
diction slangy, and their rhythms broken; the
mysticism *du Verbe* is again in full swing. M. Faÿ's
book, coupled with my own observations, convinces
me that the chief mark of post-war literature in
France and England is its Romanticism; not *un
nouveau*, but now *un vieux moyen de jouir de soi-
même et de se défendre contre le dehors*; only it is
carried to-day to the point of severing nearly all
connection with what is without. But to continue.
We next come to Rimbaud. " He is responsible for what has happened since." (I quote M.
Faÿ, who thinks him even greater as a man than as
a poet, though it is well to remember that, from the
romantic point of view, this is no antithesis; since,
according to that point of view, because he was what
the Germans call a " God-struggler " he was also a
great poet.) It takes a short time to read all
Rimbaud has written, but a long time to understand
him. I believe I have read all, but I have understood very little. With my dark lantern and jemmy
I can sometimes break into an obscure poem in my
own language, but the difficulty of mastering, say,
a Gerard-Hopkins-cum-Eliot poet in a foreign
tongue is too much for me. All I can say is that in
reading Rimbaud I am often aware that I am in the

presence of genius, and if I have some Frenchman whom I respect to back me up, I am often willing to assert that such and such a poem is wonderful. After Robert Bridges included " *O Saisons, O Châteaux* " in his fastidious anthology, I was prepared to swear that that was a perfect lyric. I do not pretend, however, to have an opinion on Rimbaud's poetry worth imparting; but from the point of view of the subject we are now discussing, I can assent to several things in M. Faÿ's account of him. His poems " are not born of contact with things, and do not aim at reproducing them, as had all that had been imagined by poets up till then; they issue from a place where there are no things, but only desires." . . . " Rimbaud plants himself in the world within him, he speaks only of and for himself." . . . " He has smashed eloquence, discovered new kinds of images and comparisons, taught a new melody, and above all, animated all that with an immense ambition: the will to repulse the exterior world—the enemy which must be conquered." After a brief literary career of nihilistic and ferocious individualism he threw up writing, engaged in commerce in Africa, and died young. No one who has read what he left behind will be surprised to learn that before his death he was received into the Church of Rome. No man can for long assert successfully his private world against the world outside; that " immense ambition " leads either to madness or to submission to authority; and then the more thorough-going the authority the better for such self-centred victims of that fruitless effort. No one ever tried more desperately than Rimbaud to live alone, completely alone, in his own inner chaos; but of course he failed.

II

The next influence considered is that of Mallarmé, whose object was to purify poetry of all interests except the aesthetic one. This also implies withdrawal from the big, common world. Very little of the traditional store of great poetry is purely aesthetic in its appeal; just as very few of the world's famous pictures are independent of the interest of representation and of emotions not strictly aesthetic. Mallarmé wished to use words not primarily to convey a meaning but to convey a poetic mood. Words in his technique ceased to be symbols with a fixed meaning. Of course the meaning of words is modified enormously by context, still traditional writers have always used them as more or less stable entities, not as symbols with a value which might be different for each writer. Some of our own modern poets have followed Mallarmé in this respect. When Miss Edith Sitwell compares the dripping rain to " wooden stalactites," the image calls up in the mind an object like a tent peg. This is not her intention. The word " wooden " has a private meaning for her. She is using it to describe some quality of light she has noticed; just as in the same poem she speaks of the light " creaking " and " whining." Mallarmé taught that a poet had a right to a private language of his own; but language which is only understood by the person who uses it is, of course, not language at all.

M. Faÿ might well have quoted this sentence in which Mallarmé tells us his poetic aim: " *Instituer une relation entre les images, exacte, et que s'en détache un tiers aspect fusible et clair présenté à la divination.*" Mallarmé trusts that the flash of chance analogies, succeeding each other instantaneously, will somehow reveal the pervasive idea in his

poem. The reader may, or may not, discover what
that is after many readings. His melody is exquisite, and definitive; and rich, romantic phrases
gleam and vanish in his opalescent style. M. Paul
Valéry, whom M. Faÿ calls *la voix du silence*, and who
now stands so high in the estimation of his contemporaries, is Mallarmé's direct descendant. M. Faÿ
quotes from him two passages which show how
closely M. Paul Valéry is related to those two masters
who taught that poetry is the voice of an isolated
spirit talking to itself:

> *Et qui donc peut aimer autre chose*
> *Que soi-même?*

(The second is a sigh of regret):

> *J'ai perdu mon propre mystère;*
> *Une intelligence adultère*
> *Exerce un corps qu'elle a compris.*

Mon propre mystère—that is what the " new "
young writers, both in France and here, are endeavouring to express in literature. It is bound to
lead to obscurity, and in natures of the coarser sort
who are attracted by the free play the doctrine gives
to egotism, it often leads to pretentious triviality and
silly arrogance. Is it not, after all, as a matter of
creeping fact, possible to be interested in and to
love something besides oneself and one's own emotions?

True, the state of the world has not encouraged
lately in sensitive minds an expansive, generous
objectivity. In the course of his essay M. Faÿ
makes a remark about the effect of the War which
is worth thinking over. He is talking about the
gulf between the older generation and the younger.
Those whom it surprised in their maturity, he says,
regarded it instinctively as a catastrophe which

would pass and leave things as they were, but those whom it caught in their first youth felt it as a revelation of the nature of life itself; and between these two there can be no complete understanding. Thus, to me, who belong to the first category, what seems the undue exaggerated subjectivity of the new literature, and the feebleness of its exponents, may appear to my juniors as the best kind of reaction to the world and as a fruitful act of spiritual courage.

III

M. Faÿ's attitude towards the Symbolists is the same as his attitude towards the Parnassians. He regards them as barren. Why it should be an adverse criticism of any writer or group of writers that they have not had any direct influence upon the literature of the last five or ten years I do not understand. No literary decade, even the latest (view it with what partiality we may), can be regarded as the crowning flower towards which the centuries have been striving; and in this case the blossom is neither of a size nor richness to justify, even for a second, such a delusion. Heredia may well be a better poet than Rimbaud, though he has not influenced the young of to-day. But M. Faÿ is certainly right in his explanation why the Symbolist school has not appealed to our young contemporaries: " They (the Symbolists) did not see that their masters (Verlaine, Rimbaud, Mallarmé) really proposed a crusade, ' a spiritual chase.' They produced literature and tried to found groups, when what was necessary was to work upon oneself." In short, they were free from this mysticism of the inner life, which is, of course, the only thing which can in the long run give intense, exaggerated subjectivity, confidence against the whole world.

I have spoken hitherto as though M. Faÿ's book were concerned only with verse, but it deals with prose also. Naturally, he regards Renan and Taine as bad, dead influences: from *le démon de la certitude* can spring no good work. He chooses Zola as the great exponent of realism, because (one cannot help thinking) Zola is a poor artist. This suspicion is confirmed by a curious omission in a little book which claims to be a survey of French literature from 1870 onwards; M. Faÿ does not mention Flaubert and barely names Maupassant. He has an indulgent chapter on Bourget, who seceded from the Naturalists, and a highly eulogistic one on Maurice Barrès, in whom the *culte du moi* enlarges into a semi-religious nationalism. It struck me as characteristic of Barrès that in his beautiful book, *Un Voyage en Sparte*, he should conclude that the Parthenon was less beautiful than his own pet little church in Lorraine—very amiable of him, but slightly provincial. That is the worst of the *culte du moi*, however enlarged and refined: it leads to provincialism. And finally, as might be expected, M. Faÿ is very severe upon Anatole France. It is the fashion of the moment to decry him, but there is more in such attacks than that. If the literary qualities of Anatole France are remarkable, then much modern prose is back-water prose and out of the main current. I have no space in which to argue with M. Faÿ here, but there is just one more remark I wish to make. M. Faÿ points out that Anatole France attacked the Symbolists, yet was feted by them; vilified Zola, yet was asked to speak at his grave; sneered at the Republic, yet was honoured by republicans; undermined tradition and faith, yet was hailed by reactionaries as a powerful ally. Now, instead of taking these facts as indications that Anatole France is probably an important writer, M. Faÿ draws from them the opposite conclusion:

I do not follow him. That Anatole France has not influenced the prose of *les jeunes* seems to me neither here nor there. I cannot see, for that matter, that Homer has had much influence on their poetry either.

NOTES ON THE NOVEL

I

I READ few novels because few novelists write the kind of novels I care to read. If I were an Oriental Potentate, however, I should from time to time order a novel to be written on a theme of my own choosing; and since it would be a trouble to find the proper author, I would select, say, twelve of the best, and set them writing on yearly salaries, beginning with a very large sum, halved each successive year to make them hurry up. Perhaps one would succeed, perhaps all would fail. In that case, I would either select another twelve, or insist on the old competitors trying again, after careful study of each other's manuscripts and cribbing from them freely. Perhaps every third or fourth year of my reign would thus be marked by the issue of a good novel. To allay all jealousy I would then publish it under my own name.

II

Sometimes writers much younger than myself discuss with me their ambitions. It may happen that a dialogue like this results:

" What do you want most to do? "

" I want to write—to write novels."

" Do you care about making money? Do you want to be rich, to have fine houses and motor-cars, and that sort of thing? "

" Oh, no; I want to write."

" Do you ever feel a longing to show mankind that all those ends are vanity and dust and ashes? Have you ever felt that the most splendid thing in the world would be to be God's mouthpiece—or anything like that? Are you interested in Religion? "

" No; I am interested in the novel as an art form. I feel that as an art form it has never . . ."

" Did you ever think of standing for Parliament? What about politics? Have you ever tried to make speeches? Do you ever dream how splendid it would be to be eloquent? "

" No; I've never taken any interest in politics; I want to write."

" What about trying, not as a politician but in other ways, to improve civilization? "

" I know nothing about social questions and care less; I want to write."

" Do you want to climb socially, to visit fine houses and people? "

" No; thank Heaven, I am no snob! "

" When you see beautiful women, do you long to make love to them? "

" I have got through all that. My sex-life, thank goodness, is arranged; I am free now to devote myself to writing."

" Do you want to ride the winner of the Grand National? To climb Mount Everest? To become a prodigy of learning? To be exceedingly charming? To give parties? To have children? To retire from the world? To collect pictures, butterflies, remarkable friends? "

" *No!* I keep telling you—I want to *write novels.*"

" Then what will you write about? It looks to me as though your only subject will be the desire to write. The world, which it is your business to reflect in your novels, is made up of people running after things which seem to have no attraction for

you; how on earth, then, are you going to understand the passions, triumphs and disappointments
of these men and women? How are you going to
fill with the breath of life people in your novels who
do *not* want to write? "

III

I have often noticed that those most contemptuous of literary estimates which are based on
morality, cannot disentangle their own moral convictions from their literary judgments. One who
flushes with indignation on hearing the adjective
" foul " applied to *Ulysses*, will the next moment be
heard applying the same epithet to Kipling. His
objection is, of course, also moral. Nor do I blame
him. But it deprives him of the right to despise
(except, of course, as an indignant moralist) those
who condemn other books on moral grounds.

A moral interest is the backbone of all fiction
which deals with reality. The main interest of all
novels which offer us a picture of familiar life is and
must always be: Is this man or woman good or bad?
Did life treat them badly or well? I cannot distinguish between my response to beauty of character
in life and my response to it in literature.

Literary criticism must therefore be largely
a " criticism of life," and it is thus that the best
critics have understood their function. Goethe,
Coleridge, Sainte-Beuve, Baudelaire, Arnold—if you
examine what they have written with an eye to that,
you will be surprised to find how much of their
criticism is discourse upon human nature and upon
good and evil.

IV

When a novelist presents his characters and
their surroundings in such a way that his sense of

values is implicit in the account he gives of them, he is called "impersonal"; when he stops to point a moral, he is not. It is generally held that the "impersonal" method is alone artistic; and on the whole it is the better way. But aesthetically this is a matter of minor importance. The important thing is that an author's text should convey what he loves and hates in people, institutions, customs, surroundings, in such a way that the reader can make a shrewd guess why he does so. If he chooses to add a gloss as well, the reader may be grateful or he may not. Trollope for instance has a most friendly way of putting himself on his reader's level. This is pleasant because he is himself utterly honest, and his comments are entirely consistent with the spirit of the text. With Thackeray I do not always feel this to be so; sometimes the narrator, sometimes the commentator claims to be the wiser, Thackeray's asides being often intended to mitigate the pessimism of the picture.

V

I once compared the novel to a hold-all into which odds and ends of experience, observations and ideas could be crammed. As a description of the practice of modern novelists that comparison was only too just. This habit of regarding the novel as a sack in which to thrust psychological curios, vivid vignettes, generalizations too trivial to make an essay, speculations too shaky to make a treatise, is the prime source of much unsatisfactory serious fiction, which nevertheless is obviously the work of alert, sensitive minds. The value of separate details and ideas may add very little to the value of a novel; and if structure is abandoned in order to include as many of them as possible, they may even spoil it.

153

Fiction is digested experience, and a great novel is the reflection of a great man's sense of the world and of the people in it. It might seem from this to be a matter of indifference whether he conveys this discursively by trumpeting it through mouth-piece-characters and interpolated comment, or by presenting his sense of life pictorially and dramatically, making the characters and story the vehicle for expressing his profoundest reactions to experience. And in a sense it is indifferent. Only, if it is natural to a writer to express himself discursively, he had better think twenty times before using the novel as his vehicle. If discursive writing is his bent, then, whatever kind of writer he is, he is certainly not a novelist; and however beautiful, elegant, acute or timely his commentary, epigrams and discussions may be, the people in his book will go the way of all waxwork.

Carlyle could draw a portrait in a few sentences, even if it were only that of a man who had sat opposite him in a railway carriage or of someone he had read about, so that we now not only see that man (how tamely inexpressive seem engravings and photographs beside the text!), but are brought into touch with the very core of his being—at least, as it was conceived by Carlyle himself. In addition to this unrivalled gift for vivid static presentment, he had also the power of revealing the dramatic clash of temperaments and aims, the incongruity between a man and his casual surroundings, and above all, everywhere and at all times, the novelist's sense of the inexhaustible picturesqueness and significance of detail. Carlyle could make the cut of a man's coat or the colour of his shoe-heels seem profoundly symbolic. He could orchestrate the passions magnificently. Yet fiction was not his medium and he knew it.

He did as a young man try his hand at a novel

in order to pour out that spiritual turbulence and that criticism of things in general, which in a wild, free, unprojected, unparticularized, subjective torrent of reflection found release a few years later in *Sartor Resartus.* (" And when ye come to think o't, a varra *bad* book! " I have enjoyed that grim dinner-table snub he administered to latter-day adorers.) He stopped *Wotton Reinfred* in the middle of Chapter VI. I have read it; I am not astonished. It contains some enviable, not to say magnificent, sentences, but it is, though bursting with intellectual and emotional energy, dead, inert, worthless. It is a bad novel. Ruskin and Carlyle both possessed in a remarkable degree the whole cluster of talents which may help to make the novel glorious, except (and they both knew it) the one all-important, absolutely essential talent. They could not invent.

Carlyle wanted his facts, his situations, his characters given him; he wisely became an historian. Ruskin required a work of art, a castle, a cloud, a mountain, a tree, to release his imagination. Let him catch sight of a palace or a church, of a clear stream polluted with broken pots and tins, of a ragged little girl tripping to the public house in her elder brother's clumping boots, of a couple of boys spitting over a bridge into boats passing beneath, or of the municipality's new lamp-post on the sea-front (suppose he had heard rag-time proceeding from its green and golden band-stand!), then he could describe and discourse; then he could give us his sense of life and of values. And in discoursing he would show so vivid an apprehension of the honourable merchant, of the artist's intense experiences, of the noble gentleman, of the dignified mechanic, of the contented cottager, and also of the opposites of all these types, that it would seem he must have been able, had he chosen, to project them as living figures in a novel, expressing his vision of the world. But, like Carlyle, he could not invent.

Invention: that is the master quality of the novelist. A great novel, as I have said, is the reflection of a great man's experience of life; but it cannot be conveyed in the form of a novel unless the writer has this specific faculty of invention. He must be able to devise a constant flow of incidents which will exhibit his characters. This may seem a commonplace, but it is one usually overlooked by reviewers and entirely forgotten by many intelligent authors who take to novel-writing. Invention seems rather more common in novelists who make no pretence to be artists or critics of life; and the result is that their novels are often better than those of writers endowed with aesthetic sensibility, ideas and psychological insight. Reviewers and critics are seldom people with a talent for invention; on the other hand, they are usually appreciative of literary ability and cleverness. Consequently they overvalue those qualities to the prejudice of the storyteller's specific faculty, and they do not even discuss stories which exhibit that faculty, if those stories do not contain fine phrases or arresting comments. Until it becomes an accepted fact that a vivid enumeration of particularities is not the same as creating character, and that psychological analysis is only a means to making men and women seem real in a book, never an end in itself, writers who are not novelists will continue to write novels.

The prevailing defect of serious modern novels is a lack of interest in the normal, and an artificial heightening of moments in the lives which they describe, either because those moments illustrate some theory, or because they are queer. Nothing evaporates so quickly as the fascination of the queer, or dies sooner than a theory.

VI

How far is a writer justified, if he is a novelist, in putting real people into his books, and how far may a memoirist go in reporting the conversation of those who are dead? The victim who is thrown into the novelist's ink-pot often cannot protest without intensifying the very injury of which he, or she, may justly complain; while the dead, of course, cannot challenge the accuracy of reported conversations. Now the number of sufferers at the hands of both novelists and memoir-writers is on the increase. Novelists claim that they must get their material from life, and that love of " art " properly over-rides any scruples they might otherwise have felt about giving pain. There is a great deal in this plea. But it is based on a claim to be an " artist," which in the majority is of course an absurd impertinence. Those whose wares are as ephemeral as pastry are often the worst offenders, not only because they are incapable of inventing characters or circumstances, but because they could not themselves believe in the characters they portray unless they included details which they associate with their models. Of course such fortuitous details do not make a character in a book live for others, but they cheer the writer up with the illusion that his characters are alive. Otherwise, in nine cases out of ten, he (or she) would never have the heart to push through to the end of the rubbish. This is the explanation (malice apart) why peculiarities which act for others as labels of identification but are irrelevant to the story, are so often left dangling from characters in fiction. Unless the bungler states that his person-age has a wart under his left eye and two Chinese dragons on his dining-room mantelpiece, and was born, oddly enough, on Spion Kop in the Transvaal, he cannot himself believe in the reality of his own creation. But it is hard on the original to whom these statements apply, if in addition to finding his private life the theme of the " artist," such unmistakable clues to his identity are also given to the public. The novelist must take his themes from life either in a modified or unmodified form; but where it has been impossible for him to improve on fact he is bound in honour and decency to conceal, rather than emphasize, the sources of his story. That seems to me indisputable. If he finds he cannot give up the wart, the dragons or Spion Kop, without spoiling his book in his own eyes, it is an almost certain sign that it matters little whether it is spoilt or not. The question, however, is too delicate for the Law. We cannot have the Law stepping in, as in a case of breach of promise, and awarding damages for " wounded feelings." It is a matter to be dealt with by " social sanctions "; certain novelists should be marked down as too treacherous to be associated with. Society can protect itself. It shows, however, little disposition at present to do so.

VII

A would-be novelist once wrote asking me whether this was a good way of beginning a novel: " It was on a blusterous windy night in the early part of November, 1812, that three men were on the high road near to the little village of Grassford, in the south of Devonshire. The moon was nearly at the full. They appeared, all three of them, to have been indulging too freely in ale at the public-house about half a mile from the village. Two of them, however, were comparatively sober, and they supported between them the third, who could hardly use his legs. On coming to a bridge over one of those rushing streams so common in that country, they propped him against the parapet and paused to recover their breath. . . ." It is an old-fashioned way of beginning a story, but it is not at all a bad one. If you are writing a story full of incident, I recommend it. Only remember that such an opening rouses expectations, and you must not keep the reader waiting long. He expects something to happen to the three men, or, at any rate, that their condition, their presence on the moonlit high road together, will turn out to have a bearing on the main story. Note that the writer puts his readers at once in possession of two main facts—date and place. Note, too, that he does not begin by writing graphically. He describes nothing; neither surroundings, nor the lurching progress of the men along the road. He merely makes statements. In this he is wise. Keep your powers of description in reserve for the vital moments; they will tell with double effect if the narrative in which they are set is a little bleak. Don't stimulate the reader's optic nerve before you really want him to *see* something. Modern novelists constantly make this mistake. In their novels the station platform at which the heroine alights is often more vividly described, and actually remains more clearly in the reader's memory, than the important scenes in the story. Your powers of description may not enable you always to rise to your great moments, but that would not be so painfully obvious if your portrayal of a cat on a hearthrug on the preceding page were not a miracle of word-painting. You at least can abstain from describing the cat. The art of the novelist does not consist in descriptions so much as in making statements in the right order. If they are in the right order the reader will do a surprising amount of visualising for himself.

When David Copperfield is just settled into his rooms at Adelphi Terrace, and he is quivering with excitement and a sense of adventure, Dickens does not describe his view over the Thames. He merely tells us that David went to the window and looked out . . . and there, sure enough, was the river. How inferior in effect would a description have been of the big brown flood, of the strings of black barges and the tugs punching up against the tide, of the silhouettes of the grey buildings beyond! The central fact was David's excitement. " Here I am. . . . This is London! London!—There is the Thames! " The reader does not need to *see* anything. " And there, sure enough, was the river "—we want no more. After all, the most effective visions which the pen paints in the darkness of the mind are not really pictures. The art of description is to make the reader feel as though he had already *read* a description, and the best phrases of all are those which achieve this. I remember making a fool of myself once by instancing the meeting of Lise and her lover at night in *Une Nichée de Gentilshommes*, as an example of Turgenev's success in describing a moonlit garden. My interlocutor was doubtful about that being a particularly fine piece of description. On taking down the book all I found was " *Elle se détacha de la porte et entra dans le jardin.*" The simple statement which had preceded this sentence had evoked the scene for me without describing it. I knew that Lavresky was in the garden and that Lise's candle had just appeared first at one window, then at another, of the dark house; the moonlight, the stillness, the garden itself, were all in the words of the lovers.

VIII

" The Rev. William Neggit sat at his kneehole table facing the window, shielding his eyes from the light with one hand, while he wrote with the other.

Outside the window lay a lawn sprinkled with daisies, and beyond it was a small kitchen garden, with gooseberry bushes and currant bushes bordering an ash-path that divided it and ended abruptly at a privet hedge. The afternoon was mild and the sliding lid of his cucumber-frame was half open. Some distance off three poplars rose against the sky. Though the country was flat, it could not be said that the vicar enjoyed a view from his study window; nor was his 'little sanctum,' as he called it effusively when introducing one of his wife's visitors to its modest comforts, well lighted—in spite of its door-window. On his right, half in shadow, stood a bookcase, the contents of which, uninviting to the layman, were apparently, judging from their dusty condition, also little used by their owner. Here and there a brighter note was struck by the purple back of some comparatively new theological work, or the red binding of a novel by Temple Thurston or Miss Beatrice Harraden; but the dingy greys of the Cambridge New Testament Texts or the obfusc brown of *Cruden's Concordance* predominated. The brightest objects in the room were the yellow tiles of the fire-place, on which leek-coloured fleur-de-lis were shallowly embossed—the brightest, if the eye were not first caught by the painted rose-bunch on the lid of the coal-scuttle, the low brass rail of the fender, or the arms of St. Catherine's College, Cambridge, mounted on wood, which hung immediately above the china bell-pull to the right of the fire-place."

(Now, if I were reading this novel, here I should stop; but as I am writing it I must continue.)

" The silhouette of Mr. Neggit's back and round head against the light of the window gave the impression of a larger and possibly more formidable man than he revealed himself to be face to face. He was nearing fifty " (I must drive my pen along—

this is a psychological experiment) " nearing fifty;
his black hair showed very little grey as yet, though
the tonsure of middle age had begun to appear
beneath the long thin locks brushed back from his
forehead. His features expressed capacity for
energy overlaid by indolence; they had thickened
and coarsened with advancing years. His nose was
unremarkable; the nippers of his gold pince-nez
permanently pinched up a little ridge of flesh, and
his bushy eyebrows (he frowned frequently, even
when not angry) carried a suggestion of choler,
though his eyes, behind their quivering glasses, remained pathetic rather than fierce, even when he
wished to threaten or expostulate. The choir-boys
had soon discovered that there was nothing behind
the vicar's eye. He was carelessly shaved. His
mouth was large and lipless; a small speck of foam
was apt to appear at the corners of it for no apparent
reason. Though Mrs. (What is her name? Oh, yes,
Neggit)—though Mrs. Neggit hardly realized it, this
white speck was one of the serious trials of her
married life. There was no train of thought, no
subject of conversation, no social pleasure, no
domestic argument, which the sight of it did not
instantly interrupt. For the first year or so of their
marriage she had not only uttered the words,
' Willy, your handkerchief! ' whenever it appeared,
but invariably dabbed the corresponding corner of
her own mouth with her fourth finger, to show
where the handkerchief should be applied. In the
course of years the formula had reduced itself to
' Willy! ' and a rudimentary upward gesture of her
hand. The vicar always instantly obeyed; though,
if the domestic weather was not absolutely clear, he
often pretended to blow his nose at the same time.

"Mr. Neggit's usual manner was that of a man
who mistakenly believes that dignity and cheerful-
ness are the modes of feeling most becoming to him,

but in reality he was most attractive when he was
tired and discouraged, or had eaten too much.
Then, his natural slovenly kindliness was lit by
quaint gleams of humour—the rarest though the
least valued, in his own and everybody else's eyes,
of his modest gifts.

" At this moment the vicar's eyes were more
than usually pathetic, for he could not fix his mind
upon his sermon. He got up, took two heavy steps
which brought him to the mantelpiece, and after
blowing through three or four of the dusty crusted
pipes lying there, selected one and began meditatively
to stuff it. He was patting the side-pockets of his
short black coat for matches, when his eye
caught." . . . Time is up. Now I will explain the
experiment.

I had complained in an article that many
modern novelists ruined their work by over-loading
it with circumstantial detail, and Mr. Hugh Walpole
had protested in a letter. I had at the back of my
mind the feeling that nothing was easier than circumstantial description. Story-telling is hard, compression is difficult, to write beautifully is very hard;
but to fill in circumstantial detail, and to insist upon
the reader fixing his attention on that, was, I expected, as easy as shelling peas. I determined to
try, and I laid down the following conditions for
the experiment: (1) I would write for an hour; (2)
I would not describe any person or any place I was
conscious of having seen. I would then see how
many circumstantial details occurred to me in that
time. You have read the result and I have read it.
It seems to me as good as the average respectable
novel—the bit about Mr. and Mrs. Neggit (it may
be the vanity of authorship) even a little brighter
than usual—only I swear I had never thought of
Mr. Neggit before I sat down, or of his room. I

opened a dictionary; the word " Nefarious " caught my eye, and beneath it " Negate." I said to myself, " Negate, Noggate, Neggit "—and off I started. The glare from the window opposite the table where I had sat down to write gave my imagination a jog: I thought of a man at a writing-table, his coat would look black, seen from behind—a clergyman? The rest reeled out. It is fatally easy. Hundreds of plausible details occurred to me which I had not space to describe.

But try the experiment for yourself. Imagine a woman just finishing arranging her hair for a party. You will find (if your patience holds out) that you have no difficulty in filling three pages of print with describing the mirror, her dressing-table and what was on it, how she half-turned her head when the maid came in, and so forth; but try to describe in a sentence the placidly - critical expression of a pretty woman giving the last pat to her hair before slipping off her dressing-gown, and you will find it extremely hard. Still, if you succeed in finding that one sentence, the reader will know without your telling him that there are rings and cream-pots on the table. Now, modern novelists strike me as shirkers; they go the long, dull way about it, forfeiting the claim to be artists in their work. And the same applies to whole scenes just as much as to details. It may be as pointless as it is easy to mention that your heroine dressed for dinner. But it is understood now that a novel is good if, as Mr. Walpole said, in the course of " a long, slow narration of the lives of certain persons the reader obtains that real sense of living in other existences "; consequently we are flooded with circumstantial detail only too easy to provide.

IX

Arnold Bennett once asked, and answered in the negative, the interesting question, " Is the Novel Decaying? " He was not pessimistic, he said, about the future of the novel, for the reason that we never can recognize great novelists when they begin writing. " It is almost certain that the majority of the great names of 1950 are writing to-day without any general appreciation. . . . Few or none recognized the spring of greatness in the early Hardy or in the early Butler or in the early George Moore or in the early Meredith. And there is scarcely a permanently great name in the whole history of fiction who was not, when he first wrote, overshadowed in the popular and even in the semi-expert esteem by much inferior novelists." He added that the first books of great novelists had often been rather clumsy.

No doubt the preludings of famous novelists have sometimes been either weak or ignored; nevertheless, I do not think Bennett's generalization is as sound as it looks at first sight. The anonymous first novel *Waverley* became instantly famous, also *Tristram Shandy*, another first work of fiction; Kipling's *Plain Tales from the Hills* (1888) and *Soldiers Three* (1889) secured that prestige which Mr. Bennett defines as " first class "—*i.e.*, they " impressed both the discriminating few and the less discriminating many "; *The Pickwick Papers* began to be issued the year *Sketches by Boz* appeared in book form (1836), and Dickens was at once immensely famous; Tolstoi's first book, *Childhood*, followed by *Boyhood and Youth*, brought him at once to the forefront of Russian writers; *A Sportsman's Sketches*, a few years before, had done the same for Turgenev; *Madam Bovary*, another first novel, instantly made Flaubert a novelist of the first importance; *Boule de Suif* (a single short story) won complete and gratifying recognition for Maupassant; Defoe was well known as a political writer before he wrote his first novel, but *Robinson Crusoe* instantly leaped to success; Fielding had written a good number of unsuccessful plays, but his first novel, *Joseph Andrews*, almost equalled the furore roused by another first novel, *Pamela*, by an obscure printer. *The Ordeal of Richard Feverel* (1859) was practically Meredith's first novel (*The Shaving of Shagpat* hardly comes under that head), and *Richard Feverel* was made the subject of a leading article in the *Times*, then a notable honour for a novelist. It did not win for the author what Bennett called " first-class prestige," but it did impress " the discriminating few," and until Meredith became a Grand Old Man he never enjoyed any other prestige. George Eliot's *Scenes of Clerical Life* received instant recognition; and Charlotte Brontë had not long to wait. Of Hardy's first novel, *Desperate Remedies*, all that can be said is that it was not, and did not deserve to be, wholly unsuccessful; his second, *Under the Greenwood Tree*, a year later (1872), brought him recognition from writers like Leslie Stephen, and two years later, with *Far from the Madding Crowd*, he began to capture the wider public. Certainly, he did not write long in obscurity.

I protest against Samuel Butler (philosopher and essayist) being included as an instance of a novelist whose promise was invisible to his contemporaries. Butler was a literary Ishmaelite whose views and peculiar tone made no popular appeal. His first book, *Erewhon* (1872) (I do not count his letters to his family from New Zealand, published at their expense), was the only one he wrote which had any success at all during his lifetime, and that was immediate. It is the book of a critic, not of a creator. That left Arnold Bennett with the case of Mr. George Moore as the sole ground for his optimism, and personally, I challenge the claim he implicitly makes for him, that he enjoys even now that double prestige, both select and popular. With the exception of *Esther Waters*, Mr. Moore has never written anything which has come near impinging upon the mass of readers. If *Abélard and Héloïse* or *The Brook Kerith* survives, it will be with readers of such books as *Marius the Epicurean*.

X

The important thing in fiction is that whatever we are told in it should convince us, whether those facts are internal and invisible or external and observable.

What have I really felt? What are men and women really like? What do they really feel? Wherein lay the charm and significance of that object, that place, that person, the exquisiteness or the horror of that moment? What sort of stuff is our life made of? If I take a strip of it called a day, an hour, can it be called happy, miserable, good, bad—anything? How much of it was tolerated, mechanically! Yet if I put it under the microscope, how complicated its texture seems! What delicate things there were in a morning's boredom, what excruciating ones in my delight! And those emotions which snatch me out of myself? Love? What is really happening to me when I " love "? Am I myself when I " love "? Am I in pain, or is this happiness? When the pain stops, do I still " love "? In what way do I care for someone else? Have my feelings any relation to the object? Do I ever really see her or him, or only my own feelings? Is it all imagination and desire? Imagination? Why was I so disappointed at *that* moment? Why did that other event fill me with such secret and complete satisfaction? Why have I ceased to care for what seemed a moment ago so immensely desirable? Why does my soul ache for a past, spent perhaps in longing for the present? Are others possessed by the same hunger which catches at what must disappoint, clutches at what it would rather let go? Is the reality always a cheat? Is it only distance which lends enchantment to the view? What do I really care about? *What?* Art? God? Men? Myself?

In a work of literary art these questions, and a hundred more, find an answer, though they are not necessarily asked in it. But on the pertinacity with which the artist has put them to himself depend the clearness and depth of his vision; and if he can only reach down to what he has really felt himself, that vision will carry with it an imposing authority for others, possess also a kind of unity which, though philosophically it is no pledge of truth, is nevertheless capable of giving much greater satisfaction to the mind than piecemeal observation of separate truths ever can.

" Sincerity " is one of the vaguest words in the critic's vocabulary, or indeed in anyone's vocabulary. Any emotion which is felt at the moment, and for a moment, may be described as " sincere," and yet the writer who merely speaks out of shifting moods is just the sort of writer we call " insincere." In contrast to him there is the consistent writer who only expresses ideas to which he assents. Is he " sincere "? Only if his assent implies the collaboration of his temperament, of his whole being; that is absolutely necessary if he is to make literature out of his convictions and perceptions.

There is another curious thing about the psychology of authorship. Often a kind of fetch or double, not the real man, uses the pen; and if the man yields to his double he may gain enormously in facility. The penalty he pays is a loss of richness of thought. The fetch or double often writes more smoothly and eloquently; but what he writes, whether it be vehement or benign, becomes monotonous. The danger is that this second fluent expressive self is only discovered at a certain depth in a personality, so that the writer himself is beguiled into thinking he has at last found his true self. He has certainly reached one who can learn nothing new. Something of this kind happened to Swinburne, and perhaps to the old Carlyle—prophets and preachers are particularly liable to this corruption of " sincerity."

XI

The young-generation novel tends to be an elaborate inner monologue rather than an objective picture of life, and its character-drawing is apt to dissolve into tracing psychological processes which may be human, but are not distinctive. Consider, for a moment, the development of the novel from this point of view. It is rather interesting. First, we have the story in which action and events are the main sources of interest. Of course, since stories are about human beings, and human beings think and feel, we are told at intervals what the characters thought and felt; but their thoughts and feelings are conventionalized and always germane to events. Presently, especially in love romances, feelings become more and more minutely described, but they are still prompted by what happens, has happened, or is about to happen. Then comes a change. Tolstoy made special use of a fact about human nature so obviously true that it has become part of every ambitious novelist's stock-in-trade. That fact is the frequent irrelevance of our thoughts to our acts and circumstances. Artistically introduced, used as he used it, irrelevant thought gives us a vivid sense of living *in* a character, and therefore of actuality. Thus Anna Karenina, at the moment of flinging herself under the train, is reminded of diving; and her last thought is not of her lover or her own tragedy, but of being hampered by her bag. You will remind me, perhaps, that the opening of *Tristram Shandy* also deals with irrelevant associations. That is a different matter: Tolstoy introduces the irrelevant thought not to amuse, but to heighten our belief in the reality of the moment. It undoubtedly does so. And from then onwards novelists began to try to get closer and closer to the actual content of the mind at any given moment, and to surprise emotion at its source. All sorts of mechanical devices have been recently employed to that end: dots, isolated words, broken sentences. We have travelled very far from the eighteenth century or the Victorian convention of soliloquies in neat, essay-like periods. In the latest kind of novel—Virginia Woolf's for example—events have become merely interruptions in a long wool-gathering process, a process that is used chiefly to provide occasions for little prose poems, delightful in themselves; as when the tiny gathers in some green silk which Mrs. Dalloway is sewing on to her belt remind her of summer waves gathering and collapsing on the beach, waves described in a passage of delicate and rhythmical prose. And, last of all, the attempt (endless and hopeless in its very nature) to reproduce in print the very texture of consciousness leads Mr. James Joyce to record, in page after page, the jabberings— I cannot call them sub-*human*, but they are certainly sub-*rational*—of the idiot or flat-headed savage who talks unheard in the backward abyss of our minds, and sometimes screams audibly in delirium. Why should enterprising fiction (of course, it is only a small section of modern fiction which betrays these characteristics) be turning now towards this extreme subjectivity? One can think of many reasons: mistrust of sentiment, moral scepticism, lack of interest in the big common world—due to the fabric of society having had such an ugly shake, and things being in a bewildering mess, old types losing their definiteness, prestige values being questioned at every turn and no one quite knowing where he is, either on the social ladder or the moral ladder. Take away interest in recognizable types, the noble-man, the soldier, lawyer, squire, clerk, parson, doctor, shopkeeper, mechanic; take away gusto in expressing moral indignation and confident joy in melting over goodness; take away interest in getting on and in social prestige; and how much of the stock-in-trade of the older novelist goes with them! No wonder the younger writers are driven to putting moods under the microscope and to relying more and more upon dreams, fantasies, and queer momentary experiences for their subject-matter.

XII

In modern novels we are constantly asked to follow streams of thought. The moment we dig down to the semi-conscious thought-stream in human beings, individuality tends to disappear. It is in actions, gestures and habits of speech that character is revealed.

In recording the thoughts and emotions of his characters, a novelist must be consistent in stopping his analysis at the same point. This is a most important factor in achieving what is called " unity " in fiction. It is fatal to " unity " to be superficial in analysis on one page and dig deep on the next.

171

Psycho-analysis has had a bad effect on fiction because it offers easy short-cuts to psychological profundity. Smatterers in human nature, after a passage or two of scientific acuteness, calmly proceed to describe life on another level. But to write a love story in which the " complexes " of one lover are analysed, while the other's feelings are described in terms, say, of Turgenev or Henry James, is to commit an artistic howler of the worst description; nor can the mole-burrowings of Dostoievsky or the subtleties of Chekov be introduced into stories which afterwards proceed on a George Eliot level.

Any talented duffer can in certain directions nowadays be psychologically profound; what no duffer can do is to put a world together in which such profundities are appropriate. Not a few novelists recognize this, and show a tendency to shirk even as much of the general survey of life as anything resembling a story implies, confining themselves to what is going on in the head of one character during a given space of time. Such novels resemble mines rather than landscapes; depth and panorama can be combined in the novel, indeed perhaps that is its great point as a form, but it needs an artist to do it.

I am uneasy myself about the future of the novel. Of course, if the novel as a literary form continues to attract first-rate minds, the novel will continue to flourish; but are they going to devote themselves to fiction? Are they doing so now? I have a strong impression that alert, original men and women are getting heartily sick of the novel. I observe, too, that the alert among novelists are also becoming mistrustful of the novel as a form. Bennett discussing the novel's future mentioned Mrs. Woolf's *Jacob's Room*. " It is," he says, " packed and bursting with originality and it is exquisitely written, but it fails," he added, " in the essential—

it fails to create vivid characters." Now, the significant thing about that book was that it was an attempt to find a form which would offer the same opportunities as the novel for the suggestion of reality and comment upon life, *without* employing the novelist's usual methods. Instead of unrolling a story, or of presenting a character, Mrs. Woolf gave us, as it were, not the train itself, but the draught a train makes as it flies by—the mere bits of paper and dust that rise behind as it rushes past; not the man himself, but, so to speak, the impression of his body upon the bed where he has lain. Such a book was a symptom of discontent with the novel itself on the part of a writer who had written two good ones. Consider the immense vogue of Proust: I am convinced that one reason why Proust's book has been hailed with such delight is that it tastes different from fiction. It is, indeed, not a novel, but half a memoir, and half a notebook of a poet-psychologist.

XIII

H. G. Wells has treated the novel as a hold-all. It is improbable that we shall bury him in West-minster Abbey, improbable that posterity will find among his many works one so impressive that they will reproach us on that account. Yet if the effect of a writer on the ideas and feelings of those who read him (in his case they are millions) is a measure of his importance, then Mr. Wells must rank very high indeed, not only among his contemporaries, but in English literature. Wide influence, even when distinguished from popularity, is not of course the only, or even the chief, criterion of a writer's greatness; but that it is, in estimating the life-work of any literary man, a very important fact indeed, can only be denied by the exorbitantly aesthetic.

When it becomes necessary to find an epitaph for
H. G. Wells, *si monumentum requiris circumspice*
will serve; only the words must not be engraved
on stone, but spoken in the streets. The minds of
the passers-by to whom these words will refer may
themselves be unconscious of their truth, for when
ideas are once " in the air " they are attributed to
nobody in particular; but it is impossible to believe
that the historian will not hold that the books of Mr.
Wells contributed largely to the moral and intellectual make-up of the average early twentieth-century
man and woman. Mr. Wells would ask no better
tribute, for this has been his aim, and to it he has
subordinated the fruits of the richest endowment
bestowed upon any contemporary novelist—unflagging vitality and invention.

And there is another fact about him, so obvious
that it is seldom mentioned, which is bound to
secure for his work an historic position: he is the
first novelist in a scientific age whose imagination
has been saturated with scientific ideas. Whether
Science proves the greatest disappointment or the
greatest blessing to mankind, any future scholar or
philosopher, who looks back to find traces of its
early effects upon the imagination, will inevitably
discover H. G. Wells—an average man of his day in
many respects, but one with strangely delicate
aerial attachments and of extraordinary force.

We often discuss which books will survive, as
though the answer would settle their comparative
value. We are ready enough, especially when we
are among the few, to admire a neglected author, to
believe we belong ourselves to a purblind generation;
and though we marvel with complacency at the
blindness to merit of those who preceded us, yet we
continue to trust the verdicts of the future. It does
not occur to us that posterity also may be an ass. It
seems to me that we may anticipate the interest of

future generations with more safety than their taste, and, in my opinion, the fiction of H. G. Wells has the mark of being likely to excite their interest.

He has been obsessed by himself and by the problems of his own times, but the history of literature shows that this is frequently the way to interest other times. Yet a natural impetuosity, encouraged, I believe, by his theory of the artist's function (Literature, according to him, is the Soul of the World doing its thinking), has often prevented him from making any particular book nearly as good as he could have made it. So long as this thought or that emotion impinged somehow on someone, he has not cared about bringing its expression to perfection. Once, in a phrase apparently modest but concealing an enormous claim, he compared the writer to a telegraph-boy who delivers a message— by implication, from on high. He has in consequence been contemptuously impatient of the novelists who thought their work their own affair, and who held that form was important (Henry James and George Moore, for example). His method of constructing a book has often been to take the back out of the cart, tilt up the shafts, and let the contents fall with an exhilarating rumble. From time to time the richness and variety of the contents of the cart have been surprising; fragments in the heap are always of rare value, though buried in a rubble of what he has himself described as " provisional thinking." Ideas, and the communication of ideas, *ex hypothesi* bubbling up from the Soul of the Universe, have alone seemed important to him. As a novelist he has stuffed them in anywhere in his stories. He glories in being " a journalist," but he is quite aware, when others take him at his word, that if he chooses he is enough of an artist-craftsman to be supremely indifferent to the jibe.

His best fiction has always been written after

he has emptied his discussions into other and more fitting receptacles; having written *Anticipations* and *Mankind in the Making*, he gave us *Kipps*, and, having emptied the cart into *New Worlds for Old*, he wrote *Tono Bungay*. Although *The New Machiavelli* contains some admirable things and is a fine analysis of the later Victorian period, indeed almost as valuable as that wonderful contemporary account of middle-class England during the war, *Mr. Britling Sees it Through*, it belongs on the whole to that inferior portion of his fiction in which he projects himself into a story as a gifted young man with a mission—and, of course, with embarrassing though triumphant love affairs. It is when he portrays himself as an ordinary forgivable, muddled, impulsive hampered creature—a little man, not a dignified servant of Mankind—when he projects himself as Mr. Polly, Mr. Lewisham, Kipps, Mr. Britling, or Mr. Preemby, and allows the comic spirit and the crosslights of the grandeur and pettiness of human destiny to play round those figures—it is then that he comes nearest to being an artist; and it is then, though I hear him protest, that he has probably taught us most.

PSYCHO-ANALYSIS AND FICTION

Miss Sinclair's *The Life and Death of Harriett Frean* is an admirably concentrated novel. There are few superfluous words in it and, what is rarer in fiction, no superfluous episodes or descriptions. Some years ago this short life of an old maid would have been more than a notable novel; it would have been a literary event, followed by prolonged reverberations. But now the psychological theories (Infantilism, Suppression) which have stimulated the novelist's imagination, and given her confidence to concentrate upon certain aspects of her heroine, are too familiar for the book to have any such effect. Miss Sinclair has surveyed the ground of Harriett's life from the cradle to the grave with the help of the psycho-analyst's theodolite, triangle, compass. It is a narrow strip of country, so flat that the reader can descry from afar the heroine's tombstone at the end of it. There is, however, a gracious absence of impatience or of anything like contempt in the author's attitude towards her, which permits a certain wistfulness to veil at times that short, bleak vista.

Harriett Frean is the first of Miss Sinclair's novels I have read; it will not be the last. I infer from it that she belongs to the camp of novelists who side with children against parents, with impulse against convention. Well, it is no use pretending I am yet (Heaven knows what years will bring one to!) definitely upon the other side, but the way novelists and dramatists (especially dramatists) load the scales against the elderly and conventional has occasionally exasperated me into wanting to spring to the rescue. I should like to strike a blow upon the stage for nonconformist ministers, curates, country parsons, philanthropists, methodical papas, comfy mothers, retired colonels, churchwardens, elderly stockbrokers, old-fashioned noblemen, squires, schoolmasters, successful tradesmen and maiden aunts. I should make the maiden aunt in that play, if ever it gets written, a sympathetic character. Though she bristle with knitting-needles and complexes, wear cameo brooches and crochet shawls, prefer reading about Princess Mary's marriage to reading Dr. Marie Stopes on marriage, have a temper and a twitch, yet she shall be, like Betsy Trotwood, a life-enhancer. On the other hand, the young people round her will be drawn as selfish without being sensible, high-spirited without being funny, pert and not at all pointful, enterprising though not intelligent, careless and not brave.

"Yes, yes," I said to myself, closing the book after my brief, absorbed perusal of it, and taking off my spectacles and shaking out a large handkerchief to wipe them (for the story had made me feel old, broken and resigned), "Yes, even so; that *was* the life of Harriett Frean, and that is what it came to." It was all the fault, it seems, of her mild idealistic parents. They it was who taught her to renounce marriage with a man she loved in order to be loyal to her conscience; and then—well, by doing so she doomed herself to gradual desiccation. "The point of honour. . . . Ay di me!" And slowly rubbing my veiny hands twice up and down my pointed knees and speckled shins, I stared upon an ashy fire. "Repression . . . her parents' fault . . . I see what we are meant to think."

Harriett's parents loved each other with an all-trusting reverence, bending together over their only child with a ceaseless protective tenderness, so that she never knew anything more dreadful than a brief look of alarmed disappointment in her mother's face, or the shadow of concern upon her father's placid dignity. Once, a tiny child at a children's party, she allowed herself on the evidence of another child's crumby plate before her to be snatched without protest from an overcrowded tea-table laden with delicious things, before she herself had eaten anything. So young, so thoroughly, had Harriett learned it is not good to grab at what you want, or even what you ought to have. The maternal sunburst of affection which greeted her self-control was as thrillingly gratifying to her then, as years later the private joy she felt at her father's quiet approval, when she told him she had refused her friend's betrothed, who had so suddenly turned his passion towards herself. But time flies; father dies and

178

mother dies. Father's modest literary reputation
dies also, long, long before Harriett notices looks of
polite but blank bewilderment in those to whom
she introduces herself as " Hilton Frean's daughter."
Life is dull now and not without worries, but it has
its consolations: her memories, her knick-knacks,
her garden, and an occasional glance at that moral
bank-book she has always kept, in which, thanks to
one huge item on the credit side—that great renouncement—the balance is still satisfactory.

Here the novelist of a less psychological age
would have left her, gently rocking in her little bay
till the sun went down. Not so Miss Sinclair. The
worst is still to come. " She gave Robin to Priscilla "; yes, but Miss Sinclair queries that great
item in Harriett's moral bank-book, shows that
against it must be set the crinkum-crankums her
nature developed. Harriett discovered, too, that to
those she meant to benefit, the value of that great
renouncement was doubtful. Priscilla, feeling Robin
did not lover her, unconsciously developed, in order
to centre his attention upon herself, chronic, hysteri-
cal, invalidism; and Robin, his unselfishness at last
exhausted, and worn out with waiting on her, married her nurse and fretted himself into an exacting,
peevish valetudinarian. Thus life goes on, cruelly
teaching Harriett lessons long after she can profit
by them, when ("Ay di me!") all she can do is to
try to stop her ears and run, run and be gathered in
imagination to her mother's arms again. She dies
of cancer. It was of that disease her mother died,
and Harriett's fate thus borrows augustness in her
own eyes. Queer bubbles of suppressed sex-in-
stincts rise from memories of childhood—that
dangerous lane below the garden, that dirty blue
fence and the squatting man behind it; and in her
last conscious moments she greets from her hospital
bed old, eupeptic " Connie " of lewd conversation,

179

with a sigh of ecstatic recognition—" Mamma " she says, and dies. (Compare the end of Flaubert's *Un Cœur Simple*.)

" There is *Cranford*," I said dolefully to myself when I had finished. But it was so long since I had read *Cranford*, I could not tell how good it was; yet my spirits rose a little. I could not deny *Harriett Frean* was a convincing story—but its moral? Was, after all, Connie's life, if one subjected it to analysis, worth more? Certainly in Connie nothing was " suppressed "; but could I not (if the task were one which tempted me) make a very drab picture of " The Life and Death of Connie Hancock "? Connie was married and had children, true; but think of Connie's kraal, think of Connie's mind! Then I saw the Freans by firelight, reading the poets, glancing at each other over the loveliest lines. I saw Harriett's father waiting in the moonlight to fetch her from her uneventful little dances, tucking her arm in his and walking home, well content and proud of her, though to most young men she was not attractive; I saw them standing side by side when the financial crash came, shaken, but conscious they had not lost the best in life. Poor Connie, on the other hand, though nothing was suppressed in her, had had no good things like these. The fag-end of any life is apt to be dismal. It is not education which makes it so.

PROUST

I

IN *A la Recherche du Temps Perdu* Proust found himself; that work has the authority, irony, and security of one who has come to terms with himself and the world. It is, perhaps, the longest novel in the world—more than twice the length of *War and Peace*, *Clarissa*, or *Don Quixote*, and yet there is no reason why it should not be ten times as long as it is. Its opening sentence: " For a long time I used to go to bed early " and the unpacking of the implications in that statement might have occurred at any point in its development. Though the characters are old in the last volume and the transformations wrought in them by age are wonderfully described, there is nothing in the author's method to have prevented him, had he lived, from then harking back and describing scenes in which they were all rejuvenated again. They have been described at dates out of chronological order before this point is reached. Sometimes the narrator who records his impressions is a child again, long after his childhood has been left behind. Proust's method (in this it is entirely original) rests upon a postulate that the whole of every life, not only his own, but those of others, lies spread out before the observer; so that while he is contemplating a situation, say, in someone's middle-life, the artist can look before or after, and see both what had happened and what was about to happen to that person or to himself. Life in the Proustian world is like a book, and to any particular page in it we can turn whenever we choose. It is already written. We do, as a matter of fact, often read the present in the light of the past, and then our impressions are immensely enriched; the interest of any situation is intensified by remembering what has happened. But in life we do not know what is going to happen to anybody, and therefore we cannot enhance the interest of the moment by also contemplating it in the light of the future. But suppose the whole of life were really spread out before us like a picture, it might sometimes be a gain to consider incident F not in its place between E and G, as it actually occurred in time, but between say B and Z. There would often be a gain in irony, often in the understanding of character and of life itself, through such arbitrary juxtapositions. This is Proust's method; and this is what is meant by his constructing his story out of " blocks of time." Some critics leave the reader to suppose that the book is architecturally constructed; that it has a unity which can be grasped when one stands back from it. As a matter of fact, *A la Recherche du Temps Perdu* resembles anything rather than a building, a pattern, or a picture; it is more like a plant, and such a plant as the prickly-pear, in which leaves grow out of each other instead of from the branches attached to a stem. The novel is shapeless. If it be criticized from the point of view from which such novels as *Persuasion*, *Adolphe*, *Eugénie Grandet* appear as masterpieces, from the point of view of form, it is a thoroughly bad novel. Such unity as it possesses lies in the temperament of the author and the trend of his intention.

His intention is to explore to their farthest recesses the mysteries of sensibility *as a means of penetrating to an absolute knowledge of human beings.* Proust's aim is knowledge, not in the first place the creation of " form." That nevertheless a " work of art " would be the by-product of seeking knowledge in a certain spirit, was a belief which, after it had constantly eluded him, he did at last attain; and having once attained it, he never lost the faith that if only he stared hard enough at any object, examined carefully enough any fragment of experience, these things would deliver up their meaning, and that this truth would be equivalent to a work of art.

Resting as it does on personal intuition and sensibility, careless of form and proportion, and indifferent to external standards of value whether of common-sense or current morality, the work of Proust is entirely and extravagantly romantic.

II

His style is composed of immensely long sentences, crammed with parentheses (much longer than those of Henry James), and with comments upon comments. Few of these long sentences are " periods," for the statements they contain are not arranged so that the most important stand out; nor does the delayed conclusion usually add weight to the whole sentence, though sometimes it does. As a rule, however, a page of Proust is no more " composed " than the volume in which it occurs. Proust has been too much set upon catching every association as it wings its way across his mind and upon pinning it down *at once*, to care how much he is complicating the drift of his sentences.

He refuses to employ those orotund rhythms which are an aid to clarity, and which Henry James trusted to carry him through a press of metaphors and hints. Nor are Proust's digressions artful like Sterne's; they are purely explanatory. But " the stuff " contained in them is usually subtle, exact and exciting in a high degree, and the justification of this style, which would otherwise be abominable, is that it carries so much along with it. If Proust were a thin writer he would be a bad writer; and in places where he does run thin he is bad: but in these great drag-nets of words, all sorts of lovely and strange impressions are hauled into sight, such as the angler with his line could never have captured. Like the later style of Henry James, it is a thinking-aloud style, and that is always more difficult to follow than one addressed to an audience. And since it is easy to lose one's way in these long sentences, we should be grateful for Scott-Moncrieff's excellent translations—in one's own language it is easier to find again the noun or verb which one has forgotten. Frenchmen themselves often complain of being obliged to read a sentence of Proust's three or four times. But the reward of reading him attentively is great. Some French critics also assert that there is a fine rhythm in his prose; others defy them to read certain pages aloud so as to prove it. On this point very few foreigners are competent to take sides.

Will Proust's style lose him many readers in future? Probably. It is the style of a volatile but extraordinarily retentive mind. True, when once we become interested in the movement of his mind, we cease to want him to write otherwise than parenthetically and digressively, but following him is fatiguing. There are long descriptive passages of marked idiosyncratic beauty; his pages are crammed with marvellously exact notations of character and manners, accompanied by subtle analysis. We read on and on (I speak, I think, for the majority) groaning under the strain and yet constantly excited and charmed.

III

A la Recherche du Temps Perdu presents us with a new view both of the external world and of the

world within us.   Obviously this is the reason why
the book has made such a tremendous stir.   It has
influenced and stimulated to a rare degree.   In fact
no book has been written in the twentieth century
which has mattered more to aesthetic and intellectual readers.   In its focus of attention, in its scale of
values it is as " new " as, say, the work of Tolstoy
or Dostoievsky once was to Europe outside Russia.
The originality of its content therefore justifies the
originality of its form, for when content has no
precedent it is impossible to be sure that it could
have been presented otherwise.

When *Du Côté de chez Swann* first appeared
there was a silence.   But once appreciation began,
it increased at an unheard-of rate, being echoed and
re-echoed from quarters of the literary globe most
opposed to each other in taste and philosophy.   Mr.
Middleton Murry, in his contribution to *Hommage
à Marcel Proust*, remarked, in commenting on the
comparison of Proust to Saint-Simon (the resemblances are superficial), that it would be more
pointful in one respect to compare him to Rousseau:
the salient fact about him was that he had discovered
new forms of sensibility.   Rousseau made people in
the eighteenth century attend to emotions and
impressions they had felt, but ignored as unimportant, and thus discover new sources of interest,
satisfaction, and excitement.   Proust also revealed
to his contemporaries, and especially to his juniors
whose sense of proportion was not already fixed,
new ways of responding to experience.   They
suddenly became aware of interesting and subtle
complications in what had seemed flat, colourless
bits of life.   They not only found themselves in its
pages, but discovered that to read him was also to
learn how to intensify the pleasures of self-consciousness, and make the very pains involved in sensitive
self-consciousness sources of new interests.   Whether

185

Proust's interpretation of experience is better than others is a different question; but it is a new interpretation, and one which has already influenced profoundly other interpreters.

Personally, nothing would induce me to *live* in Proust's world, but I like to visit it. And just as one can sharpen one's perceptions of certain aspects of things by gazing attentively at the pictures of some modern artist, without necessarily holding that he saw more beauty than some familiar master who ignored those aspects, so can one learn to observe and feel like Proust without believing that he has interpreted life better than writers who ignore what was to him so important.

IV

Proust's world is that of the searching, inquisitive, intellectual artist. This will make his work survive, in spite of his delusion that mankind has unlimited time for reading. His book has no story; what happens next is comparatively unimportant. Nor is it his object, though the form of his book is more or less that of a memoir, to draw a picture of himself. He himself as a character, with an outline to be clearly apprehended, is perhaps the most indefinite and shadowy figure in it. His book is a voyage of discovery in his own soul. He is an artist who believes that the external world can only be seen clearly and understood by examining, with the most minute attention, the reflection of things in his own memory. He is a Lady of Shalott who never takes her eyes off a magic mirror. He has little communication with the external world except through this converse with reflected things and people. The peculiarity of Proust is that he does not check his own impressions by the common stock of experience which mankind has accumulated. He trusts only his own. It is a question of degree. Every novel is of course made out of memories and impressions, but Proust is the most extravagantly " subjective " of all novelists; only a few poets have exhibited an equal degree of subjectivity. " No one is wiser than everybody "— such a saying as that would be complete nonsense to Proust. A great part of an artist's life, of his labour, consists in working through the impressions and judgments which he has taken from others till he reaches what he alone has felt. To record and convey that is obviously his only chance of being original, and of contributing anything new to the common stock of experience. But it is equally obvious that such contributions may be worthlessly idiosyncratic. Most writers and artists have been aware of this horrible danger, and have striven to keep in touch with the reports of mankind as to the nature and importance of what they describe. It is possible to produce fine works of art by never going beyond the common experiences which are generally accepted and immediately recognized; perhaps the greatest are those in which the strictly personal element is small, and the most blessed artist the one who, apart from his shaping power of imagination, is born a man like ordinary men. Proust was far from being such an artist.

His sensitiveness is extraordinary, often morbid; but what prevents his sensations being either so idiosyncratic or so morbid as to be uninteresting, is that this peculiar sensitiveness is accompanied by an equal intensity of intellectual attention. The whole of this vast piece of fiction vibrates and quivers with a passionate intellectual curiosity, and this brings the author into touch with readers who would not otherwise share in his peculiar aesthetic and emotional experience. Another curious characteristic in him is the way in which his emotional re-

sponses are retarded. It is only afterwards, sometimes long afterwards, that he knows, or thinks he
knows, what has happened to him. Of most of us
it is certainly true that we only see clearly on looking
back; but in Proust's case seeing is much more a
matter of understanding than it is with normal
people. In the last volume of *Le Temps Retrouvé*,
Proust says, " *les vrais paradis sont les paradis
qu'on a perdus.*" That, or its equivalent, has been
said before, but the significance of it in his case is
peculiar. It is not remembered happiness that has
for him this thrilling beauty in retrospect, for that
is a phrase which implies that happiness has actually
once been experienced. With the exception of certain childish memories and a particular class of
experiences—purely aesthetic, musical and visual—
the narrator has never tasted the happiness which
he remembers. He is never conscious of the value
of anything till its absence or destruction informs
him that it was very precious to him: love is experienced poignantly only in the form of jealousy
or estrangement; death, when suddenly, perhaps
on some trivial occasion, such as undoing his boots
a year afterwards, some association brings home to
him overwhelmingly his loss. Hence the principal
and most pervasive defect in Proust's picture of life.

The description of the death of his grandmother
has been greatly admired; it is terrible and extraordinarily vivid. But compare it with, say, the death
of Levin's brother in *Anna Karenina*, and it will be
seen at once that something very important is
absent. Tolstoy's description of the death of a
beloved person is as completely observed, but it is
a description by one who felt the tragedy and
awfulness *at the time*. In Proust's death-bed scene
there is, by contrast, something disconcertingly un-
beautiful and cold—something one does not like.
And this defect is still more noticeable in the love-

affair of the narrator and Albertine which takes up such an enormous space in the book. When Albertine is with him he feels nothing. Even his physical relations with her are of the most trivial importance to him, and he does not care a straw about her as a human being. He has just informed her casually that they had better part, when her mention of a particular woman suggests to him that she may have had relations with her of a sinister nature; instantly he feels he cannot lose Albertine. This is one of the dramatic turns in the book, and it is a passage of which, I have heard, Proust himself was particularly proud. *La Prisonnière*, which follows, is chiefly composed of the agonies of jealousy and uncertainty which he suffers henceforward on Albertine's account. The greater part of that volume contains a minute account of sufferings similar to those attributed to Swann in *Du Côté de chez Swann*, where jealousy, if not " done " better, is at least described more briefly. Albertine herself brings him no happiness, but when she is asleep by his side there is a halcyon lull in his torture. (The passage which describes her asleep and his feelings at that moment is justly famous.) But how can we care greatly, or be interested for so long together, in the sufferings of a man who has lost what, when he possessed it, was of no value to him? Wordsworth's sonnet:

Surprised by joy—impatient as the Wind
I turned to share the transport—Oh! with whom
But thee, deep buried in the silent tomb?

is moving because we believe he had shared transports with her who was dead. Proust shared his transports with nobody; we cannot therefore be deeply moved by his bereavements.

189

V

There are very few novels which deal directly
with the inner experience of an artist, although
novels in which one of the characters is a writer,
painter, musician or poet are exceedingly common.
The artist, especially in relation to his love affairs,
seen from outside, is one of the commonest types in
fiction. Yet to form an idea of what it *feels* like to
be an artist and of the relation of a day's experience
to the creative faculty, we have usually to go to the
autobiographies, diaries, and letters of artists, and
these are usually scrappy. For instance, we can
learn much more of what it means to be ridden by
the twin demons of observation and imagination
from reading Henry James's *A Small Boy and Others*
than from reading his *Roderick Hudson*. One
characteristic which makes *A la Recherche du Temps
Perdu* a permanently interesting book is that it is an
extraordinarily complete account of the life of an
intellectual artist; of his unceasing efforts to comprehend experience and discover what it is that
moves him most profoundly. It is the life-story of
a man whose business in life is to define impressions,
whether these are visual or emotional, and this
makes it a thrilling, stimulating, and supporting
book to those who feel stirring in them the same
impulse to understand and define. We all have a
something of the artist in us, and therefore Proust
appeals to those also who have no talent for expression or only an inadequate one. Even when the
object which Proust succeeds in revealing seems
unimportant to the reader, Proust's pursuit of any
particular gleam of beauty, or hint about human
nature, is in every case an object-lesson how to make
the most of those moments when we are contemplative artists ourselves. This, to my mind, is the

most important aspect of his work; more important than his own picture of life.

With that picture of life I have myself many faults to find. There are enormous gaps in it. It has often the pettiness of the man who has been debarred from all action, of one whose sensitiveness is so acute that his responses are abnormally retarded, so that no painful impression impinges on him directly but sinks at once into his subconsciousness, from which he has to fish it out long afterwards. His own temperament made him exaggerate the importance of certain phenomena, homosexuality for instance; although, in his introduction to *Sodome et Gomorrhe*, he notes that those who are born with this propensity tend either to regard themselves as solitaries, or else to conclude too readily that others, if they dared admit it, are really like themselves. Such perverts see cryptic perverts everywhere. His own picture of society suffers from this distortion. His interest in this subject is not so entirely detached and artistic as his interest in other aspects of life. He allows it to sprawl over his book; and the reader, who keeps his head, can often catch Proust falsifying probabilities in this direction. Yet it is natural, apart from his bias, that this subject should have had a peculiar fascination for him: he is always searching for the particular thing that makes every human being different from every other, especially when it is implied in what they do rather than openly expressed. Such propensities as these are, of course, typical of what excites him most as an observer. His skill as a novelist is never more clearly shown than when the narrator at last grasps the key to M. de Charlus's erratic behaviour, so puzzling before. Suddenly, all Charlus's inconsistencies become coherent; he is understood.

VI

Was Proust a snob? This is a minor point, but not an unimportant one. It does not matter if a writer is a snob in private, but it does matter if that weakness distorts his picture of life. People who deny that there are differences between an aristocrat and a well-behaved member of the professional classes, and that it is the mark of a snob to suppose that there are, must necessarily think Proust an outrageous snob, for he spends much ingenuity in defining such differences. They interest him enormously. I think, however, we get nearer the truth in saying that *A la Recherche du Temps Perdu*, though it is the most complete manual for snobs ever written, could never have been written by a snob. The author has, of course, experienced snobbish emotions himself, or he could not detect them so acutely in cryptic snobs (Legrandin, for instance); but he has seen all round his own emotions, with the consequence that he is quite as ready to see vulgarity in a Guermantes as in a Verdurin or a Bloch. He delights in noting differences of behaviour, speech, and tradition, not only between members of great families and the *bourgeoisie*, but between " specimens " within classes generally supposed to be homogeneous; within the aristocracy itself, and within the *bourgeoisie*. His picture of French society is that of a society quivering with social competition and spitefulness; but Proust himself moves about in it as detached himself as a classifying entomologist, with his net, his little boxes and his pins. His delight in the magnificent markings of, say, a Prince de Guermantes, and in the difference between the bloom upon the wings of " Oriane," of a Mme. de Villeparisis (slightly rubbed), and of a Mme. de Cambremer (definitely shabby), is half aesthetic and half scientific. When, as a boy, the hero of the novel begins his investigations in the direction of " *le côté de Guermantes*," the owners of historic names have a romantic glamour for him; the duchesse de Guermantes seemed to him then an inhabitant of a far-off fairy world, different from other women. On closer acquaintance he discovers that both she and her set *are* different from the people he was brought up with, but even more different from what he first imagined them to be. He no longer sees Mme. de Guermantes as he saw her in the church of Cambrai, when she was kneeling in the chapel of her ancestors, the dukes of Brabant. She turns, on closer acquaintance, into an exquisite creature inhabiting a world which in many respects is petty and spiteful, ignorant and unfeeling—certainly not a world of romance. Glamour is replaced by curiosity. His observation of her and her peculiar code of manners becomes then as detached as his observation of his servant Françoise and her ways of looking at life. The resemblances between the speech and social code of servants and those of the Guermantes interest him as much as the differences between them. Nor does he give the palm to the aristocratic conception of what is dignified behaviour compared with that of his own class.

When a critic is arguing against what he believes to be a false diagnosis, he is always apt to overstate his case; but what, to my mind, refutes this charge of snobbishness is that Proust's picture of " society " is entirely free from contempt for people who do *not* possess the characteristics of those at the top, while those characteristics never for a moment blind him to the insensitiveness and stupidity which may accompany them. If in this respect he is compared with most other novelists, the comparison will be found to be greatly in favour of Proust. Balzac's picture of society is a more beglamoured one; it is even ridiculously and vulgarly so, besides being ill-informed. If you compare Proust with some English novelists, W. H. Mallock for example (no mean novelist by the by), the difference is startling. In Mallock's books the identification of " good " with " good form " is carried to a pitch at times painful; either all his well-born characters are superior beings, or it is obvious that the author loves them much more than the others. Now that is the snobbish point of view. Even Meredith and Henry James never succeeded so completely as Proust in dissociating elegance and the marks of rank from virtues and qualities which do not necessarily accompany them. They were not nearly so much interested in studying such distinctions as Proust was, but neither were they so detached when they did so. Proust has the preoccupations of the snob, but is peculiarly free from snobbish prejudices.

I admit that most of those who figure in his novel appear as ferocious and impassioned snobs, but Proust himself, though he responds to every quiver of emotion in them, is detached. The people who seemed wonderful to him when they were inaccessible, on closer and closer acquaintance prove more and more ordinary and vulgar. It is part of the whole " moral " of Proust's view of life, that the social world, like love and everything else, is best enjoyed in memory and in imagination.

VII

In one respect, Proust's picture of the French aristocracy strikes the English observer as strange. We are looking, it must be remembered, at only a small section of it, whose sense of their importance separates them in their own eyes, not only from other classes, but from many people in their own class.

Charlus informs the young Proust that there are, perhaps, a dozen families in France who count; the rest are as insignificant, from the Guermantes point of view, as the middle-class. There is no difference between Charlus's attitude towards Proust himself and towards the Cambremers, who are an ancient and noble family. I have never set foot myself in the Faubourg St. Germain, and therefore I cannot check Proust's account of the people in it; but what strikes any one who has come in contact with people in a similar relation to the rest of society in England is that, if Proust is not exaggerating something, the social atmosphere of the aristocracy in France must be markedly different from what it is in England. The " note " of English aristocratic society is self-confidence; in France it seems to be a restless anxiety to make others aware that they are themselves entitled to peculiar respect by behaving either with an exaggerated affability, or with covert or open insolence. In England, this is rather the mark of those who are on the climb, than of those who were born at the top. Similar people in England may snub those whom they think too familiar or pushing, but they are not perpetually preoccupied with protecting or with flaunting their own pride. It would be difficult for an English aristocrat not to think of the world which Proust describes as rather ignobly and nervously diffident. The English equivalent of Mme. de Guermantes would not bother her head whether she could emphasize her own social distinction by going to, or not going to, a particular party: she would go if she wanted to, or stay away if she didn't. That an English aristocrat in the position of Charlus should, at the close of the Verdurins' party, boast with radiant self-satisfaction that no other man in France could have induced so many exclusive people to come, is nearly inconceivable. Can you imagine, say, a Duke of Devonshire swaggering to Mme. Verdurin in that way? I may be wrong, but Proust's aristocrats strike me as having the social outlook which, in England, is the mark of the *déclassé* snob of good connections, who has to be always hinting that he is more important than he appears, for fear nobody will believe it. I cannot think that this is an accurate picture of the Faubourg St. Germain. But it makes most excellent comedy, so one cannot regret it. It gains plausibility, perhaps, from the fact that in France the set which Proust describes are only *heraldically* distinguished from the rest of mankind, not by any effective importance. The English aristocracy, though they have lost nearly all their power, have still no small share in the life of the nation; their traditions, too, are rooted not only in the far past but in quite modern history; coalmines and misalliances have repeatedly saved them from impotence, and they are perpetually recruited from the successful of all classes. But in the modern world, a group of people who settle among themselves their relative importance by the order in which their ancestors went out of a room in Louis XIV's reign, and judge outsiders by their knowledge of these distinctions, are merely playing a game. It is one with amusingly elaborate rules, and therefore excellent sport for the Comic Muse. Proust watches them with sympathy for their romantic pride, with incessant curiosity, and with a smile. He also has an unerring eye for elegance and grace of bearing, whether accompanied or not with dignity of feeling.

VIII

Readers of Ruskin's *Praeterita* may have been astonished at Ruskin's claim to be the possessor of " the most analytical mind in Europe." If I remember right, he does not put this forward as his own judgment of himself: (that would be very unlike him). But he quotes it as a tribute which, however exaggerated in expression, emphasizes what he himself considered to be his master quality as a writer. Proust was a great admirer of Ruskin. The qualities which appealed to him in Ruskin were a capacity for rapture, and his acute faculty of analysing the impressions made upon him by material objects. Proust possessed both these gifts himself, otherwise two men could hardly be more different. His analysis of his impressions is more patient and minute than Ruskin's; the impetus, in his case, is never moral fervour; yet there is a real resemblance. Both make an extraordinary intellectual effort to discover what is behind the impressions which have excited them. Proust traces to the last tiny filament-root the sources of his impressions of joy, beauty, or disgust. He never rests until the confused ideas which have exalted him have been dragged up into daylight. Describing one of his walks as a boy, and his literary ambitions, he says: " *Alors, bien en dehors de toutes ces préoccupations littéraires et ne s'y rattachant en rien, tout d'un coup un toit, un reflet de soleil sur une pierre, l'odeur d'un chemin me faisaient arrêter par un plaisir particulier qu'ils me donnaient, et aussi parce qu'ils avaient l'air de cacher au delà de ce que je voyais quelque chose qu'ils m'invitaient à venir prendre et que, malgré mes efforts, je n'arrivais pas à découvrir. Comme je sentais que cela se trouvait en eux, je restais là, immobile, à regarder, à respirer, à tâcher d'aller avec ma pensée au delà de l'image et de l'odeur. Et s'il fallait rattraper mon grand-père, poursuivre ma route, je cherchais à les retrouver, en fermant les yeux; je m'attachais à me rappeler exactement la ligne du toit, la nuance de la pierre qui, sans que je pusse comprendre pourquoi, m'avaient semblé pleines, prêtes à s'entr'ouvrir, à me livrer ce dont elles n'étaient qu'un couvercle.*"

It was thus, too, that Ruskin looked at a church, a street, a picture, a face; he stared at the object till he believed he had discovered the secret of its exciting power in something else behind it.

IX

I have already drawn attention to those passages in which Proust describes his effort to understand the meaning of some experience, or the message some particular object seems to have for him; that is to say, those passages which illustrate most clearly an artist's life. These moments of torturing happiness, in which there is almost more distress than happiness until expression has been found for them, are the passages which make *A la Recherche du Temps Perdu* a unique book. Proust, like many artists, is inclined to be mystical about them. There is no religion, no God in his book, and the place of religious emotion in it is taken by these artist's emotions. This is an unbelieving age, and I am inclined to think that one reason why *A la Recherche du Temps Perdu* has been taken so very earnestly by some people, is that it refreshes the hope in them that aesthetic experience may, after all, fill the place of religious experience in their own lives—probably a vain hope. Certainly aesthetic experience led Proust to a kind of philosophy which was to him a sufficient support; but it is a philosophy difficult to state and difficult to make one's own, and in so far as it was mystical it strikes me as resting on a confusion of thought: Proust identifies a method of handling experience as an artist with a method of becoming one with Reality. I despair of making it clear to any one who has not read Proust, without an apparent digression.

X

The importance of memory in Proust's work I have already touched upon; and this passage from Emerson, in which he is writing about memory, is worth quoting for comparison:

" It is the raw material out of which the intellect moulds her splendid products. A strange process too, this, by which experience is converted into thought, as a mulberry leaf is converted into satin. The manufacture goes forward at all hours.

" The actions and events of our childhood and youth, are now matters of calmest observation. They lie like fair pictures in the air. Not so with our recent actions—with the business which we now have in hand. On this we are quite unable to speculate. Our affections as yet circulate through it. We no more feel or know it, than we feel the feet, or the hand, or the brain of our body. The new deed is yet a part of life—remains for a time immersed in our unconscious life. In some contemplative hour, it detaches itself from the life like a ripe fruit, to become a thought of the mind. Instantly, it is raised, transfigured; the corruptible has put on incorruption. Henceforth it is an object of beauty, however base its origin and neighbourhood. Observe, too, the impossibility of antedating this act. In its grub state, it cannot fly, it cannot shine, it is a dull grub. But suddenly, without observation, the selfsame thing unfurls beautiful wings, and is an angel of wisdom. So is there no fact, no event, in our private history, which shall not, sooner or later, lose its adhesive, inert form, and astonish us by soaring from our body into the empyrean. Cradle and infancy, school and playground, the fear of boys, and dogs, and ferrules, the love of little maids and berries, and many another fact that once filled the whole sky, are gone already; friend and relative, profession and party, town and country, nation and world, must also soar and sing."

This is exactly Proust's doctrine of the relation of memory to Art; and—since Life is to him the life of an artist—to Life itself. Proust is a man for whom the present does not exist in any important sense, except one—as a means of evocation. But he also lays special stress upon the importance of a particular way of remembering. When you sit down to recall the past you can remember much, but this deliberate process is no good; you will find out nothing from it. He would agree with Emerson that it is impossible to " antedate " the revelation; you must wait till some, perhaps trifling, actual incident makes the past unfurl itself and come to life. Proust has described minutely how the taste of a cake, the tinkling of a spoon against a cup, the unevenness of the pavement, led him to such sudden revelations. The past came back to him transfigured, because it was now experienced by a godlike observer, detached from the grip and confusion of actualities. To live as far as possible for such moments, and in them, is the Proustian philosophy, his remedy for the sadness and imperfection of life. As a philosophy it has the drawback that to live in the present, and even for the future, is an instinct so strong that only the profoundest disillusionment can subdue it; and besides, the less we live in the present as it passes, the less we will have to remember. The magnitude of Proust's achievement can be measured only when we take into account that his book, besides being the most careful record of an intellectual artist's experience, is also a panorama of social life; full of figures as unforgettable as

Balzac's; built up from the observation of minute traits and peculiarities of speech, without the help of those crucial events on which most novelists rely to reveal character to the bottom.

A la Recherche du Temps Perdu can be criticized as shapeless, overloaded, digressive, ill-proportioned. It began as a story of Swann's love and jealousy, which then sprouted in both directions, backwards and forwards; the book thus became a formless collection of curiosities and beautiful things, full also of the very essence of an artist's experience. The Swann episode is far more self-contained than the book itself. It lies like a half-digested lump in the middle of a sort of protoplasmic monster which has wrapped itself round it. I like that invidious comparison; after all, protoplasm is the basis of life, and Proust's work is astoundingly alive. And if it is asked what service his novel has done us, the question can be answered in his own words:

" Once the novelist has brought us to that state, in which, as in all purely mental states, every emotion is multiplied tenfold, into which his book comes to disturb us as might a dream, but a dream more lucid, and of a more lasting impression than those which come to us in sleep; why, then, for the space of an hour he sets free within us all the joys and sorrows in the world, a few of which only we should have to spend years of our actual life in getting to know, and the keenest, the most intense of which would never have been revealed to us because the slow course of their development stops our perception of them. It is the same in life; the heart changes, and that is our worst misfortune; but we learn of it only from reading or by imagination; for in reality its alteration, like that of certain natural phenomena, is so gradual that, even if we are able to distinguish, successively, each of its different states, we are still spared the actual sensation of change."

No novelist has ever done such complete justice to the great fact that all things pass and change, or has pointed out more clearly how the artist can turn his experience of mutability to his profit. But what about people who are not artists? Has he anything to say to them? If no experience has any meaning beyond itself, and at the time is invariably disappointing; if the universe is godless and without meaning; if no moral judgments have any validity, and individuality and responsibility are delusions; if human beings are merely a congregation of thoughts and sensations in perpetual flux—if life is so empty, what is the use of intensifying our consciousness of it? It will only mean more pain. More pain, yes; but according to the philosophy which emerges from the central pages of *Le Temps Retrouvé*, also attainment, the only kind of experience worth having. It is for this reason that some of Proust's readers have found comfort in his book. Analysis certainly could not go further in destruction, but something—what is it?—remains—something that makes the world for them a world in which it is after all worth while to live. Yes, amid all the dross and copper of life there comes now and then a slip of gold. These moments are the stuff out of which true works of art are made, but all may capture them who can attend. Proust's experience is thus in harmony with the doctrine of " essences " as expounded by Santayana, who wrote, in commenting upon this novel:

" Such an essence, when it is talked about, may seem mysterious and needlessly invented, but when noticed it is the clearest and least doubtful of things—the only sort of thing, indeed, that can ever be observed with direct and exhaustive clearness. An essence is simply the recognizable character of any object or feeling, all of it than can actually be possessed in sensation or recovered in memory, or conveyed to another mind. All that was intrinsically real in past time is accordingly recoverable. The hopeless flux and the temporal order of things are not ultimately interesting; they belong merely to the material occasions on which essences recur, or to the flutterings of attention, hovering like a moth about lights which are eternal."

XII

In his ninth year Proust was first attacked by that torturing intermittent malady, asthma, which afflicted him all his life. He was the son of a busy successful doctor; his mother was a Jewess, *née* Mlle. Weil. They were well-off. In spite of his delicate health he entered the Lycée Condorcet. His prodigious memory and passionate curiosity enabled him to do well there, although he was often absent owing to ill-health, but he failed to distinguish himself. History, especially the history of the Court of Louis XIV, fascinated him. He was interested, too, in botany and natural history. His bad health did not prevent him from serving a year in the army. Afterwards, to satisfy his father, in spite of his longing to write, he set about preparing himself for the Diplomatic Service. He entered the Sorbonne, where he was much more interested in metaphysics than in the faculty of Law and Political Science. Bergson's first treatise had just appeared. It is said that the influence of that philosopher, his manner of envisaging time, his insistence upon the importance of the unconscious and of intuition as opposed to intellect, permanently impressed itself on Proust's mind and can be traced in his work, though I do not myself quite understand what is meant by this.

Having money, the young Proust founded a literary review called *Le Banquet*, which did not live long, but had contributors who afterwards became well-known writers. His contemporaries seem soon to have made up their minds that Proust was too fashionable to become a proper man of letters. In 1896 he published a pamphlet, *Portraits de Peintres*, and *Les Plaisirs et les Jours*, a short collection for which Anatole France wrote a preface. It was well written and there were charming things in it, but it seems to have only confirmed the impression that the author was incurably a society man. The social world became the source of his keenest pleasures. "Salons, cliques, the small heroes of these groups occupied in his conversation an almost exclusive place." From 1900-1905 he contributed occasional articles to the *Figaro* on the houses and hostesses he frequented. He also translated Ruskin's *Bible of Amiens* and, oddly enough, *Sesame and Lilies*.

Marcel Proust at the age of twenty had large black eyes with heavy lids drooping at the corners—very bright eyes with a look of extreme gentleness in them, which dwelt long on what he looked at; a still more gentle voice, a little breathless and trailing, almost affected, but never quite suggesting affectation; long thick black hair, sometimes falling forward, hair which was never to show grey. It was to his eyes, however, that attention always returned: large, tired, nostalgic eyes, surrounded with dark rings; extremely animated, they seemed to follow the hidden thoughts of any one talking to him. A smile, amused, receptive, hesitating, would play about his lips for awhile and then remain fixed. His face of dull pallor, once fresh and rosy, suggested, in spite of a black moustache, that of an indolent and precociously acute child. His clothes were those of a fashionable dandy, but not tidy. When he entertained, he liked to eat beforehand so as to be free to talk.

He had an astonishing gift for intimacy and an astounding memory. He could repeat pages of prose and verse by heart, and his memory for emotions and exact circumstances was even more surprising. He had the memory of the heart. The attention he bent upon anyone who was with him was extremely flattering in its complete concentration; at the same time it was never cloying, because his conversation showed a clairvoyant detachment. His address and compliments were, if anything, over-flattering, and his sympathy, which made him fantastic over little matters, was perhaps more completely agreeable to women than to men. A sharp irony, which was to develop later, was perceptible behind his expatiation upon trivialities. He was an excellent and most amusing mimic. He chose his friends; they had to be either devoted, intelligent, or aristocratic. His money enabled him to organize a manner of life which suited his ailments and his excessive sensibility, and also to satisfy his impulses of affection or sympathy. He was superbly, absurdly generous. Such was the young man who, during the first, the " active " part of his career, as opposed to the productive, devoted himself to intimacies and society. He had every gift necessary for such preoccupations except the power of making plans and the habit of punctuality. All appointments were surrounded for him with insuperable difficulties. Dressing, eating, catching a train, finding a cab, were matters requiring strategy of the most elaborate kind. His attention moved like an insect across every page of the book of life, shadowing one letter at a time. As he grew older he became more and more eccentric in his habits.

XII

I should like someone to analyse Proust's treatment of time in his book. We get a curiously strong impression of time from it, a feat which few novelists accomplish satisfactorily. That impression, by the way, is the essence of the tragedy of *The Old Wives' Tale*. Arnold Bennett did it, so far as I can suggest the process in a few words, by somehow making time fly with the sister in Paris and crawl with the sister in the Five Towns, and then, when Sophia's Paris life is over, by suddenly presenting Charlotte Povey as an old stout woman, when the sisters are at last about to meet again. I shall never forget the shock it was when I suddenly saw Charlotte slowly making her way up the hill, an elderly, placid old body, her life practically over. *The Old Wives' Tale* was the first book which made the prospect of old age really alarming to me. Until I read it I had envisaged the process of growing old with perfect equanimity. Tolstoy, of course, is a master of this art. There is nothing more wonderful in that most wonderful of all novels, *War and Peace*, than the way in which the transition from one generation to another is managed.

But with Proust I am perplexed. I do get most strongly the sensation of time; yet it is not a stream of time bearing all away with it and changing human character. It is rather a whirlpool in which people and incidents revolve, vanish and come back, are whisked away and return again. He treats time as though it were almost a static element, in which he juxtaposes scenes arbitrarily, as though they were rather in space. For my own part I am constantly mystified as to the age of the hero himself. Sometimes, when he has seemed not only adult but independent, he will appear the next

206

moment as a child requiring nursery care. Another puzzle to me is why the hero makes such an impression on others. The extreme subjectivity of the book is shown in this, that while his impressions of others, of their smallest gestures, of the minutest incidents connected with them, are extraordinarily vivid, he himself moves through the action like a bodiless percipient. He is adored, sought after, petted. His conversation, it is suggested, is extremely impressive, yet we are very seldom given it, though the talk of others is recorded with a skill unmatched, and goes on for pages and pages. In fact the hero of the book is almost silent. Again, we know he is very delicate, but have we any idea of his appearance? It may be said that this characteristic is common to all books told in the first person—the hero himself is invisible. Nevertheless we do as a rule get a much clearer idea of the kind of impression his presence makes on others. In this case we only gather that that impression was profound, which makes us all the more conscious of our vagueness about the nature and manner of the impression.

Then there is another aspect of Proust's book that I should like to see investigated. It is realistically convincing, down to the minutest details; yet it is also full of glaring improbabilities which are recounted with the same careful circumstantial detail. The account for instance of the hero's relations with Albertine is riddled with difficulties. No young girl could visit a young man's room at all hours of the day and night, at an hotel or at his house, as she is made to do. There is something fundamentally incredible about the framework of their relations. The immunities and freedom they enjoy are more characteristic of a relation between two people of the same sex, and once the idea has entered the reader's mind that there has been a transference of sex in this character, it will continually strike him that Albertine has been incompletely feminized. Many of Proust's women are drawn with the last perfection; compared with them Albertine is a botch.

To take another case, the hero is a youth of no importance, no achievement. When he is first invited to a grand dinner-party at the duc de Guermantes' house, he arrives rather early and asks to see the pictures. He is shown into a room which is not the room where the guests are to assemble, and there, lost in contemplation of these works of art, he remains so long that on returning to the drawing-room he finds that the party, among whom is a royal princess, has been waiting three-quarters of an hour for him. His host, anxious not to embarrass him by making him feel that dinner has been postponed on his account, keeps them all waiting another five minutes. Such an incident is impossible.

XIII

Proust, as I have said, gives us an account of the life of an intellectual artist. But what indifferent creatures the artists in Proust's book turn out to be, when known in the flesh: Vinteuil, the agitated and timid musician; Elstir, the idol of a vulgar little clique; Bergotte, who wrote like an angel and talked like poor poll; Berma, the great tragic actress who was commonplace in life. The young hero of *A la Recherche du Temps Perdu*, so exquisitely sensitive to Vinteuil's sonata, Elstir's line and colour, Bergotte's prose, Berma's acting, so capable of communion with them as artists, felt acutely the contrast between that communion and what he could draw from them as people whom he knew. His disillusionment with those whose names trailed the glories of history across his imagination was not

greater than with those artists. I am not at all
sure, from the peeps at him which biography and
reminiscence have given us, that I should not have
felt the same about Proust himself. I mistrust in
many matters, though not in all, the delicacy of the
delicate. I suspect Proust of intricate and dulcet
treacheries, of exasperating and petty self-absorp-
tion. I question even his fine, extravagant *bonté*,
as being partly a device for keeping others at a
distance and having finally done with them. How
I should have missed in him, as a man, contact with
the common massive satisfactions of life, and the
steadiness of fundamental good-nature! But when
he speaks to me as an artist, when I am in communion with his mind, how little that matters!

RICHARDSON AND PROUST

THE story of *Pamela, or Virtue Rewarded*, is a minute circumstantial description, given in letters which purport to be written by an exceedingly sententious young servant-girl, of her dominating and elegant master's repeated attempts to seduce her. Pamela, as Mrs. Barbauld put it, is " the conscious possessor of a treasure which she is wisely resolved not to part with but for its just price "; and at the end of volume two, after resisting incessant persuasion and persecution, and sustaining on at least two occasions an excitingly close siege, she accepts the offer of his hand and heart.

Of this famous novel, the full title, characteristically part puff and part description, runs as follows: " Pamela, or Virtue Rewarded. . . . A Narrative which has its Foundation in *Truth* and *Nature*, and at the same time that it agreeably entertains, by a variety of *Curious* and *affecting Incidents*, is entirely divested of all those Images which, in too many Pieces calculated for Amusement only tend to *inflame* the Minds they should *instruct*." It was published in November 1740, and was instantly swept to success by a wave of collective sensibility. It was equally popular with mistress and maid. Discriminating males also revelled in it. At Ranelagh elegant ladies held up copies to each other to show what they were reading; clergy recommended it from their pulpits, and at Slough, where the local blacksmith had been reading it aloud to the villagers, his audience rushed to ring the church-bells at the point where the heroine succeeds at last in bringing

her would-be seducer to his knees with an offer of
marriage. All of which goes to show that the
eighteenth century was a more excitable age than
we sometimes allow for, and that a theme which
delights the prurient while lulling their consciences,
when treated by a gifted author who aims at improving our morals, is ever sure of a prodigious triumph.
In December, 1741, Richardson followed it up by
a two-volume continuation, describing Pamela's
life after her marriage. These volumes are in-
tolerably tedious. But although *Pamela* is greatly
inferior to *Clarissa*, and even to *Sir Charles Grandison*, no one can call the first two volumes dull.

As a rule I find myself in agreement with
orthodox opinion upon great writers, and tend to
feel uneasy when I am not. But with regard to
Richardson I differ jubilantly. The mind behind
these famous books is repellent to me. When I
read him I feel that I am in mean company, which
is a great deal worse than low company. Yet no
one can fail to see that Richardson must be ranked
as a great English novelist, though his influence has
worked itself out. He has left an indelible mark on
the literature not only of his own country but of
Europe, though he is now commonly neglected by
the incurious, and regarded by those not anxious to
hold instructed opinions as a tedious writer.

This, however, is not the stone I would throw
at him. Dr. Johnson once replied to an observation
of Thomas Erskine to the effect that Richardson was
dull: " Why, sir, if you were to read Richardson
for the story, your impatience would be so much
fretted that you would hang yourself. But you
must read him for the sentiment, and consider the
story only as the occasion for the sentiment." If
for the word " sentiment " the phrase " intellectual
and aesthetic curiosity " were substituted, Johnson's answer would meet equally well modern

objections to Proust. In his *Biographia Literaria*, Coleridge speaks of " the loaded sensibility, the minute detail " of Richardson's work, of " the morbid consciousness of every thought and feeling in the whole flux and reflux of the mind, in short, its self-involution and dream-like-continuity "; and these phrases are applicable to the work of Proust also. Richardson performed in his day much the same service for his contemporaries and successors as Proust has done for us. He, too, fixed attention upon the texture of experience, while extracting from it a sense of values which was equally welcome to contemporary sensibility, though it is old-fashioned now.

In one of his letters, the late Sir Walter Raleigh drew up a general scheme of the plot of Richardson's novels on the principle of *The House that Jack Built*— it applies chiefly to *Sir Charles Grandison*.

" This is the next to nothing that happened.

This is the young lady who wrote to her friend describing the next to nothing that happened.

This is the friend who approved the young lady for the decorum of the manner with which she described the next to nothing that happened.

This is the admirable baronet who chanced to find the letter to the young lady approving the decorum, etc.

This is the punctilio of honour that prevented the admirable baronet from reading more than the first thirteen pages of the letter to the young lady, etc.

This is the company of brilliant conversationalists that discussed the punctilio of honour, etc.

This is the marriage in high life that resulted from the meeting of the company of brilliant conversationalists that, etc.

And so on."

" The house that Proust built " is very different in substance, but between the impression made by both writers on contemporary critics there is a resemblance. Recall Johnson's comparison of Richardson and Fielding: " There was as great a difference between them," he said, " as between a man who knew how a watch was made and a man who could tell the hour by looking at the dial-plate." " Now, at last," exclaimed the critics on reading *A La Recherche du Temps Perdu*, " we are allowed to watch the very pulse of the machine; hitherto novelists have merely contented themselves with reporting the movement of the hour-hand." Both writers discovered a new manner of writing—detailed, long-winded, exact. The picture of life is in each case all foreground; both dwell continually upon trifles because they are significant of the important feelings which they desire to communicate; and in the quality of their observation and interests there is a marked femininity. (Lovelace, at the moment of Clarissa's elopement, will stop to describe her gown to Belford with the zest of a dressmaker.) The method of both, though prolix and digressive, has this great advantage, that it permits them to scrutinize every character the moment he or she appears, with the result that their pages are crowded with small vivid portraits. Both novelists moreover confirmed and directed the sensibility of their day. That this sensibility was, in 1740, emotionally lachrymose and sentimentally moral, and in 1920 was predominantly sceptical, aesthetic and amoral—this fact does not affect the relation in which, with their preternaturally minute imaginative faculties, they stood to their times; though it does alter, of course, their comparative value for us.

Both had valetudinarian temperaments. " His perpetual study," Johnson says of Richardson, " was to ward off petty inconveniences, and procure petty pleasures." Life also compelled Proust to take continual precautions, and narrowed the range of his responses; but there was a stoical detachment in him born of great suffering, and this removes from his work every trace of that smug timidity which is so trying in Richardson. Richardson's world is, after all, the world of a thoroughgoing muff, and the absence of all virility in it is not compensated by that aesthetic sensibility, which with other authors, and most notably with Proust, often more than makes up for such a deficiency. Feminine is not a term of abuse, but there is something about masculine-femininity in literature which is apt to produce, in the male sex at least, a curious exasperation.

Fielding felt it, and though his authorship of *An Apology for the Life of Mrs. Shamela Andrews*, which appeared in April, 1741, just after the third edition of Pamela was issued, has been disputed, his *Adventures of Joseph Andrews* was inspired in the first instance by a strong desire to strike at what he despised in Richardson. But he also learnt, as is not uncommon, something from the author he mocked. There seems to be a reluctance on the part of critics to attribute *Shamela* to Fielding because the satire in it is blunt and coarse; but when we take into consideration that Fielding was capable of both bluntness and coarseness, and that certain malapropisms which occur in *Shamela* are repeated in *Joseph Andrews*, the case for Fielding's authorship seems fairly strong, especially as he returned to the attack. A critic can obtain a verdict of non-proven, but that is all.

To borrow a phrase from Walter Raleigh's talk, Fielding, when reading Richardson, must have felt like a dog reading a book written by a cat. The streak of uneasy servility in Richardson (the expression is Austin Dobson's, who admired his genius) must have been peculiarly repulsive to Fielding, especially when he found it combined, as it was, with an excitable sanctimoniousness. Fielding, of course, was an observer—not a subtle one, but direct and sure, while Richardson belonged to the spider class of creators, who spin their work out of their own consciousness. Being three-parts woman, he understood the inner workings of women's minds incomparably better; and dipping, as he occasionally does, in the concealed turbid sediment of his own sympathies, he succeeds sometimes in producing a thoroughly convincing female villain. If one compares Mrs. Jewkes in *Pamela* with Mrs. Slipslop in *Joseph Andrews*, one is struck at once with the contrast between a really sordid nature known from within and the portrait of a rather similar woman drawn with good-natured and amused contempt from without. Mrs. Jewkes is the most real character in *Pamela*, for Mr. B. is waxwork, and Pamela herself only comes alive at moments when her creator is unconsciously aware that she is really a minx, and neglects the moral which he wishes us to draw. *Pamela* is a curious work, in which the conflict between unconscious hypocrisy and the impulse of a genuine artist is visible on every page.

To portray Richardson himself would require a subtlety almost equal to his own. His influence was rapid and immense. It extended to France, Germany, and Italy. Diderot compared him to Homer, and, indeed, he was the master of that *sensiblerie* in which Diderot himself unfortunately and incongruously revelled. " Oh, Richardson, Richardson," he exclaimed, " a man unique in my eyes, you shall be my reading at all times! " For many years Ossian, Richardson, and Sterne represented British genius in the eyes of Europe. For Musset, too, *Clarissa* was *le premier roman du monde*.

DEFOE

I HAVE been re-reading *Moll Flanders*. When I was a boy it was not an easy novel to come by; it was on the moral index. From second-hand sets of Defoe's works that volume was frequently missing. The first copy I ever succeeded in securing, execrably printed, was bought at one of those dingy little shops which attract by making a show, as far as they dare, of purveying pornography. Happily, *Moll Flanders* has now been rescued from the society of *The Adventures of Maria Monk* and *The Works of Aristotle*. It has been often reprinted since then, and men of letters have written prefaces to it. I mention these facts because they show a change of mind in the reading public itself. They are beginning to learn the difference between lubricity and plain decent speech upon " improper " subjects.

Moll Flanders is an autobiography of a woman who was a prostitute and a thief. It is, perhaps, the best written, and it is certainly the best constructed, of all the novels of Defoe. Defoe's attitude towards his subject and his public is characteristic. The closer we look at him as a man the more we are struck by two contradictory elements in his nature; his genius is clearly inseparable from straightforward honesty of vision, yet this superb honesty was combined with a taste for devious devices. Of no man's life, too, could it be more pointfully said that " his honour rooted in dishonour stood." His standards were those of an honest, modest, respectable tradesman, one in whom simple truth seems his utmost skill; yet he could not deny himself the excitemenι of dubious and risky undertakings. One cannot read a page of Defoe without being convinced that it is written by a man of exceptional trustworthiness, yet we find he always kept one eye askew on the main chance.

This " plain dealer " was also one of the most brilliant circumstantial liars who ever existed. Indeed, as Walter Scott and Leslie Stephen pointed out, even his methods as a novelist are closely akin to the dodges of the liar; that is to say, he was an adept in introducing into bogus statements adventitious details of such a nature that no one could believe that he had taken the trouble to invent them. He slid gradually into writing fiction through the practice of embellishing in this manner what purported to be accounts of actual events. As a reporter he acquired the art of blending fact and fiction so that it was impossible to disentangle them. *Moll Flanders* sprang out of his work on *Applebee's Journal,* for which he interviewed condemned criminals in Newgate. Now, such confessions truthfully taken down seldom make good reading. Because a man is going to be hanged tomorrow it does not follow that he has anything interesting to say about it; Defoe was master of the art of improving upon the poor words and scanty facts usually obtainable at such crises. It was not a long step to inventing the immortal Moll Flanders.

After the Restoration there seems to have been a marked trend of taste in the direction of books about low life; interest in criminal adventurers increased. In this line Defoe had several predecessors whose names are now almost forgotten, of whom Francis Kirkman was perhaps the most successful. Kirkman wrote the story of a disreputable woman, one Mary Carleton, known in her day as " The German Princess," whom Pepys visited in prison on several occasions. She was arrested for bigamy, acquitted and re-arrested for theft, and then transported to Jamaica. She foolishly returned to England, and was hanged at Tyburn in January 1673. Readers of *Moll Flanders* will at once perceive some resemblance between the careers of these two heroines. Kirkman, however, went a great deal further than Defoe in the direction of licence.

Defoe, in his preface to *Moll Flanders*, professes that he writes in order to counteract the effect of such books. He is careful throughout to emphasize Moll's repentance and to garnish her story with moral and prudent reflections put into her mouth. " To give the history of a wicked life repented necessarily requires that the wicked part should be made as wicked as the real history will bear, to illustrate and give beauty to the penitent part, which is certainly the best and brightest if related with equal spirit and life." He points out that " there is not a wicked action in any part of it but is first and last rendered unhappy and unfortunate; there is not a superlative villain brought upon the stage but either he is brought to an unhappy end or brought to be penitent; there is not an ill thing mentioned but it is condemned even in the relation, nor a virtuous just thing but it carries its praise along with it."

Note how cunningly this preface is calculated at once to excite the interest of the prurient and to allay the scruples of the moral. Defoe was a master of this kind of dexterity, for both impulses were equally genuine in himself: the desire to edify and the desire to secure the largest sales possible by exploiting the interest of low life. Indeed, Defoe's conscience became a subtle organ of his business instinct. He had only to ask himself what would " do most good " in order to discover also what would pay best.

The extraordinary thing is that this characteristic never clouded or confused his gifts as a writer.
His natural matter-of-factness was so superb that
it triumphed over everything. He is one of those
writers who are impressive thanks to their apparently possessing no " imagination " whatever.
When Wordsworth complained of a man that

> A primrose by a river's brim
> A yellow primrose was to him,
> And it was nothing more,

he described the type to which Defoe belonged. A
fact was a fact to Defoe and nothing more, and his
power over his readers lies in his incapability of
doing anything but leave facts to speak for themselves. Thus he attains, by grace of his limitations,
an impartiality after which great artists have often
striven in vain. He was so unimaginative that he
could not conceive that a story could be interesting
to others unless they believed it; and so was the
middle-class public of his day. To them also what
they read in print was of no account unless it could
be read as a description of things which had actually
taken place. Defoe therefore in all that he wrote
aimed first at supplying the appearance of authen-
ticity.

Of *Robinson Crusoe*, he said, in introducing
the story, that it was " a history of fact "; *The
Life of Moll Flanders*, he alleged, was " written
from her own memorandums," and he complains
" that the world is so taken up of late with novels
and romances that it will be hard for a private
history to be taken for genuine where the names and
the other circumstances of the persons are concealed."
When taxed with " forging stories and imposing
them on the world for truth," he replied, in the case
of *Robinson Crusoe*, that the book was an allegory
of his own life, and therefore true—a fantastic

quibble which has led some critics to see in the story a parable of spiritual isolation.

The fact is that, as a journalist, Defoe had practised all his life the art of " forging stories and imposing them on the world for truth." He began by writing biographies with real names attached to them; memoirs of Charles XII, Peter the Great, the Duke of Shrewsbury, Captain Avery: the King of the Pirates, Rob Roy, Jonathan Wild, Jack Sheppard. It was a small step, so much did he draw on his imagination in these, to sit down to write biographies of fictitious people. His methods were the same in both cases, and there is a great deal in Minto's remark that, though Defoe is usually spoken of as the inventor of the realistic novel, " realistic biography would, perhaps, be a more strictly accurate description."

The paragraphists and newsmongers in those days of imperfect communication could take liberties with facts to an extent incredible to us. They could, indeed, only satisfy the demand for news by inventing; there were no special correspondents to send accounts of events from the spot. Defoe, besides being a most energetic and forceful pamphleteer, was an extraordinary master of the trick of supplying this deficiency and of describing things as though he were himself, or had been himself, on the spot. Thus, when, late in life (1719), he turned to fiction, it was not a sudden change of vocation; nor, with his lifelong practice, was it odd that the result should be of supreme excellence in the matter of circumstantial invention. As early as 1703, Defoe, while imprisoned in Newgate, had written an account of " the great storm " of that year, in which a large part of the British Fleet went down and London itself was severely damaged, an account which is unmatched for vigour and verisimilitude; yet he had not seen even the wrecked houses round his prison. This feat, as much as his later success in novels, was due to long training in a style out of which, as Mr. Whibley has said, the last particle of literary pretence has been squeezed; that style which Defoe himself described as due to his " natural infirmity of homely plain writing." The classical writers of Queen Anne's time regarded him as a vulgar scribbler, which makes one wonder whether the censure of the fastidious upon the style of some popular writers to-day will in all cases be corroborated.

To say that a man capable of describing a storm which happened while he was in prison has no " imagination " seems a flat absurdity. But let me explain. Defoe's prodigious faculty of inventing facts and incidents and circumstances was so far in excess of his power of describing the emotions which they might inspire that the statement is no worse than a paradox. He can recount in the most convincing way possible what his characters did next or what happened next, and the endless fertility of his plausible invention makes *Moll Flanders* an absorbing story. But though he may occasionally use a few strong phrases to describe her misery or contrition, these are merely statements *about* her feelings—he does not attempt to make them real to us. The result is that, however wicked or good his people are, they are all exactly the same inside. Moll, with her prudent apprehensions about her future both in this world and the next, her courage, forethought, and resourcefulness, would have made a perfect mate for Robinson Crusoe; indeed, she *is* a Crusoe in petticoats. Moll's " governess," as she calls her, who is baby-farmer, pimp, abortionist and " fence," is as amiable as Moll herself; a more loyal, sensible, kindly woman never breathed. Nor can one distinguish, except by their actions, Moll's bad husbands from her good ones. The result is oddly refreshing. Defoe's sense of evil is so entirely that of a formalist that we have all the excitement of moving in a wicked world without any of the unpleasantness of coming into contact with a single wicked person; while the author's moralizings leave us blandly undisturbed. While reading *Moll Flanders* we seem to share a point of view as equable as the extreme impartiality of perfect Christian charity, combined with a very comfortable, almost comically matter-of-fact sense of values.

DAVID GARNETT

I

I INTEND in this article to use a more informal
mode of address. I often enjoy myself what is
called " the personal note " in criticism, but as a
critic I also despise it. To begin with it is so easy.
You need not weigh your judgments carefully if
you plump them down as expressions of individual
opinion. For instance, I want to say that Mr.
David Garnett's story, *The Sailor's Return*, is one
of the best long-short stories in English literature,
and I have been held from writing about him and
his last story, *The Grasshoppers Come*, for several
hours, by a reluctance, half nervous, half conscientious, to make so positive a statement. It expresses
what I think, but I am not sure whether I am right
in so thinking.

Now, if a critic adopts the personal mode of
address, he rids himself of such scruples; instead of
criticism he can then offer without disguise a scrap
of mental autobiography, which the reader is free to
regard as a whimsy, amiable or otherwise; and the
writer is usually most careful to see that it shall
be thought amiable; another reason why I despise
this method. Winsome exhibitionism is disgusting.
Personal confession in print, real intimacy between
reader and writer, should be reserved for occasions
of vital importance, for matters so urgent that in
connection with them egotism ceases to be egotistic,
or else for the essay which is creative as fiction is
creative, when an author is no longer on his honour
to speak literally his mind.

Nevertheless, I shall adopt "the personal note" for David Garnett, because he happens to be one of my favourite authors. But his peculiarities and his good qualities give me so much pleasure that I cannot trust myself not to over-praise him. The scruple may seem foolish to many, but those with a dash of the critical spirit in them will understand. For real criticism is a compromise between the reports of the individual critic with his preferences and those of the clear, cool percipient whom men can find, if they hunt for him, residing in themselves. The critic, too, is under some obligation to attend to the voice of tradition, and he must take past verdicts into account; besides delivering *obiter dicta* he must interpret "case-made" law. The literary babbler is free of all such obligations.

II

When *Lady Into Fox* appeared in 1923 it had a most enviable success. Spreading from that small core of literary persons which is found within the wider reading public, its fame expanded to an imposing circumference. The author was awarded both the Hawthornden Prize and the James Tait Black Memorial Prize of that year. Mr. Wells, forgetting for the moment his own theory that literature is the World-Soul thinking hard, said that *Lady Into Fox* was so perfect he could only accept it, not criticize it. There were most flattering squabbles about it too; one member of the same family or group declaring that it was exquisite, another that it was repulsive. I remember a conversation with a serious-minded friend, who happened then to be more than usually serious. He was infuriated at the fuss made over such a trivial production. "Remember my words," he said, "it will be soon forgotten." "Forgotten?" I replied. "Of course it will be forgotten—and remembered again, forgotten again, and remembered. It is not a work which ' enriches the life-blood of the world,' nor will it make the smallest difference to the emotional life of anyone at any time on this planet: but for all that it is a perfect literary nick-nack, and I should not be at all surprised if Father Time kept it on his mantelpiece. He has a habit of clearing out of his house the beds on which thousands have found rest, and the huge chests where they stored their intellectual treasures, and of sticking instead to some little object because it is complete and amusing. He has always had his frivolous side."

Some people with morbid noses could not get over the author mentioning that when poor Mrs. Tebrick turned into a fox, one of the distressing results was that she smelt like a fox; and the triumph of Mr. Tebrick's tenderness over that defect only upset them the more. Others could not stomach his devout solicitude for her litter of cubs. But these were Mr. Garnett's unduly literal readers; their horror was, indeed, a tribute to his powers and imperturbable gravity as a narrator. Apart from the excellence of the style, to which Defoe contributed his matter-of-factness and Mr. Garnett himself a queer meditative slyness such as gleams sometimes in the eyes of old rustic gaffers, what made *Lady Into Fox* a trivial masterpiece was the author's power of following out, not only logically but emotionally, the minutest consequences of his preposterous fancy. The gradual conquest of the poor lady's humanity by her increasing foxiness was traced by him step by step with exquisitely deliberate circumstantiality. In short, Mr. David Garnett opened his literary career—bang!—with a gratifying success.

In his next book he tried the same sort of thing over again. The hero of *A Man in the Zoo* did not

225   Q

become an ape, but when crossed in love he resolved
to permit himself to be treated as one. If this book
had come first it would have been hailed enthusiastically as fresh and delightful. It contained admirable
passages; and the story, without being an allegory,
was nevertheless a small private whisper in the ears
of those whose feelings have been humiliated. It
was written in the same clear, slow, bright, concise
prose, and in the same self-amused yet perfectly
grave, not to say tragic, manner. But the *Zeit-
Geist*, let alone Father Time, does not want two
specimens of the same kind of literary oddity, and
Mr. Garnett caught on to that. He fell back on his
excellent eighteenth-century gift for narrative and
his admirable powers of concrete statement. He
wrote next *The Sailor's Return*, the story of which
I think so highly. How stupid the clever were about
this touching, solid, beautiful story!

What charms me about Mr. David Garnett is
that he is a Peter Bell of letters; to him a primrose
is a primrose, nothing more. He is fond of it, but it
suggests nothing to him. This is a rare and refreshing peculiarity in a literary man, and it gives a delicious prosaic poetry to his descriptions. He likes
things in the way a smoker likes his pipe, or a child
something pink. His invention is fantastic, but his
imagination is matter-of-fact. The characters he
thoroughly understands are those who have the
same kind of absorption in things as he has himself.
One-idea-at-a-time-people, who are resourceful, even
sometimes in a simple way subtle, but never think
round about or into things, suit him best. Targett,
the sailor, and Tulip, his black wife, and their tragic
attempt to set up together as host and hostess of a
village inn, were perfect subjects for him. When,
later on, he took to describing more sophisticated
characters, as he did in *Go She Must* and *No Love*,
his best faculties were not fully used. Now in his

226

last story he has returned again to his proper
line.

III

The Grasshoppers Come is full of that originality
in handling familiar situations and things which is as
marked as his power of pretending that there is
nothing extraordinary about incredible events. It
is an account, excellently vivid and matter-of-fact,
of a long-distance flight of two men and a woman
from an aerodrome in England to Hong Kong, an
attempt at record-breaking which ends in disaster.
An oil pipe bursts; Mr. Beanlands Shap (observer)
and Wreaks (pilot and Mr. Garnett's hero) and their
passenger are deposited in a stony gully (fortunately
there is a trickle of water) in the desert of Gobi.
Wreaks twists his ankle badly in the fall; the other
two are unhurt, and they leave him with his share of
the meagre provisions and walk off in the hope of
meeting help. We never hear of them again.
Wreaks is marooned. It is a " Robinson Crusoe "
situation, and Mr. Garnett treats it with Defoe's
circumstantiality plus a dash—nicely measured that
additional ingredient—of modern nervous sensibility. We identify ourselves with Wreaks's expedients and sufferings, his practical timidity and his
stolid ingrained powers of endurance. If I said they
thrilled the reader I should be missing the whole
point and beauty of the method. The author never
heightens anything, never gives an extra turn to the
verbal screw. He achieves a level impressiveness.
Wreaks is saved by a locust-swarm, which is described with the calm of a naturalist and the vividness of a practised man of letters.

Like John the Baptist, he lives on locusts. But
they come at last in such horrifying numbers that
he is maddened.

"He could no longer see the sun even as a radiance in a sky which was as brown as the thickest London fog: against its dimness the descending rain of living bodies was only feebly outlined; as it grew thicker it became darker, until in the brown light it was hard to see the insects when they had fallen on the reddish-brown carpet of their fellows. A sour, dirty smell sickened him; the shrill whirring of millions of wings deafened him.

"Shouting oaths, Wreaks stood by the air-screw and slashed at them. But the sound of his own curses only maddened him, and roused in him a lust for massacre and destruction which he could not gratify. What was the use of striking down a hundred when the sky was stained bronze by billions of them? An insect alighted in his open mouth as he uttered a last curse and he spat it out, suddenly sickened."

He is rescued by a Chinese airman, who—it adds to the quaintness of this tiny astonishing world of ours—has been to Cambridge. The story has opened with an admirable description of grass-hoppers in a marsh; the scene changes to the aerodrome, and an analogy is felt, without its being emphasized, between the short, erratic flights of the insects and the wheeling and crawling of the air-planes round their home. Then comes the description of the long-distance flight; impressions of ten-sion, boredom, and moments of beauty, then the marooning, the rescue, and Wreaks's return to hum-drum routine. It ends with a short—what shall I call it? — prose-poem by a naturalist upon locusts:

"When they fell in waterless desert places they died; where they passed they left desert;

they sprouted wings and flew. Their seed sprang again in wingless armies from the earth. They had no reason and little that might be called instinct. All their movements are due to the heat of the sun. They are thermotropic."

UNITY OF EFFECT

ANYONE in search of an example in the art of conducting a story to its proper and foreseen close could not do better than study the construction of *Persuasion*, though such unity of effect presupposes something else not necessarily within the reach of other writers, however eager they may be to profit by Jane Austen's example. The consistency and confidence of her attitude towards every character, every event and every detail in her stories, cannot be imitated. Moreover such confidence must ever be as much the product of a period as of individual effort. It is the fruit of corroboration. Private conviction does not produce an equal stability, for human beings cannot possess the unself-conscious calm of complete assurance unless their judgments are confirmed by others. Here and there some passionate solitary may succeed in asserting consistently his own sense of proportion in the face of surrounding dissent, but inevitably in doing so he will feel a need to defend his views. He will be explanatory, and, almost inevitably, explanatory with that over-insistence which is liable to upset at any moment the subtle spiritual balance upon which so much depends in art. How distressing—and in the end how unconvincing—it is to find oneself catching continually the compelling but strained glance of the novelist's eye as one turns his pages! How blest, on the other hand, the writer of fiction who, if his reader should stop to ask, What is your point of view? can reply with mild surprise, " Why, of course, that of all sensible men! " But it stands to reason that such writers can only exist when sensible people do as a matter of fact agree; and it follows that works which possess the solid, restful quality of Jane Austen's must be the product, in a sense, of many minds and not of one. *Daphnis and Chloe* could only have been written at a time when all sensible men conceived the pleasures of sensuality to be one of the blessings of life; when they felt no need to dress up or disguise young desire to make it charming. But when, in an age in which all sensible people are not agreed on this point, Mr. George Moore, for instance, attempts to write in the same vein, consciousness of being naughty or daring inevitably creeps into his work. The benign and careful lubricity of Anatole France is not free from a taint of malicious awareness; he may have been sure that he was right to be on the side of Venus, but he was all too conscious that there was another. *Securus judicat orbis terrarum*; and it is a huge help to the artist to feel that " the verdict of the world is conclusive "—and on his side. It is hard for a rebel to attain the peace of assurance.

This complete harmony and confidence contributes enormously to our pleasure in reading Jane Austen; but since it comes by grace and fortune, let us consider her imitable qualities. *Persuasion* is, in my opinion, the most perfectly constructed of her novels. The theme is definite, and limited with great discretion: it is the story of the re-engagement of two lovers after a parting which took place seven years before. The reader anticipates their reunion and there are no external obstacles to it: Captain Wentworth is still unmarried—even heart-free; and he is now well-off; Anne still loves him, and she has no obligations of loyalty or duty elsewhere which could prevent her from becoming his wife. In the heart of such a straightforward situation, how then does the author manage to create the suspense and

complication so important in exciting intense interest
in the happy ending to a love story? She does so by
telling it from the point of view of the one who is
compelled to be entirely passive throughout, partly
owing to her sex, but above all, owing to her previous conduct. It was Anne who broke off the
engagement. It is only Anne's feelings that we
follow; every other character is seen from outside.
We watch Wentworth only through her eyes (he is
never on the scene unless she is there), and his
behaviour in her presence, until near the end, is so
adjusted to the purpose of creating suspense that it
never conveys more than that his resentment may
possibly be changing into temperate good will.
Anne cannot hope for more than that. The reader
is made to identify himself entirely with Anne, so far
as Wentworth's behaviour is concerned, and to her
each stage in their relations is full of pain, perplexity,
and suspense, which the reader shares.

Henry James had a theory that it was necessary
to get rid of the omniscient observer; that everything recounted in a novel should be seen through
the eyes of some character in it; not necessarily the
same, and perhaps through one character after
another. *The Golden Bowl* was written on these
lines. It seems to me a fallacious general principle.
Let us test it by seeing what we should have lost had
Persuasion been constructed in obedience to it. Let
us suppose that everything, all the incidents, all the
characters, Sir Walter Elliot, the Musgroves, Admiral
Croft and his wife and Wentworth had been seen
through Anne's eyes alone. Well, either Jane
Austen's own delightful view of them would have
been lost to us, or Anne would have become Jane
Austen herself, with her intellect, irony and critical
detachment; in which case we could never have
felt the same poignant sympathy for Anne and her
predicament. Suppose, on the other hand, that

the business of reporting had been transferred later on to the brain of Wentworth; we should then have known every stage of his affections, and consequently followed Anne's misreading of them with indifference. Henry James would probably have then turned, say, Lady Russell and Charles Musgrove into a pair of gossips of genius who would, by exhibiting at once an extraordinary clairvoyance and an odd blindness to obvious probabilities, have complicated considerably the situation. But what a loss such a transfiguration would have been! Charles Musgrove, while doubtless keeping his gun, his riding-breeches and his good temper, would have been endowed with his creator's restless analytical curiosity—in short, have become unrecognizable as a normal young English squire. Here lies the fatal flaw in Henry James's theory. If the narrator is abolished, the characters who narrate in his place become inevitably endowed with the novelist's own peculiar faculties and intellectual temper. This happened in his own later novels, in which the characters were often so steeped in the colours of their creator's mind, that their individual tints barely showed through the permeating dye.

Contrast this method with the instinctive tact of Jane Austen in such matters. Her characters are introduced briefly and objectively. At first her heroine is a mere background figure, a member of the Elliot family: " Anne Elliot had been a very pretty girl, but her bloom had vanished early "; that is all we hear about her in the first chapter, which is devoted to exposing so amusingly the vanity of her father and sister, and those financial family embarrassments, incidentally the initial causes of bringing Anne and Wentworth together again. How quietly and inevitably it is done! The letting of Kellynch Hall is the first step in the love-story, yet we are not aware of it as such, but

233

only as part of the comedy of Sir Walter. This is the art of construction. Gradually Anne comes to the front as the most sensible and honourable member of the family. The novelist continues to present scenes, to describe thoughts, and feelings, and characters objectively. She uses the privilege of omniscience only in the case of Anne's emotions; and that these are centred upon her old lover gives him a special prominence in the eyes also of the reader. Although Wentworth says and does very little, that little has peculiar weight because it reaches us through Anne's feelings about it. He alone is seen subjectively, emotionally; and this gives him a unique position among the other characters. Thus he need not do much or say much to make an impression on us; he is a man who is loved, moving among other men and women who are observed. This gives an intensity to all the scenes in which Wentworth appears which links them together in the reader's mind, so that the surrounding comedy never for a moment destroys, though it may suspend, the continuity of the love-interest.

ALDOUS HUXLEY

MR. ALDOUS HUXLEY'S last volume of stories, *Brief Candles*, met with a tepid reception from reviewers who a few years ago would have praised enthusiastically, but their comments will only influence opinion in so far as these reflect an already existing discontent or satiety in his many admirers. There is no falling off, quite the reverse, in Mr. Huxley's penetration and execution; the merits of these stories must, indeed, have been embarrassing to those who wished to convey their disappointment. Each story is a complete expression of its theme, and the words in which every detail is described are precise and, when occasion requires, charming. The style is his own fine blend of intellectual curiosity and æsthetic sensibility; at the same time it is faultlessly correct. It is not, it cannot be, the craftsman who has disappointed his critics. His reviewers must have started by asking themselves another question: Are these stories worth telling? That an inclination to underrate his aims should appear already asserting itself is due to a common phenomenon—satiety. All authors are musical-boxes which play a limited number of tunes; sooner or later their readers become aware that they are listening to variations on tunes heard before; and the crucial period in the history of every literary talent occurs when an author's merits are thus taken for granted while his limitations are discussed. Mr. Aldous Huxley is on the edge of it. Yet every real talent survives it, and not infrequently after the ordeal by satiety those books which were received with indifference are recognized as the flowering of that talent. Even the letters of the inexhaustibly resourceful Dickens betray now and then an uneasiness lest readers of some forth-coming number will exclaim: " Hullo! the same old stuff "; *David Copperfield* was a tremendous effort on his part to draw from a fresh and deeper spring.

With Aldous Huxley this period was bound to occur early in his literary career, because the attitude towards life he has hitherto compelled us to share is one in which no one can remain contented for long together. It is detached, exacting—and inconclu-sive, and we find ourselves perpetually looking down on human nature; we never have the exhilaration of looking up. To share his detachment is, for a while, flattering; for though we may often recognize our own failings and ignoble predicaments in his pages, these facts exist in our own lives, we know, in contexts which are omitted from his books and relieve them of much of their meanness. It is primarily, therefore, other people who appear to us to be mercilessly exposed. This is agreeable until we realize that, after all, it is as necessary to respect and like at least a few other people as it is to respect ourselves. And this Mr. Aldous Huxley seldom, or never, allows us to do. True, there is one character in *Point-Counter-Point* in whose behalf our admira-tion is claimed. But Rampion is unconvincing com-pared with Kingham in *Two or Three Graces*, who was suggested by the same model. In the case of Rampion we were asked to take the fineness of his nature on trust: in that of Kingham we were acquainted directly and cogently with the obverse side of that same nature, its histrionic, suspicious, ruthless egotism. How well that was done! But what is Rampion? A point of view, a conduit-pipe of theories upon life.

It is not true, as has been said, that there are

no amiable people in Mr. Huxley's stories; there are. But the aspects of them to which he attends are seldom admirable, and either chill or make us despise them. Take, for example, Lord Edward Tantamount, the elderly peer whose enthusiasm for science came to him on the wind of a revelation of the obvious, namely, his solidarity with the world and the interconnection of all things: " It's all like music" (he said to himself), " harmonics and counter-point and modulations. But you've got to be trained to listen." And who thenceforth, and with a singleness of mind only possible to the pure in heart, sits down to correlate phenomena—especially connected with newts. Lord Edward's concentration and his ignorance of the world outside his laboratory were, no doubt, fit subjects for ironic observation; but in the hands of Mr. Huxley he grows gradually into a grotesque old noodle. We forget as we read that he is also worthy of affection-ate respect. Take, too, another figure from *Point-Counter-Point*, Bidlake the painter, twice married, in whose life there had been one relation, broken by death, so perfect that when it ended he could never bear to recall it again, but lived for ephemeral satis-factions on the hypothesis that he would live for ever. In the book he appears as an honest, roughish sort of sensualist, and at last as a hapless victim, whose roots are gradually and painfully wrenched by disease from the common compost in which he had imbedded his talent. That most significant passion in his life is confined to a sentence, while what is presented in the novel is his depressing de-feat: *Sanitas sanitatum omnia sanitas*—so much for robust old Bidlake, who was good at seeing feminine contours in the landscape. The same point could be illustrated by Mr. Huxley's handling of his flibberty amusement-hunters such as Mrs. Viveash. They are not so bad as they appear in his pages.

I can imagine the author interrupting me here by saying: " Well, since my characters have apparently suggested that to you, I don't see ground for complaint." To which I would reply: " It is a matter of emphasis. You always leave to my imagination to supply what is amiable or exhilarating, while employing your skill in fixing my attention on what is not." What is the explanation? This is a question which the analyst, confronted by Mr. Aldous Huxley's work, must attempt to answer.

II

Before making the attempt it is necessary to define his position in the world of letters. For although his limitations are not inevitable consequences of his peculiar gifts, they are affiliated to the qualities which make his work important.

No one can deny its importance to his contemporaries; and the interest which it has roused confirms it. He has succeeded in recording modes of feeling and thinking characteristic of his own generation which have never been described before. He has made his contemporaries more aware of their own responses, moral, amoral, æsthetic and intellectual; their indifference, impatience, obtusity, disappointment, sensibility. He has diagnosed subtly and mercilessly the diseases of modern self-consciousness, and described the ignobly comic falsifications of emotion which result from them. But this is not for the critic the central fact about him. His distinguishing mark is that he stands out as the most deeply and widely cultured of modern novelists. I am not sure that even in the past one can point to any other writer of fiction who has illumined his picture of life with cross lights drawn from an equal familiarity with contemporary knowledge and theory. George Eliot only comes near to him. It is one of the great merits of Mr. Wells that his imagination has absorbed his knowledge of science, but Mr. Wells is far from being a man of culture in other respects. The peculiarity of Mr. Huxley's work is that not only science in all its branches is frequently laid under contribution, but also the history of art, music, poetry, medicine, society and philosophy. What is disconcerting is the contrast between the extraordinary many-coloured richness of the light he pours upon his subjects, and that these subjects are taken from small and often stuffy corners of the big common world of experience. He is the most universal of novelists in his references and one of the most limited in focus. His constant theme is love and sex, and the result of his investigations is dissatisfaction, or more positively disgust. The two questions which he continually asks are, what is the right attitude towards sex-attraction, and is it all-important, or unimportant, or of moderate importance? This preoccupation he shares with his age, which is thinking as hard and confusedly about sex as the one preceding it thought about religion. Hence the peculiar interest of his fiction to his contemporaries. No one in his senses could say that sex was a small corner of experience; it is, after all, the staple theme of fiction. But it is either the falsifications of emotion by self-consciousness, or the dullness of mere promiscuity, that he studies. The failure of the intellectually honest to fall in love romantically, and the failure of the frankly canine to get satisfaction without romance, are aspects of sex he has made his own; and he has done them extraordinarily well—the lovers who try to drag their feelings up to emotional heights, and those who, no less fatally, endeavour to satisfy instinct without committing their emotions. He is a merciless analyst of emotional play-acting in love; that tendency to pretend one feels like someone else or like

some character in a book. He is the student of
" Bovaryism " in all its forms. Those who are not
interested in his drift either enjoy, or detest, his
careful lubricity, for his skill in the rapid suggestion
of such scenes is equal to that of Anatole France.
To those scenes he owes not a little of his popularity,
though they are not the substance of his work.

III

Point-Counter-Point is the most ambitious of his
novels, but he does not achieve in it more than he
had done in *Antic Hay*. That book also took us
from scene to scene in which different characters
were interpreting experience, chiefly amorous, according to their different sense of values. The effect
was desolating, though often amusing. The title
Point-Counter-Point suggested that he had hoped
in this later book to make the music of humanity
audible: " It's all like music; harmonics and coun-
terpoint and modulations." But we heard only
distressing jangle. The author had not pulled the
world together in his own head any better than
in *Antic Hay*. That feat so necessary to the artist,
who if his work is to have balance must pretend, at
any rate, that he has done so, is one of enormous
difficulty to him. To begin with he cannot pretend;
and no novelist is more sensitive to the inconsequent
queerness of life, and the inconsistency of what is
happening simultaneously in every moment of experience. His scientific awareness makes it harder
still for him to unify his impression of life, except
as a patternless confusion in which any sense of
proportion is as good as another, and all moral
judgments equally valid. Intellectually, therefore,
he is entirely sceptical, but temperamentally he
seems to be one who is driven into making passionate, not to say acrimonious, distinctions. It is this

perpetual discord between the indulgent scepticism of his intellect and the severity of his uncorroborated reactions, that is responsible for that acrid discontent which emanates from his fiction, shot though it is with gleams of beauty.

In *Point-Counter-Point* he has borrowed a device from M. André Gide, an author who is in a similar predicament. Mr. Aldous Huxley introduces a novelist into the story who resembles himself. Like the uncle in Gide's *Faux Monnayeurs*, " Philip " is both an actor in the story and a spectator. The passage in which " Philip " meditates on board ship upon his own art is instructive to the critic.

" The heart was Burlap's speciality. ' You'll never write a good book,' he had said oracularly, ' unless you write from the heart.' It was true; Philip knew it. But was Burlap the man to say so, Burlap whose books were so heartfelt that they looked as though they had come from the stomach, after an emetic? If he went in for the grand simplicities, the results would be no less repulsive. Better to cultivate his own particular garden for all it was worth. Better to remain rigidly and loyally oneself. Oneself? But this question of identity was precisely one of Philip's chronic problems. It was so easy for him to be almost anybody, theoretically and with his intelligence. He had such a power of assimilation that he was often in danger of being unable to distinguish the assimilator from the assimilated, of not knowing among the multiplicity of his rôles who was the actor. The amoeba, when it finds a prey, flows round it, incorporates it and oozes on. There was something amoeboid about Philip Quarles's mind. It was like a sea of spiritual protoplasm, capable of flowing in all directions, of engulfing every

241   R

object in its path, of trickling into every crevice, of filling every mould and, having engulfed, having filled, of flowing on towards other obstacles, other receptacles, leaving the first empty and dry. At different times in his life and even at the same moment he had filled the most various moulds. He had been a cynic and also a mystic, a humanitarian and also a contemptuous misanthrope; he had tried to live the life of detached and stoical reason, and another time he had aspired to the unreasonableness of natural and uncivilized existence. The choice of moulds depended at any given moment on the books he was reading, the people he was associating with. Burlap, for example, had redirected the flow of his mind into those mystical channels which it had not filled since he discovered Boehme in his undergraduate days. Then he had seen through Burlap and flowed out again, ready, however, at any time to let himself trickle back once more, whenever the circumstances seemed to require it. He was trickling back at this moment, the mould was heart-shaped. Where was the self to which he could be loyal?

" The female missionaries passed in silence. Looking over Elinor's shoulder he saw that she was reading the *Arabian Nights* in Mardrus's translation. Burtt's *Metaphysical Foundations of Modern Science* lay on his knees; he picked it up and began looking for his place. Or wasn't there a self at all? he was wondering. No, no, that was untenable, that contradicted immediate experience. He looked over the top of his book at the enormous blue glare of the sea. The essential character of the self consisted precisely in that liquid and undeformable ubiquity; in that capacity to espouse all contours and yet remain unfixed in any form, to take, and with an equal

facility efface, impressions. To such moulds as
his spirit might from time to time occupy, to such
hard and burning obstacles as it might flow
round, submerge, and, itself cold, penetrate to the
fiery heart of, no permanent loyalty was owing.
The moulds were emptied as easily as they had
been filled, the obstacles were passed by. But
the essential liquidness that flowed where it would,
the cool indifferent flux of intellectual curiosity—
that persisted and to that his loyalty was due.
If there was any single way of life he could lastingly
believe in, it was that mixture of pyrrhonism and
stoicism which had struck him, an inquiring schoolboy among the philosophers, as the height of
human wisdom and into whose mould of sceptical
indifference he had poured his unimpassioned
adolescence. Against the pyrrhonian suspense of
judgment and the stoical imperturbability he had
often rebelled. But had the rebellion ever been
really serious? Pascal had made him a Catholic—
but only so long as the volume of *Pensées* was
open before him. There were moments when, in
the company of Carlyle or Whitman or bouncing
Browning, he had believed in strenuousness for
strenuousness' sake. And then there was Mark
Rampion. After a few hours in Mark Rampion's
company he really believed in noble savagery; he
felt convinced that the proudly conscious intellect
ought to humble itself a little and admit the
claims of the heart, aye and the bowels, the loins,
the bones and skin and muscles, to a fair share of
life. The heart again! Burlap had been right,
even though he was a charlatan, a sort of swind-
ling thimble-rigger of the emotions. The heart!
But always, whatever he might do, he knew quite
well in the secret depths of his being that he
wasn't a Catholic, or a strenuous liver, or a
mystic, or a noble savage. And though he some-

times nostalgically wished he were one or other
of these beings, or all of them at once, he was
always secretly glad to be none of them and at
liberty, even though his liberty was in a strange
paradoxical way a handicap and a confinement
to his spirit.

'That simple story of yours,' he said aloud;
'it wouldn't do.'

Elinor looked up from the *Arabian Nights*.
'Which simple story?'

'That one you wanted me to write.'

'Oh, *that!*' She laughed. 'You've been
brooding over it a long time.'

'It wouldn't give me my opportunity,' he
explained. 'It would have to be solid and deep.
Whereas I'm wide; wide and liquid. It wouldn't
be in my line.'

'I could have told you that the first day I
met you,' said Elinor, and returned to Schehera-
zade."

Clearly there is little that the critic can tell Mr.
Aldous Huxley about his work that he does not
already know himself; but this passage contains
much that his critics should remember. They must
accept him as a writer not " deep " but " wide."
They must accept his novels and stories being disquisitions illustrated by characters, since his supreme
merit lies in width of reference, and in putting facts
in juxtaposition which his omnivorous reading and
perpetual reflection have assembled. The deep pleasure in reading Mr. Huxley lies in following the movement of his mind. He is aware also of the irritation
produced in some readers by his inevitably discursive
methods. There is an amusing self-critical bit of
dialogue on this point between " Philip " and his
wife. They are driving in a motor and they have
just run over a dog.

" ' It was his fault,' said Philip. ' He wasn't looking. That's what comes of running after the females of one's species.'

There was a silence. It was Philip who broke it.

' Morality'd be very queer,' he reflected aloud, ' if we loved seasonally, not all the year round. Moral and immoral would change from one month to another. Primitive societies are apt to be more seasonal than cultivated ones. Even in Sicily there are twice as many births in January as in August. Which proves conclusively that in the spring the young man's fancy.... But nowhere *only* in the spring. There's nothing human quite analogous to heat in mares or she-dogs. Except,' he added, ' except perhaps in the moral sphere. A bad reputation in a woman allures like the signs of heat in a bitch. Ill-fame announces accessibility. Absence of heat is the animal's equivalent of the chaste woman's habits and principles....'

Elinor listened with interest and at the same time a kind of horror. Even the squashing of a wretched animal was enough to set that quick, untiring intelligence to work. A poor starved pariah dog had its back broken under the wheels and the incident evoked from Philip a selection from the vital statistics of Sicily, a speculation about the relativity of morals, a brilliant psychological generalization. It was amusing, it was unexpected, it was wonderfully interesting; but oh! she almost wanted to scream."

Not unnatural; still Elinor's " desire to scream " was not a good criticism. Mr. Aldous Huxley's loyalty is committed to " a cool indifferent flux of intellectual curiosity." It is his point; it is that which makes him unique among English writers of fiction.

He is an Anatole France, only far more learned, who has not attained to the suavity of indifference. He is therefore more interesting, but less successful, as an artist.

D. H. LAWRENCE

I

IT is certainly the duty and it should be the delight
of a critic to examine his contemporaries. This is
the most difficult part of his work. Critics are most
at home with old books; it takes apparently many
minds to measure a good writer. The collected
works of critics show they have been at their best in
expounding " case-made law " on classics, in refining
upon and combining the judgments of others. I
was aware of Lawrence for fifteen years, also that to
understand contemporary thought I must tackle
him. Yet I put it off and off, writing upon him at
last, and for the first time, shortly before his death.
Why did I shirk it so long? Chiefly laziness. I
knew Lawrence to be a large and difficult subject,
and even now I am not in a position to deal with
him, though I have read him with some assiduity
since he died. He is a difficult subject, partly
because he was a seer, and originality in that kind
is difficult to place in any sort of perspective; and
still more because, though his pictures were vivid,
they were not hung on a wall, so to speak, as
finished products, but rather carried on the retina of
his own eyes, into which the reader was forced to
gaze in order to see them. And when the reader did
look into those eyes, he was conscious also of a profound internal confusion behind, often the more
confused thanks to the excruciated efforts of the
artist to account in abstract terms for what was
inside him. These explanations and generalizations,
too, were thrust before the reader with an arrogance
which spoke more of the author's own dark distress

than of his certainty that he had succeeded in saying
at last what he felt to be so important.

He harangues us like Carlyle, whom he resembled in many aspects, the artist in him was
doubled with the rhetorician. He too sprang from
a poverty-cramped, sullen, illiterate fighting-stock;
he too was the favoured child of a mother who represented in those surroundings a superior and
pious refinement; he too was born with a suspicion of any sort of agreement, and with a
conviction, often agonized, that everybody must
be wrong except himself; he was born too with a
faculty for exquisite sympathy with individuals and
an almost sadistic relish for the sufferings of people
in general—" the mostly fools " of Carlyle being
translatable in Lawrentian terms by " all corpses
or swine "; he too was a humorist whose sense of
fun sprang from a constantly tragic sense of life;
he too was a prodigious egotist, yet in himself
strangely lovable and fascinating, his egotism finding relief in minatory " uplift " diatribes, and showing itself in his intolerance of the smallest self-
assertion on the part of others. For Lawrence the
egotist, to whom the experience of " love " was the
crucial test of individual excellence, egotism, legitimate or illegitimate, in that relation, was a central
problem. He too was, in the sense in which that
phrase has a meaning apart from accomplishment,
" a great man," one whom to be near, whether
through his writings, or directly, meant for others
an enhancement of life; he too was an aesthete
who constantly mistook himself for a moral teacher.
(Not a fundamentally fatal mistake, since in individual life aesthetic and moral judgments are often
indistinguishable, but fatal when the moralist pre-
tends also to legislate for society at large. Thus the
political philosophies of Carlyle and Lawrence are as
weak as they are emphatic.) The prose of Lawrence

was marred, too, by the same defect; like Carlyle he valued earnestness, a state of feeling in himself, more than truth. Both, as writers, were the victims of their own passionate garrulity. Both abounded in insight and in unforgettable phrases; but there was a certain headiness (how violently Lawrence himself would have repudiated that word!) in all they wrote. They had the same fault of letting their feelings run on without thinking of the reality of their object. Indeed, Lawrence's temper of mind was extraordinarily like Carlyle's, lending itself to histrionic gestures, to sweeping contempt, harsh laughter with aerial overtones, dramatic projections of his own emotions into things animate and inanimate, and a dangerous and lonely pride. Though his gospel that we ought to return to a more instinctive way of living is entirely different from Carlyle's, who was terrified of the body, Lawrence was just as dogmatic, just as sure that everyone round him was either sick or dead. In Carlyle this certainty often took the form of lofty commiseration—" poor " so-and-so was his favourite adjective; in Lawrence it took the form of indignation and terror of contamination.

Carlyle's rhetoric has become mere noise to this generation, intolerable because his " message " seems to concern nothing vital to them. It helps no one, yet it is delivered as though it were of the utmost moment. Most fatiguing. But that does not prevent the critic from recognizing Carlyle as a great English writer, or the historian from admitting his past influence. To many of his contemporaries his ideas were " seeds of creation lying burningly on the Divine Hand." They are cold now, while those of Lawrence are still glowing, and if I understand the times in which I live, they are likely to grow brighter in the years immediately ahead. Lawrence has something of vital importance to *us*. This, however, is not the only interesting fact about Lawrence to the critic of to-day, any more than the appeal of Carlyle's message was the only interesting fact about him to the critical temperaments of his own time.

Lawrence is a great figure, and one likely in the near future to loom larger still. Except some of his short stories, his construction was faulty, though this is also true of most novelists admitted to be great.

The novel is of all literary forms the one in which perfection is rarest; and it can be, if successful, the most artistic of all forms, precisely because its aesthetic equilibrium lies deep within it and is independent of all rules. Coherence so complicated can only be achieved by mind and heart working together better than the author knows. His intellect and heart (his responses to what he loved and hated) did not always work together. His intellect was apt to run theorizing ahead of his perceptions and responses, or, turning back, to over-emphasize them or add a gloss with a view to propaganda. His will to live and write in the condition of an absolute earnestness confused as often as it sharpened his insight, and the results in his pages exhausted readers already tired by the excessively *physical* impact of his images and impressions. But how incomparably vivid those impressions were, how packed with vital experience those pages! His inspiration was unmistakable; he trusted to it to pull him through every difficulty, his violent temperament supplying a unity which he scorned to achieve also as a craftsman. That, no doubt, was an error. But how refreshing the results were compared with the works of novelists to whom Mr. Roy Campbell's epigram applies:

You praise the firm restraint with which they write—

I'm with you there, of course:
They use the snaffle and the curb all right,
But where's the bloody horse?

II

Immediately after Lawrence's death a good deal
of cautiously kind criticism appeared, written by
men who disliked his work but did not now quite
dare to damn it, his fame having entered on that
posthumous stage in which an author's having
flouted conventions counts less against him. (No
one really minds acutely a dead man having shocked
society.) In contrast to these pronouncements Mr.
E. M. Forster wrote a letter to *The Nation* declaring
that Lawrence had been, among his contemporaries,
the greatest of imaginative novelists. Mr. T. S.
Eliot then wrote a letter saying that two others
(unnamed) had as much right to be so described,
and complaining that the statement was meaningless
unless the words " great " and " imaginative " were
defined. Now all assertive terms of praise are apt
to be vague. Unfortunately, I missed Mr. Forster's
reply, if he made one; but since I agree with him
and might easily have used those vague terms myself, let me explain what I should have meant by
them. By " great " when applied to a novelist, I
should have meant to suggest that the writer in
question was chiefly concerned with some of the
most important things in life, and had a power of
conveying his preoccupation with them adequate to
their importance; by " imaginative," that the merit
of his work at its best was akin to poetry, and that
the world which he had created was subjective and
every detail of it saturated with emotion. Both
these statements hold good of Lawrence. There is
the literature that lends the charm of imagination
to reality (this is the kind I prefer myself at its best),

and there is the literature which adds the force of
reality to the imaginary. Lawrence's work on the
whole belonged to the latter class. Neither his
characters nor his stories owed much to observation.
He was a seer rather than a fashioner. To read
him is to be steeped in his personality, and his
creations are projected, but never separated, from
himself. He was one of those artists who do well to
be absorbed in the salvation of their souls (so boring
a preoccupation to others whose souls are different),
because it was only in relation to that perpetual
inner conflict that he could invent imaginary figures
or be interested in imaginary events. His invention
was entirely dependent upon that interest. He had,
for example, a curious contempt for the eye and
the reports of the eye. The eye apprehends from a
distance, and the value of its reports depend on the
mind. Lawrence yearned after closer contacts.
The sense of touch, which can be so overwhelming,
seemed to him to possess a mystic power of divination. But it was not through touch or sight, or any
one sense alone, that he strove to apprehend the
nature of things, but with his whole being at once.
His peculiarity as a writer is that he succeeds so
extraordinarily in responding with his whole body
to what is before him. He interprets animals,
plants, landscape, gestures, through his sex as well
as his senses. Only of the judgments of the mind
as to the nature of things was he distrustful, and he
distrusted them because analytical observation and
reason interrupted and destroyed that deep vascular
response to them which he most valued. It is
certainly a very serious limitation in one who set
out to respond to life as a complete man that he
should have omitted, as far as was consistent with
sanity, to use the human reason. And he did his
best not to use it. Possessed as he was by this
imaginative craving for the closest contact with life,

it was inevitable that the act of physical union between man and woman should be for him the central
experience, and seem to him the closest and purest
form of communion possible between human beings.
Hence his fury against any ideas, prohibitions,
habits, morals, or theories which either prevent or
spoil or degrade it.

III

I began by comparing Lawrence with Carlyle.
The discussion of sex fills to-day the place taken by
religious controversy in the times of Mill, Carlyle,
and Huxley. It needed then the same kind of
courage to speak one's mind about Christianity, as it
needs to-day to speak about sex; and the topic has
the same kind of vital interest for all who ask themselves the question: How ought I to live? Carlyle
was thought to be very bold, and yet somehow to
have saved the sanctions of faith. If there is a great
deal of truth in Neitzsche's epigram, " Carlyle was an
English atheist who rose to fame for not being one,"
there is also point in describing Lawrence as a religious prophet who was mistaken for a pornographer.
The other modern prophets, Shaw and Wells, have
done their work. I no longer see any trace of their
influence on the creative as opposed to the passive
section of the young generation. The young are
interested in personal, not in social problems.
Lawrence has therefore something to say on two
questions crucial to them: how to preserve an
inner integrity and hold themselves together in
spite of rejecting all rules of thumb in conduct; and
how to prevent sexual life degenerating into squalor,
now that belief in prohibitions is going. The main
drift of Lawrence's work, the strongest infection
from it, is reverence for sex. Sex is the sun which
warms and animates his whole world. What, ac-

cording to him, is wrong with civilization is that it does not recognize sex as the source of the natural warm flow of common sympathy between everybody as well as between man and woman.

In his pamphlet *Pornography and Obscenity*, an answer to Lord Brentford's *Do we Need a Censor?*, Lawrence expressed what any intelligent reader might have inferred from his novels, a loathing of pornography as " an attempt to insult sex, to do dirt on it." " This," he added, " is unpardonable . . . *the* insult to the human body, *the* insult to vital human relationship." In that pamphlet he also mentioned a passage in my review in the *Sunday Times* of his *Pansies*. It ran: " his attitude towards sex is misunderstood; it is neither ignoble nor ugly. It occupies too large a place in any possible view of the world except his own, and therefore appears obtrusive to others, but I repeat it is neither ignoble nor ugly. He has attempted to express the Lucretian poetry of lust. If he did convert the world, two things would disappear from it: the love-lyric and the smoking-room story." I had not read Lawrence then as thoroughly as I have done since. Had I done so I should not have expressed my respect merely in negatives, and I should have said that he had expressed far more than the poetry of Lucretian lust. What is interesting is his comment upon the last sentence of that review. He admitted its partial truth, adding that that depended on the kind of love-lyric the reviewer had in mind. If it were a *Du bist wie eine Blume* sentimental lyric on purity, it might as well go, but if it were a question of a sound love-lyric, such as " My love is like a red, red rose," then we were on different ground. Still, there is more in my objection than that. There is such overwhelming emphasis in all Lawrence's work upon the physical, and he so dreads to allow the contemplation or even the recognition of beauty of character in a love-relation, that I cannot see but that my comment holds good in the main. What he did achieve as a novelist and poet was to make intercourse beautiful and serious, and to come nearer to absorbing some aspects of that experience into literature than other writers before him; a daring, salutary and considerable achievement. True, in doing so he often slipped into ugliness, theoretic elaboration and over-emphasis, as in the privately-printed *Lady Chatterley's Lover*, also into defiant use of obscene words in order to compel his readers to take sex fully into their consciousness; but it must be remembered that he had to wrestle with the deficiencies of language, our sex-vocabulary being composed of two equally distorting sets of words, one scientific, and therefore useless for conveying emotion, and the other of the gutter with the wrong associations. His burning seriousness alone enabled him to accomplish what he did, and what he did has made it easier for those who follow to take into poetry and literature the whole of life.

IV

The technical peculiarity of Lawrence's later poems is that they are written in the spoken word. He " talks " his poetry. Even when he uses rhyme he nearly always does so only to give an added air of carelessness to the composition, which helps in some cases to intensify the contempt he wishes to convey. This distrust of traditional form and literary phrasing is genuine in him. It is not in his case a concession to the prevailing taste of the moment—that irrational preference for what is unfinished and incomplete in art, whether in painting, music, or letters. It is a distrust which is a consequence of his temperament and outlook. His methods happen to be in the fashion, but they belong to the body of his thought like a skin. Literary language is the most perfect creation of the civilized mind; it is the most delicate and stable means of communication available between man and man. But the civilized mind is to Lawrence an evil barrier between us and " Life "; more than that, " the mind " itself is a poison which has defiled the vital springs at which we ought to drink.

His aim is to make audible the voice of uncivilized man; and in order to interpret what he considers our instinctive and profound responses to experience, he has to use words in an extra-subtle and inventive fashion. Of this art he is a master. Consequently, though almost unintelligible to the simple, his work gives keen pleasure to the sophisticated. " Back to Nature " prophets—and Lawrence is the latest of these—have invariably found their audiences among their ultra-civilized contemporaries.

Lawrence's " natural man " is, of course, a very different creature from Rousseau's, from Tolstoy's, or from that of Whitman, whose object, like Lawrence's, was to send forth a " barbaric yawp over the roofs of the world," and to " outbid from the start all the cautious old hucksters " of literature. If this were not so, Lawrence would be an echo, not a writer of importance; and whatever you may think of his philosophy, he is important. That philosophy has been very ably expounded and attacked by Mr. Wyndham Lewis in his last book, *Paleface*, which those who wish to collate and compare scattered " tendencies " in modern literature should read. Rousseau's " noble savage " was a creature who, had he been a racehorse, might have been described as by the Savoyard Vicar out of Mme. de Warens; Tolstoy's, the religious and resigned peasant; Whitman's, any young bus-con-

ductor, hatter's assistant, or tripper to Coney
Island, provided his friend was more to him than his
wife. While Lawrence's " noble savage " is a being of
whom no conception was possible before the researches
of modern anthropologists and sex-psychologists.

Rousseau's conception of the superiority of
" the natural man " seemed plausible to his own
generation, as the stories of Marmontel and others
show; and even Voltaire, though he thought the
" back to Nature " cry fudge, used Rousseau's conception himself as a stick with which to beat
the priests in *L'Ingenu*. Tolstoy's attribution of
" grace " in a special sense to tillers of the soil—
it was partly aesthetic, they were *le vrai grand monde*
—did not to many readers seem extravagant at a
moment when a return to primitive Christianity
seemed a possible solution of all social and moral
problems; nor did Whitman's idea of the divinity
of the ordinary man jar on a generation which had
an exorbitant faith in democracy.

In the same way, Lawrence's conception of
the superiority of instinctive man now chimes
with the heart-searchings and body-searchings of
psycho-analysis. A good many people are prepared
to admit that it is far from silly to think that
the body is more important than the mind, and
therefore that this, the latest type of " noble
savage," may be the model for us all.

Such an attitude is, of course, heresy to the
religious, to whom it offers at best a mysticism of the
senses in the place of another ideal; and it is nonsense to those to whom belief in civilization seems
a first condition of sanity, since in so far as they can
place man in nature, he appears to be an insurgent
child who, in a world without justice, love, or sense,
has succeeded in introducing a measure of those
desirable things. To both the religious and the
rational Lawrence's philosophy is therefore a sum-

mons calling man back to the dark, primitive condition out of which he has slowly raised himself. Yet although the positive doctrine behind his inspiration may be utterly inacceptable, and though the highest emotion it offers may be only a sense of self-obliterating oneness with environment such as a uni-cellular being might be surmised to feel even better than man can feel it, nevertheless as a point of view from which to criticize human beings it has its effectiveness. The value of the work of Rousseau, Tolstoy, or Whitman did not lie in their positive ideals, but in the fact that these enabled them to see civilized man from outside, to examine his emotions and aims and detect their falsity and shallowness. The critical value of much of Lawrence's work is indisputable. In the collection of *Pansies*, he is mostly attacking, though in a few instances we see into a very private ecstasy of his own, still deeper than his wrath and contempt. The reader must not be disturbed by the brag and egotism of *Pansies*; there is that in it which excuses over-confidence.

Let me throw out a hint as to the best way of reading this book. I can do this because I began myself to read it in the wrong way: I treated it like a book of separate poems each of which could be judged on its own merits; and if the reader does this he will get little out of it. Many of the " pansies " will seem hardly worth while, though he may come across some first-rate descriptive passages and phrases which startle by their fine audacity; and here and there, even before he has been caught up into companionship with the writer, may discover some little poem such as this:

Desire may be dead,
And still a man can be
A meeting place for sun and rain,

Wonder outwaiting pain,
As in a wintry tree.

Nothing very remarkable? No: so I thought;
though while repeating those lines to myself I knew
that only a poet could have written them. But
when I read them again as a moment in a series of
moments—some ecstatic, cosmic, some expressing
lassitude and a mystic's dryness, many a rollicking
humorous contempt, others a wail of despairing
indignation—then even those few bare graceful
lines took on an added significance.

In reading any poet, especially one whose sense
of beauty is dependent on an unfamiliar conception
of the significance of life, it is necessary to become
for a time that poet. One must understand what
it feels like to feel like him; one can recover one's
own personality afterwards, and measure the loss
and gain which temporary surrender has involved.
You must let the moods of this poet go over you like
the tide; and then you can examine the wrinkles
left in the sand. Decided gain, definite loss—that
is my own verdict. When I began re-reading the
poems straight through, I was a dilapidated sceptical old creature, just capable, if pulled together,
of prospering placidly on good literature. After
my surrender, my imagination and vitality were
intensified to a pitch which enabled me to enjoy
not only *Pansies*, but any creative poetry. There
was something in it which it had been a decided
gain to share. I understood Blake's proverbs:
" The pride of the peacock is the glory of God; the
lust of the goat is the bounty of God; the wrath of
the lion is the wisdom of God." I say I understood, I do not say that I believed, these proposi-
tions. That would have involved the sacrifice of
beauty and values of another kind which I was by
no means willing to forgo.

GERTRUDE STEIN

I

OUR period—I am speaking of a short stretch of time which, in the history of literature, will shrink to nothing—looks to me like a period in which small things are done well, valuable experiments are tried, and muddles are exploited without being cleared up. It seems to me rather a silly period. Enterprising writers, who are also self-critical, seem more than usually doubtful whether they are pioneers or will-o'-the-wisps—and chance it. Certainly more downright nonsense will pass as wonderful to-day than ever before. Respect for the unintelligible in prose and verse inhibits readers who, in other matters, show unmistakable signs of intelligence, from recognizing rubbish when they see it. The " dread of offending against the Unknown Beauty " has never exercised a more paralysing effect on criticism.

Among the Second Series of the Hogarth Press Essays you will find one by Miss Gertrude Stein. It bears the title *Composition as Explanation*; but if the word " explanation " raises hopes, you will be disappointed. The first part of the pamphlet is a lecture on her own work, which Miss Stein delivered at Oxford and other places; the latter half contains four specimen compositions of her own, bearing the titles, " Preciosilla," " A Saint in Seven " (not in " Heaven " but in " Seven," which has the advantage of meaning nothing), " Sitwell Edith Sitwell," " Jean Cocteau," " G. Stein." You must not think, nor must Miss Gertrude Stein, that she is alone in producing this kind of composition. I happened to pick up a book the other day, and on page 6 I read the following passage:

"A jagged hedge ahead led Jill aside. She likes a side saddle; he is laid aside; he is laid aside; he is laid aside; he is laid aside; he has skill; he has skill; she is less agile; she is less agile; she is less agile; a seal likes fish; a seal likes fish; he sighs as if he is half dead; she said she had a legal lease; she said she had a lease; she asked if he liked a fiddle; she asked if he fiddled; she is glad she filed a deed; all lads like hill-sides."

I turned the page and read, " The quay was gaily arrayed with flags the quack had qualms, but made no reply. Pick a quantity of walnuts for pickling." These passages possess unmistakably the same literary quality as, " Paul makes honey and orange-trees. Michael makes coal and celery. Louise makes rugs and reasonably long. Heloise makes the sea and she settles well away from it," which occurs in " A Saint in Seven."

I am sure it will not detract from the pleasure admirers of Miss Stein's work must take in these quotations to discover that they have been written by a less conscious artist in prose. The wind of inspiration bloweth where it listeth; and the fact that these passages are from Exercises 5 and 7 in " Pitman's Commercial Typewriting Manual " cannot rob this other artist of his meed of fame. That even when intent upon an end so remote from art as exercising a typist's fingers, we may produce the kind of " modern composition " destined, according to Miss Stein, to become classical, should be a matter of rejoicing. Personally, I prefer Miss Stein in her less austere, less repetitive moods. For instance, in a little piece called " Tails," which opens with a

261

word suggested, as often happens in her writings, by rhyme: " Tails: Cold pails, cold with joy no joy. A tiny seat that means meadows and a lapse of cuddles with cheese and nearly bats, all this went messed. The post placed a loud loose sprain. A rest is no better. It is better yet. All the time." I cannot help preferring this to her austerer later work (*Useful Knowledge*, 1929), in which the words " and one " are repeated a hundred times on a page, and " yes and yes " considerably more than a hundred times on another.

" Are There Six or Another Question? " she asks in a title to a poem in that book:

> One—Are there six?
> Two—Or another question?
> One—Are there six?
> Two—Or another question?
> Two—Are there six?
> One—Or another question?
> Two—Are there six?
> Two—Or another question?

This is the first poem I have ever read which consisted entirely of the repetition of its title.

I may be misjudging the labour of the artist, but it looks as though it would be easy to write like this if one abandoned one's mind to it. I hope I shall never be tempted to make fun of Miss Stein; I would far rather make fun of those who encourage her to write.

Miss Stein is not to be blamed for indulging in automatic writing. I remember once composing a piece of prose under the influence of gas, which struck me as singularly beautiful. Alas, only the last cadences could be recaptured on waking: " I prefer snails. Long may they continue, those black, blithering and blasted animals, to salt the rainy ground of virtue." However, even as I remembered those words, they seemed to lose their magic significance. I was not to blame for having composed them, but if my friends had persuaded me to mesmerise myself back into the state in which that sort of stuff is produced, and if, when I wrote a thousand pages of it down, they persuaded me that I was doing service to art by publishing it, they would be very much to blame indeed.

"I created then," she says in her lecture, "a prolonged present naturally I knew nothing of a continuous present but it came naturally to me to make one, it was simple it was clear to me and nobody knew why it was done like that, I did not myself although naturally to me it was natural." This is one of the more lucid passages in her "explanation," an explanation which is, unfortunately, itself too much of a "composition" to be clear. She begins by saying that "it is very likely that nearly everyone has been very nearly certain that something that is interesting is interesting them. Can they and do they." There is no need here for so much caution. We may take it as true that some people have found some things interesting. "Can they and do they" is otiose. Then Miss Stein asserts that "nothing changes from generation to generation except the thing seen and that makes a composition." This is not a happy way of saying what is familiar, namely, that different generations have different points of view which determine the kind of art which interests them. She continues: "Those who are creating the modern composition authentically are naturally only of importance when they are dead, because by that time the modern composition having become past is classified and the description of it is classical." This is very ill-expressed: the meaning is that new art is only recognized as "classical" after its own period has passed away.

263

So far, her lecture has consisted of three commonplaces obscurely expressed; finally she reaches her own work. " A continuous present is a continuous present. I made almost a thousand pages of continuous present. Continuous present is one thing and beginning again and again is another thing. These are both things. And then there is using everything." She began by " groping for a continuous present and for using everything by beginning again and again. . . . Having naturally done this I naturally was a little troubled with it when I read it," she confesses. But she persevered. " I did not begin again. I just began," she says, which means that she went on in the same manner:

" In this beginning naturally since I at once went on and on very soon there were pages and pages and pages more and more elaborated making a more and more continuous present including more and more using of everything and continuing more and more beginning and beginning and beginning."

This is a very candid description of her method. We seem to be listening to a little girl who has been taught that she was a genius, and encouraged to talk about " grown-up things." We can almost see her fumbling with her frock and fixing her candid eyes upon her admiring parents. Of course " very soon there were pages and pages of it."

" It was all so nearly alike it must be different and it is different, it is natural that if everything is used and there is a continuous present and a beginning again and again if it is all so alike it must be simply different and everything simply different was the natural way of creating it then."

Alas, the stuff *was* all " so nearly alike." Alas, the idea that the repetition of the same words *must*

264

be different, and that beginning the same sentence again and again led anywhere, was her fatal delusion. It is either very malicious or very asinine of other people to encourage her in it. She confesses that " the quality in the creation of expression the quality in a composition that makes it go dead just after it has been made is very troublesome." So I found when my laughing-gas essay " went dead " on me after I woke up. You see, if people did not encourage her she might lose confidence in her piffle.

The only significant statement in her lecture is that her work would have been " outlawed " in any other generation than this post-war one. That is horribly true, and in that fact alone resides the importance of Miss Gertrude Stein.

II

I was once reproached for allowing commas to be inserted in the passage from Miss Gertrude Stein's writings. They are said to have destroyed its delicate organic beauty. Well, the harm has been done, so I will quote another passage to show her quality. The two commas in it are in the text:

" November the fifteenth and simply so that simply so that simply in that simply in that simply so that in that simply in that simply in that simple way simply so that simply so that in that way simply in that way, simply in that way so that simply so that simply so that simply simply in that, simply in that so that simply so that simply so that simply in that, so that simply in that way.

Actually the fifteenth of November.

Played and plays and says and access,
Plays and played and access and impress, etc. etc."

How, one asks in amazement, can anyone
suppose this sort of writing to have any value? It
is that fact, not Miss Gertrude Stein's work, which
is interesting.

She wrote a good many years ago, a good many,
many, many, a good many, a good many ago, she,
she wrote a good many years ago, a little book
called *Tender Buttons*, and more recently a much
larger book. I have lost my *Tender Buttons*, and
into her last book I only glanced, seeing it was in the
same form and only cut up into different lengths.
Of course, if you start with a form which can convey
no meaning, which ignores syntax, and consists in
repeating either the same word or the next that
suggests itself while the intelligence is completely
in abeyance, it is impossible to develop; and her
work has shown no development. Miss Stein
sprang, fully armed like Minerva, from that part of
the human brain which is usually inaudible in
waking life, yet can sometimes be overheard jabbering nonsense to itself. Medical psychologists have
discovered recently that this jabbering may have a
value in diagnosing mental troubles, but that it
could have any other, only a generation which
theorized itself silly could suspect. Yet Mr. T. S.
Eliot has printed her in *The New Criterion* (in good
company), and Miss Edith Sitwell once praised her
as only fine writers are praised who run some danger
of being misunderstood. I fear I shall not get to
the bottom of this puzzle; but it is possible to indicate some of the proceedings by which people
manœuvre themselves into positions from which
rubbish in art appears worthy of respect. The in-
quiry is of wider application.

The door of welcome is first left ajar by some

experimenter in a new art-form. Then the art-
snobs (those whose desire to be the first to understand what others do not, is stronger than their
power of enjoying or understanding anything), lean
their backs against the door and push till it is wide
enough to admit any enormity. The experimenters
cannot then shut the door without leaving themselves
on the wrong side of it. The solidarity of all rebels
is the first thing to take account of in studying art
movements. Whether they are genuine discoverers
or humbugs, these rebels all stand in the same relation to current convention in taste; they are in the
same boat, and the same charges are levelled against
them all. Mr. Eliot is an obscure poet; incompre-
hensible to many himself; he cannot object to
Miss Stein's writings on the score of their impenetra-
bility, or to Mr. Joyce's, who has also taken to
writing intricate pitch-dark rigmaroles. Secondly,
all new movements are defended by aesthetic
theories. Alas, if these do not prove as much as is
wanted, they can be easily made to do so by the
application of a little logic. For instance, the recent
movement in painting originally had for its defence
the reasonable theory that the merit of a picture
does not depend upon its subject: that seemed safe
and sensible. We assented. But if the subject
was indifferent, why need it be recognizable when
painted? We were reminded that pots and carpets
could undoubtedly be beautiful, and that they conveyed no information about reality. Why then
should pictures? And we were presently given portraits in which the moustache of the sitter was dis-
cernible in one corner of the picture and one eye in
another, while the rest had no resemblance to
anything at all. Logically, we could not complain.
We could only murmur that we missed badly something which was to be found in pictures which the
ages had agreed in enjoying and the innovators

themselves still admired. We were reluctant to say
with the Rev. Dr. Opimian, " I must take pleasure
in the thing represented before I can derive any
from the representation," so we were next asked to
accept the dogma that as far as aesthetic emotion
is concerned drawing and painting have nothing to
do with representation. The same thing happened
with regard to literature. Our attention was drawn
to the fact that the aesthetic value of a poem, or of
a piece of prose, had no fixed ratio to the value of
the thought it expressed. We were next asked to
admire arrangements of words which had no meaning at all. Beauty in words, like beauty in pictorial
art, was to reside in pattern.

Miss Sitwell puts the matter clearly in her
essay, *Poetry and Criticism*:

" What may appear difficult (*i.e.* in modern
poetry) is the habit of forming abstract patterns
in words. We have long been accustomed to
abstract patterns in pictorial art, and to the idea
that music is an abstract art, but nobody to my
knowledge has ever gone so far in making abstract patterns in words as the modernist poet
has. The nearest approach known to me is
Beddoes'

> Adam, that old carrion-crow
> The old crow of Cairo.

There is, of necessity, a connecting thread running
through each pattern, otherwise it would not be a
pattern. . . ."

How slender this thread, presumably of sense, may
be, we have seen.

She then praises Miss Stein " for bringing back
life to our language . . . by breaking down predestined groups of words, their sleepy family habits
. . . and rebuilding them into new and vital

shapes." . . . "The question," she continues, " of the making of abstract patterns is far more important at this time than any question of whether free verse is on as high a level as other forms of verse." I agree; it is much more important. The idea that the stuff of literature is a mass of words which can be arranged like coloured pebbles to make a pattern, undercuts almost the whole conception of what makes it valuable to man. It is not what modernists are up to that is difficult to see, but the value of what they produce.

What Miss Sitwell means by " breaking down predestined groups of words, their sleepy family habits," is simply (to employ a word which Miss Stein in the passage quoted on page 265 has roused from its sleep) using them regardless of their sense, which Miss Sitwell herself does frequently, and Miss Stein habitually. The small basis of truth upon which they have raised this theory of literature is the fact of the aesthetic quality in the sound of vowels, consonants and rhymes in relation to rhythms, images, and sense. But what we mean by " word-music " is not the mere sound of words. " Cancer " is a word with an agreeable sound, and " cellar-door " is magnificent, yet they cannot be used as notes in chords apart from their sense.

Such are the logical processes which have pushed open the door of welcome to much rubbish; but it would not have been kept open so long but for a threat.

III

The threat is a potent one. All dissidents or doubtfuls are warned that if they are not duly respectful towards the new enormities, they will find themselves numbered among the philistines who, in the past, derided and rejected " the unknown beauty." Modernist poets are never tired of pointing out that Coleridge and Keats were once jeered at; the supporters of cubist art continually remind the public that it once heaped abuse upon the now respected Impressionists. Indeed, the threat is in constant use, and it has an alarming effect upon people in whom the desire to be right about art is rather stronger than their power to enjoy it.

In its subtler forms this threat reduces the diffident to aspen-hearted acquiescence. One way is to write in an airy confident tone as though only fools, of course, and block-heads were conscious of those misgivings which are internally gnawing the would-be proselyte, and at the same time to remind him, perhaps, in the words of the Goncourts, " The Beautiful is what seems abominable to uneducated eyes. The beautiful is what your mistress or your cook instinctively finds hideous." If, at the moment of reading, the poor art-snob has any misgivings about either his cook or his mistress, such a quotation will at once open his eyes to the merits of the poet or painter in question. But, failing that, such a quotation as " *L'art n'est pas chose populaire, encore moins ' poule de luxe '* . . . *L'art est d'essence hautaine* " will surely bring him to heel.

Note the flattery implicit in it. He will henceforth feel lifted above his fellows proportionally as they disagree with him, and also be able to pass through the houses of the rich and the galleries of collectors with pleasant, supercilious equanimity. Moreover, there is something besides flattery— there is also truth—in that statement. Art, like physics, politics or tennis, *is* best understood by a few, and those few are not necessarily to be found among the rich, who are particularly apt to confuse (though we are all liable to do so) prestige values with beauty. And it is precisely the blend of flattery and truth in this statement which makes it so persuasive. What, however, we are right to resent is a truth of such very general import being used to push us into admiring any particular book or work of art. Those who put their faith in the verdicts of the few often present a comic spectacle when the many come round to their opinion. While watching the ups and downs of reputations, I have often found myself exclaiming, " Ah! The rats are leaving the floating ship."

In reading criticism it is always well to keep a sharp look-out for flattery or intimidation; unless controversy is running high, these are generally the methods of imperfectly-convinced critics.

Now with regard to that formidable threat, there are several considerations which may help us to bear up under it. In the first place, those who use the argument that the majority have been always unintelligent in the past omit to mention that they themselves often despise the same works which the majority once abused. *Hernani* was defended against mockery by a band of brothers whose smallness and compactness left nothing to be desired. Yet that Hugo's play was fustian the modernist poet would be the first to assert. The Pre-Raphaelites and Impressionists were not in favour with the very painters who recently called out loudest, " You are abusing us as you once abused Whistler and Rossetti whom you now admire." It was a good retort, but a trifle disingenuous, for they despised both artists themselves. The public is undoubtedly an ass, but not uncommonly in criticism we find the elect and progressive of a later date echoing that ass's ancient bray. And what is one to think then? Secondly, though it is lamentably true that Coleridge and Wordsworth were ridiculed, so was Mr. Bowles. Comforting thought that some

poet whom we find it impossible to admire, in spite
of the threat that we are offending against "the
unknown beauty," may be a Bowles! Lastly, there
is nothing to be ashamed of in not surrendering
quickly to what is new, or in retracting opposition
afterwards.　In short, it is equally unsafe to despise
a particular work because the many admire it, and
to admire it because it is only understood or liked
by a few.　Even when minorities and majorities
agree the corroboration may be valueless, for a work
of art may be enjoyed at different levels—Hamlet,
for example.

　　There is a passage in Mr. Santayana's *Life of
Reason* which throws light on the nature of all
" new " ways of writing;　it justifies a stiff attitude
towards them:

> " Pure poetry [he writes] is pure experiment;
> and it is not strange that nine-tenths of it should
> be pure failure.　For it matters little what un-
> utterable things may have originally gone to-
> gether with a phrase in the dreamer's mind;　if
> they were not uttered and the phrase cannot call
> them back, this verbal relic is none the richer for
> the high company it may once have kept.　Ex-
> pressiveness is a most accidental matter.　What a
> line suggests at one reading, it may never suggest
> again even to the same person.　For this reason,
> among others, poets are partial to their own com-
> positions;　they truly discover there depths of
> meaning which exist for nobody else.　Those
> readers who appropriate a poet and make him
> their own fall into a similar illusion;　they attribute
> to him what they themselves supply, and what-
> ever he reels out, lost in his own personal revery,
> seems to them, like *sortes Biblicae*, written to fit
> their own case. . . ."

A CRITIC'S DAY-BOOK

WOKE early and to my dismal situation; I am sick of journalism. I must have a change. Resolved to write a discursive diary instead. Reminded myself that a diary must be very bright—and sighed. Tried to recall the flattest entry I had ever read in a printed diary: " Oct. 23rd. Walked to Slapton with Brown," occurred to me. Couldn't well sink lower myself.

Robinson Crusoe has been my bedside book for some time. I am almost as fond of that book as the butler in *The Moonstone*, who used to refer to it whenever in doubt what to do, and wore out several copies. Robinson Crusoe's fervid thankfulness for small mercies is infectious; also his manful, forethoughtful simplicity of mind. Most complications (unhappily not all, but more than one might suppose), yield to Crusoe methods. Then, how delightful to contemplate the existence of anyone who has oceans of time! Crusoe is continually returning to this aspect of his predicament. Time is no object; indeed the longer everything takes him the better. How different the life of a journalist!

It has often happened to me to regret the invention of photography. The possession of a photograph has often weakened my power of calling up an image of the dead, for when I have tried, the familiar photograph instead has instantly presented itself to my imagination; the visible definiteness of the portrait has driven off the vaguer but far more real apparition which would otherwise have answered

273   T

my call. I would recommend separated lovers, though it is impossible to resist an exchange of photographs, to consult them seldom, and on no account to put them up where they may constantly catch an eye preoccupied with other thoughts.

I have been reading several novels by women lately. I have been struck by the enormous importance attributed in them to dress, struck into amazement mingled with some contempt and a slight distress. Indeed, I have gone about asking people if it can possibly be true that a pair of silver slippers may be a real help in time of trouble, or that the sight of a small hole in the stocking of some other woman will bring a flood of confidence and self-respect back to the heart of her who observes it. What should we think of a man whose soul withers within him because of the splendour of his interlocutor's tie! I am rather upset about it, for my inquiries have not entirely failed to corroborate the intuitions of these feminine novelists.

When the subject of booming or advertising comes up in conversation the question is often put, for what sum of money would you be willing to—well, sell, in one form or another, your dignity. People differ in this respect. There are generals, statesmen and men of letters, who would require a sum so exorbitant that it would be worth no one's while to pay it, before they would allow their portraits to appear in a patent medicine advertisement, with some pathetic legend underneath it like " I was covered with Pimples." I remember in a local paper the following announcement: "Wanted: Twelve bald-headed men who would not mind having ' So-and-So's Honey ' painted in blue on the crowns of their heads."

No doubt they were forthcoming. As a rule those who go in for self-advertisement require only reasonable remuneration for advertising the wares of others. It is fairly safe to count on any man or woman who booms himself or herself, being ready to boom anything which does not interfere with that.

The sleepless are often advised to court drowsiness by giving up their minds to some monotonous occupation, counting imaginary sheep or studying minutely with the mind's eye a piece of brown paper. In my opinion these expedients do not deserve their reputation. As Mr. Thomas observed in his delightful *Whirly-gig*, after one has counted 324,956 sheep it is usually time to get up. These devices are too dull to compete with random thoughts and recollections. To the wandering-minded sleepless I recommend more sinuous methods. Let one who lies sleepless with the ache of some anxiety at heart, or with a *faux pas* rankling in his memory (for anger and real remorse there is no poppy or mandragora—anger produces a flow of internal eloquence which murders sleep)—let such a one picture to himself a scene from the life of some character, real or imaginary, which carries with it a soothing suggestion of security. At the age of ten I discovered this dodge for myself to keep away night fears. I used to tell myself excessively humdrum stories, beginning: "Fagger was puzzled where to go for his health." It does not matter what figure or what circumstances you choose, as long as they carry with them a suggestion of satisfying cosiness. Men carousing in the belly of a fort will do, if you can call up the scene so that it inspires a sensation of thrilling security; or David Copperfield after his terrible tramp to Dover, safe at last with Miss Trotwood; or Mr. Woodhouse: surrounded by all the people he is used to, saying,

"Let us all take a little gruel together." The important thing is to get rid of fear.

At the New Prince's Theatre I once heard M. Jacques Dalcroze lecture on "Eurhythmics in Education." His lecture was illustrated by some of his pupils. With the exception of some dances at the end—"plastic realizations of music" is, I believe, the proper phrase to use—what we watched on the stage was M. Dalcroze taking a class of advanced pupils while he talked to us and explained his aims and methods. His audience was a large one, and very attentive. Most people who hear of new ideas at all have heard of M. Dalcroze and his college at Hellerau, near Dresden; many of you must have seen photographs of its spacious, simple, almost forbiddingly hygienic architecture, and of the pupils dancing barefoot in the open air. Whether the pictures pleased you or not depended probably on whether or not you are the kind of person who readily believes that the secret of a happier, better life lies quite near to hand, and that the clue to its discovering it lies in the body. A great many people do nowadays believe this. Some of them think salvation is to be found in a particular diet, others in dancing—

He who is light of heart and heels
Can wander in the Milky Way—

others, again, in wearing fewer and looser clothes, or in seeing each other, if possible, naked (this last is now a favourite theme with novelists; conversion follows upon surprising someone bathing), or in repeating to themselves "Life is perfect, I am perfect," as they brush their hair every morning, drinking at the same time a glass of fair water. Personally, my first impulse (I prefer not to think the tendency congenital, but to attribute it to a

Public School education) is to put down everyone
who declares he has discovered a new contribution
to the art of living as a cranky ass: occasionally it
has been necessary to apologize afterwards.

What an admirable compositor memory is!
Why, we are all of us artists when we remember,
though it is a different matter when we try to write
our memories out, or even to share them in talk;
then their atmosphere thins away. Have you
noticed how closely the vividness of the past resembles that of a picture or a scene in a novel?

I have always delighted in Montaigne and
thought him a wise man; and in nothing wiser than
in his attitude towards fear, a state of mind to be
gently circumvented, if it cannot be out-faced.
The literature of fear has always been repellent
to me, even when it is also the work of genius: for
Dostoievsky admiration in me is mixed with dislike
and contempt; he is too pathological, and terror too
often inspires him. " There is nothing more cheerful than wisdom; I had like to say more wanton. . . .
In fine, we must live among the living and let the
river flow under the bridge without our care, above
all things avoiding fear, that great disturber of
reason. The thing in the world I am most afraid
of is fear."
His early essays were commonplace books in
which he copied out passages which struck him as
he lazily read with his reflections upon them. But
as time went on they began to achieve more and
more completely an avowed intention—that of drawing a portrait of himself. In studying himself
minutely he drew to our great gain a diagram of our
species, while by dwelling curiously upon each experience as it passed he made his own life more
rich. Thus we learn to know human nature better

through knowing him so well, and if we can acquire his habit of self-observation we too can enrich our lives.

It is not in experience that our lives are poor, though sometimes it would seem so. If they appear to us limited and monotonous, it is because we do not watch what is happening to us or what we are feeling about it. Montaigne is a good master in the art of life because he teaches that detachment which enables us to be more conscious of life as it passes. Each day contains moments which could not be more pleasant or interesting even if our heart's desire had been fulfilled, or some longed-for piece of good fortune had befallen us. We do not wake up to this until our desires have been met or the luck is actually ours, when we are astonished to find after all how little difference that has made. The daily texture of our lives remains what it was, and in amazement we cry out that all is vanity! Since fortune is fickle and many things may come between a man and his desire, it is wise to make the most of those resources which good fortune cannot increase and only the worst calamities destroy. This is the lesson of Montaigne. Have not even the stricken sometimes marvelled to find themselves enjoying a fine day, a joke, a meal? There is comfort in this. Why dwell only on the humiliation in it? We may smile ironically with Montaigne at human nature, its " flexibility and diversity," but unless we learn from him to smile also gratefully, we have not caught his message.

The only epigram I ever made in my life, with the persuasion that I was saying something not entirely obvious, was: " In order to know yourself, you must let others know you." Since it is certainly true that to know others you must know yourself, it should follow that reserve in everyday life is inimical to the creative imaginative faculty, and letting yourself go, favourable to it. Then what about Ibsen, a shut man apparently, if ever there was one? But perhaps he was rather laconic than reserved, speaking, when he did speak, out of himself, more than most men generally do.

I still read for pleasure—that is a statement which would strike most people as hardly worth making. Yet I could assure them that if it caught the eye of a fellow-reviewer he would drop this book in astonishment. Very likely on second thoughts he wouldn't believe it. Several most capable reviewers have, I happen to know, almost entirely lost the faculty of reading. They can now only read to review. Why should a gardener take up a spade unless he is going to dig, or a dentist a pair of forceps unless he is going to pull out a tooth?

The other day I came across the following comment in Tolstoy's short story, *The Devil*. " It is generally supposed that Conservatives are usually old people, and those in favour of change are the young. That is not quite correct. The most usual Conservatives are young people: those who want to live but who do not think, and have not time to think, about how to live, and who therefore take as a model for themselves a way of life that they have seen." This strikes me as a true word. On the other hand, enthusiasm about reforming the world depends upon the belief that the world is malleable, and that belief is mixed up with the youthful feeling that one is made of malleable stuff oneself. In youth, nothing is easier than to believe that one can turn over a new leaf and begin a new and glorious existence. When one ceases to believe in turning over new leaves, one ceases to believe that the world can turn them over either. Some slight

279

improvement in both cases is as much as can be hoped for.

The peculiar character of Paris, its bright, civic magnificence combined with its general air of nonchalance, its tolerance of neglected beauty and obliterated ornament, never seems to change. The contrast between the gaiety and confident flourish of everything expressive of sociable open life, and the proud parsimonious indifference of its citizens to external shabbiness and dilapidation where their privacy is concerned, is the secret of its charm— apart, of course, from its legacy of palaces and churches, and that great natural beauty—its olive, silvery river which is divided so sweetly by the green prow of the city's island. Parsimony is not a virtue of radiant countenance, yet it is to French parsimony we owe those sombre narrow streets of high houses, with their long windows and heavy doors revealing small dim courts, the admirable proportions of which the eye at once seizes, while the imagination both pities their actual humility and recalls their ancient pride. But for parsimony, the French people with their formidable practicality would be, I am sure, too ready with the pick-axe.

The best way to form an idea of one's own character (or anyone else's) is to look for the particular mental and moral attitude in which, when it occurs, one feels most spontaneous; the moment when a voice within cries " *This* is *me*! " Important as this discovery is for all, for the artist it is discovery even more important. Compare Anatole France with Renan, how easily and quickly he levitated to his own true natural level of superficiality. Superficiality? Do not mistake me. There is a superficiality which is more comprehensive than most profundities. But there is a danger,

especially for the artist, connected with this moment
of self-recognition. To find himself may be to stereo-
type himself.   Henceforth it is not he, but a ghost,
an emanation of himself, that holds the pen; a ghost
with perhaps a happier facility of expression; or (it
is the same thing) he becomes in personal life a
" character," one who is more characteristic in all
his words and behaviour than really can be true.
Old age is ever in league with this tendency.

At the date of Waterloo there did not exist in
England outside the landed class five hundred
persons whose incomes exceeded £5,000 a year. Now
such a small cohesive class, having " the monopoly
of varied experience," united by subtle similarities
of taste, behaviour, and judgment, and with constant opportunities for meeting each other, makes
a very enviable society, especially when it is un-
challenged. There is a delicious *chez soi* feeling
when any who belong to it meet together, and this
feeling is intensified when they are conscious that
they are envied and gaped at by those outside.
No wonder our fathers and grandfathers took
" society " more seriously than we do. It was
really worth while in their days to be a lady or a
gentleman. Now the standards have got so mixed,
the privileges so precarious, and the rich class so
huge and so lacking in common traditions, or indeed
anything in common except a vague sense that they
are all perched together on the backs of the poor,
that a man or a woman who is much preoccupied
with his or her social position must be rather silly.

The decay of the country-gentleman tradition
is not merely due to smashing taxation. In old
days an heir probably inherited soon after he was
thirty, after having been brought up to be squire as
a matter of course. But now, life is lengthened,

and old age comes later, and knowing that his father
will quite likely reach his eightieth birthday, the son
naturally takes to a profession. When he comes
into his property, say, between fifty and sixty, he
has the settled interests of a barrister, broker, soldier
or banker. The death-duties fall on him like an
avalanche. He is probably urban in his habits, with
perhaps a love of sport, but not so exigent that it
cannot be satisfied by a few days' hunting and shoot-
ing a year; at any rate the difference between such
pleasures and an afternoon's golf is not very great
to him. His children don't know how to talk to a
keeper or the old woman at the lodge. To them
the family home has just been a place for Christmas
—and now they have to live in it. They are always
either taking aimless spins in the car, or two-step-
ping in the hall to the strains of the gramophone, or
sprawling in chairs and slamming down magazines
with a yawn. It may be a sentimental wrench to
the new squire (boyish memories, ancestors) to sell,
but his family are not going to help inch and pinch
to hang on. They pull in the direction of more cash
and variety. Then some man with a long pocket,
but no more idea of how to be a country gentleman
than a head waiter, makes an offer; tempted com-
mercially, by the thought that though he may have
to pay a solid price for the acres, the fine old house
itself (unless it is so situated as to be a " week-end
place ") is thrown in like a paper-weight to keep the
acres from flying away, tempted also by a vague
notion of the prestige and dignity of squires. Down
he comes, puts in six tiled bathrooms and a lift, paints
a lot of things white, abolishes the laundry, never
inquires after the soundness of fence or tree, but
treats such matters and the garden on a Napoleonic
scale. He appears utterly indifferent to expense,
yet sacks a man because the cucumbers haven't
paid; builds a much more comfortable cottage for

the carpenter, but earns the latter's undying dislike by suppressing his dog, which strayed into the hall one morning; loses his temper with the keeper because the pheasants didn't come over the important guest; shocks the village by sending £10 out to the carol-singers, without listening to them or offering them supper in the servants' hall, let alone looking in to see if they are enjoying themselves—down he comes, in short, spreading everywhere bewilderment and discontent. Then there is a slump in something; off he goes again to make room for another like him. Meanwhile the idea that the lift and those bathrooms will be thrown in with the paper-weight rankles. He'll get that money back, anyhow, and since he had no longer the gratification of being a squire on the spot, everybody on the estate endures the unfamiliar and unpleasant experience of being run on strict business lines.

The moral is that our old land-owning system is incompatible with the new longevity. Only when the new squire inherits young or has spent his life partly in sporting idleness, partly as his father's agent, is the result likely to be different. Such a one has a horror of events following the course just described. In spite of death duties he will do anything to avoid that. He will live like a weevil in a biscuit in his huge house. He will try to avoid marrying a woman who does not see eye to eye with him. His friends may wish they had taken up their great coats with them when, changed for dinner, they hurry along icy passages, meals may be served in the study, landings and wings shut up, the pheasants in the covers may change from hand-fed birds to wild, the kitchen garden into a market garden, and flower beds to turf. Sticking on may mean economy to the bone in some respects, and dismissing many indoors and out of doors. Still, these changes will not be conducted on business lines. There will be matters in which indifference and generosity on the squire's part are obligatory, and stinting or fuss inadmissible. What is more, the people about him will know all this as clearly as he himself. This common understanding is the best side of the system, but without proper squires it tumbles to bits. Now a man is not going to hang about as his father's son till he is sixty to qualify; increasing longevity will complete the extinction of the country gentleman.

An old lady told me once that she had lunched with the Dickens family when she was a child (you must imagine a table full of children) and that Dickens had sat down without a word, leaning his head on his hand in an attitude of profound despondency. One of the Dickens children whispered to her, in commiseration and explanation, " Poor Papa is in love again! "

Balzac's *Contes Drôlatiques* were written in the style of the *conteurs grivois* of the sixteenth century, and they are very good *pastiche*. Indeed, from the point of view of style, they are the best-written of his works. As a rule he is a most unnatural, pretentious, turgid, ugly writer; and since he is one of the very greatest of novelists, his work seems to show that the art of writing well is of subordinate importance in novel writing: he at any rate managed to do amazingly without it. But in the *Contes Drôlatiques* he did for once write stories in a style which had quality. Without quality the rollicking lubricity of these stories would be flat and vulgar; without raciness of phrase they would send no one's spirits up. Here lies the difference between pornography and literary lubricity, in which more than half the reader's excitement is a delight in the phrases and turns of speech such topics inspire. Cobbett in his *Advice to a Young Man* refers rather contemptuously to Shakespeare as " the punning and smutty Shakespeare," but Shakespeare's smuttiness is always leavened by this literary exhilaration, and these Tales, though the sense of fun is often lumbering and medieval, are permeated by it, too.

The *conte grivois* has few counterparts in English literature, though Mr. George Moore in *A Storyteller's Holiday* has supplied some. The Wanton Muse has inspired a great deal of English verse, but oddly enough, very little English prose, though to the definitely pornographic literature of the world England, on the other hand, has contributed largely. There is no English Boccaccio and no collection of stories equivalent to the *Cents Nouvelles*, and I do not suppose there ever will be, in spite of literary prohibitions breaking down, as they show signs of doing, for in the past English writers were free enough and yet they did not write such stories.

That *Rasselas* and *Candide* should still be living classics seems to me significant. Both are monotonous, undramatic little stories in which each short chapter repeats the same lesson, that life is always empty and happiness is impossible. Now if the pessimistic view of life were a fantastic one and had no root in experience, neither of these certainly overcharged statements of its case would have continued to appeal to men. They continue to attract successive generations because they find much truth in them. Suppose, on the other hand, that the reiterated moral had been reversed, so that each short chapter was an episode of bliss and of hopes abundantly fulfilled, not even the austere eloquence of Johnson nor the quick precision of Voltaire could have kept those works alive. Such a surfeit of optimism would have been too repulsive to the average honest mind. Books of that kind no doubt get written, but they die like flies.

Touching pessimists in general, have you ever considered why they are not depressing—I mean the good ones? *Candide* and *Rasselas* certainly cannot be said to be cheerful pictures of humanity or hope-inspiring estimates of life; the gloom of *Rasselas* is even deeper than that of *Candide*. Schopenhauer, too, is far from a depressing author, indeed, quite the contrary. And why does not Ibsen, who is certainly not a bringer of good tidings, depress us, while we often go away in wretchedly low spirits from plays which are not nearly such formidable indictments of human nature or society? The explanation is that the pessimism of good writers is not the result of dejection, doldrums, discouragement, dumps, but of an unusual intellectual activity which becomes a temporary possession of our own while we are reading. One of my favourite critical principles is that a work of art must have somewhere in it a suggestion of desirable life. Yet it is often difficult to recognize this in stories which are nevertheless indisputable works of art, until one realizes that it *is* there, all the time—in the mind of the author, whose virtues of soul and intellect are infectious, and exhilarate more than the melancholy of his conclusions can depress. The contempt of the average hearty reader for " face the facts " plays and novels is usually justified; they are seldom the fruit of intellectual power, but mildly pretentious projections of feeble, if sympathetic, moods of despondency. Away with them!

It is sometimes a critic's duty to talk about himself, though by no means as often as might be inferred from reading some critics. It is so when he is far from thinking a subject as attractive as it is to the author he is criticizing. For instance, if he is reviewing a book, say, about a seminary, and is personally affected by a priest as many people are said to be affected by the presence of a cat, he should reveal that fact early. Now there is much in Arnold Bennett's novels, for instance, which almost excuses us for believing that the modern " luxury-hotel " is his spiritual home, so often and so fervently has he dwelt upon its amazing costliness and convenience, and so invariably is he impressed by everything in modern life that it summarizes and represents. Yet there are people who prefer lodgings. I am one of them. To me the " luxury-hotel " is awful. Nor is this the sour estimate of one of the bitter excluded poor; I have entered them frequently—at the expense of others. But it is only the company of friends that makes these places endurable to me. When undistracted by talk, or when unconcentrated upon a plate (thank goodness, the food is almost always excellent!), my genial spirits droop. Misanthropy descends upon me as I watch the crowd munching to music.

From those lounges of gilt and mirrors, from those drawing-rooms and writing-rooms done up in " styles," there is no escape for the imagination, except in the direction of banking accounts and thrusting snobbery; there is not an object on which the eye can rest which does not proclaim Pretentiousness as the key to the art of living, and all the more insistently when the object itself happens to be also " refined." Arnold Bennett's *Imperial Palace*, for instance, could have hardly found a less sympathetic reader. You wonder perhaps how in that case I can even tolerate Bennett, let alone admire him as I do. Well, I said the presence of a friend makes even a " luxury-hotel " tolerable to me, and Bennett's humanity and integrity are like companions to me. Of course, I grin as I read at the ease with which he is impressed, not only by luxury,

but by what he thinks astounding instances of
" poise " in behaviour which are nothing of the kind;
but I forgive him for being taken in for the sake of
his superb plain humanity.   I may have to wait and
wade through a lot before it comes, but sooner or
later a wave of it always breaks over me.

    I have been reading the book of Mrs. Watson,
née Gillman, about Coleridge at Highgate, but I only
dare recommend it to those who love Coleridge;
to enjoy it, you must be so fond of him and so fascinated by him that you can read anything about
him.   It is a mistaken book.   It proves that Coleridge was an industrious man, that he only took to
opium as a relief from pain, and that he was a blessing, not a burden, to the good Gillmans.   I do not
mean that Mrs. Watson is wrong on these points, but
that she is mistaken in thinking them important.   It
is all very well for Coleridge to have been humble
about himself.   He would not have had just his own
peculiar, lovely sense of beauty without also a deep,
tremulous, affectionate humility; he would not
have been the damaged archangel he was without his
remorse, his shame, his abjection.   But it is quite
another matter for others to think they can magnify
the great Coleridge, or worse, clean him, by showing
he was also really a patient and industrious citizen.
What does it matter whether a man worked hard or
not, if he could compose *Kubla Khan* in his sleep?
Look at his model brother-in-law, a first-rate man
of letters too; what is the value of his gift to mankind despite his ceaseless industry, beside that of
Coleridge?   How ridiculous even to compare them!
Southey made one Miss Fricker much happier than
Coleridge made the other, but it would matter far
less now if Southey had never lived.   Coleridge
was a great benefactor, one of those who have added
to the world's stock of lovely possessions; yet we

are asked to think better of him, because he really did also put in some regular work on *The Morning Post*.

I do not want to be severe with Mrs. Watson. She loves Coleridge. She is quite right to show us that her grandmother and grandfather Gillman owed more to Coleridge than he to them, and that they, bless them! knew it; but she muddles things up which ought to be kept distinct. It is a most useful, laudable and common quality, industry; it is a somewhat negative, though important, virtue to abstain from drugs. But sometimes it happens that without the help of these merits a man achieves something of lasting value, and something much more precious than others who possess them can achieve. In such a case if evidence crops up showing that, after all, he was not nearly so lazy and inebriate as was supposed, it is a mistake to think this discovery important. Interesting such points may be, but not important; I am afraid Mrs. Watson writes as though they were. She forgets, as she writes, that there is one fact so much more important than the others that it dwarfs them all, namely, that Coleridge was Coleridge.

Is it not ridiculous that one of the comparatively few human beings who have actually achieved something should have been accused by his contemporaries, and after his death, of having wasted his life, and by people too of whom, now their day is over, it can be safely said, they were naughts among nothings? " But *he* could have done so much." That is always the plea of the censorious. But what do they know about it? Anyhow, it is not a line for those who achieve nothing to take. A little modest wonder, a little gratitude, becomes them better. (I am not thinking of Mrs. Watson, but of the professors, lecturers and biographers who patronize Coleridge.)

I saw a letter in the paper this morning suggesting that publishers should start an advertising campaign pointing out that reading is one of the cheapest and best of pleasures. The public should be urged to read books and buy books. It should be rubbed into them " that a book is very much cheaper than a theatre ticket, and that it entails no extra expenses." Certainly, reading is the cheapest pleasure, and if men and women were firmly set on economy they would read more and go out less. But unfortunately reading is not a social pleasure. It is the gregarious instinct which drives people out in the evenings, whether to restaurants, dinners or theatres, even when their cash is low, and the more worried they are the more restlessly gregarious they become. For though you cannot pretend to yourself you are enjoying a book when you are not, unfortunately it is quite easy to pretend you are enjoying yourself in a noisy, hot room, with a band playing, and in company with other people, even if you hardly like them. On such occasions there is a mutual conspiracy that everyone is having a good time and that everybody is agreeable, and though the moment the party disperses each person knows the evening was a fraud, still, while it lasts, thanks to everyone playing up and pretending, it is a relief.

" Why can't you sit quiet and read a book? *How She Hooked Him*, by the author of *The Judicious Separation*, is very good," sounds, especially to the young, like a surrender to domestic gloom. I do not think " a best up-to-date seller " is going to rival the more expensive ways of spending the evening, however vigorously reading may be recommended by the Publishers' Association, let alone the fact that in " the best up-to-date seller " the ideal way of spending the evening is seldom depicted as sitting in a chair and reading one.

It is a cold windy world for young poets, and nine-tenths of the books of verse which appear are blown shivering to oblivion as soon as they are published. To anyone familiar with the inside of a newspaper office the long array of thin but not inexpensive volumes of verse, getting dusty upon the shelves, is a depressing sight. What moments of exquisitely ardent but ineffective labour every page represents! Poetry is its own reward, but the publisher's loss. The honours of the poet are the rarest attainable. It is a mistake, usually leading to disappointment, to subsidize publication. But publishers have a duty towards literature, and this should sometimes involve taking risks; only that those risks should be heavy is unfair. The late John Lane built up his excellent literary connection largely upon his shilling poets, some of whom became well known, but all of whom were content to appear first with a few specimens of their poetry, and between paper covers. I do not think, either, that an unknown poet has the right, considering the chances from the reader's point of view, to ask much more from him than a shilling.

Looking into Professor Saintsbury's *Minor Poets of the Caroline Period* made me think what salutary reading it would be for modern poets, bringing home to them as it must the transience of fashion in thought and expression. It is clear that there was, for the contemporaries of these poets, a peculiar fascination in the quality of their diction; its intellectual quippiness and dry sparkle made them ask nothing more from poetry. Anyone who has read contemporary verse over some years will have noticed how quickly fashions in language follow and oust each other. Now it is for the rich, sensuous phrase, soon that is succeeded by " a rage " (as sweeping as those which make every boy in a private school suddenly buy a pair of stilts or a squirt) for the brisk, crackling, conversational epithet, or for the emphatic yet non-committal generalized one; skies in turn are " million-tinted," " streaky " or simply " amazing." The pleasure which the mere flavour of a slightly new diction gives is brief; while it lasts, unfortunately, it is keen enough to conceal emptiness of inspiration both from writers and readers. It is, therefore, salutary to turn up from time to time the old forgotten poets, who draped themselves so skilfully in the idiom of the moment, and see what emptiness lay after all beneath. Seventeenth-century diction is up just now, the rich associative adjective having palled; but I am soon expecting the turn of the stately, smooth, limpid style, after we have masticated hair-brushes, Christmas-trees and hog's-bristles a little longer.

The language of art criticism is the queerest and most shifting of shorthand jargons. A word or phrase is taken up for a little time and then dropped, and the imprecision of these phrases is so great that it is often impossible to tell whether, or not, the slang symbols which replace them are synonymous. A few years ago the word " amusing " was exceedingly common; it is used still but not so often. It was only in the context and in front of the picture to which it was applied that one could approach to understanding what was meant by it. It did not, of course, mean funny; a drawing of a crucifixion or of a solitary potato on a plate might be " amusing." It meant, or seemed to mean, that the critic was rather fascinated by the picture, but either did not really feel much when contemplating it or, for reasons unstated, regretted he was fascinated so much. It was the most subjective term imaginable. It is still possible, without laying yourself open to the charge of being as foolish as Ruskin, to speak of " generosity " in the handling of a head, or shoulder, or what not. But what on earth does this mean if not that something in the painter's treatment of his subject gives one the same kind of satisfaction as generosity in a human being? A great deal of art criticism is still unconsciously Ruskinian.

When I travel I like to take a book of travel with me. It need not be about the places I am going to visit. I choose a book of travel because I like, at such times, the company of an observer; he teaches me how to make the most of my time. On my holiday I took with me Maupassant's *Sur l'Eau*. This is not one of his books which are oftenest read; yet, in a sense, it contains the whole of him.

Sur l'Eau is a reflective diary of one of Maupassant's cruises in his yacht, the " Bel Ami." I chose it partly because I thought I should like on my own journeys the companionship of a strong, truthful man; partly because, being in a black mood, I thought I should prefer such a one to be also a pessimist. Things in general would soon cheer me up quite irrationally, and meanwhile I should like to keep hold a little longer of a few grim truths (so they appeared to me) about life and the world, and a sincere pessimist (none of your lurid, bengal-light and gloom effects, thank you, with the philosopher raving and cursing magnificently above the wreck and roar)—a sincere pessimist, I say, would help me, in spite of the gentle allurements of change, to keep such facts before my eyes. There is the fact of death, for instance, which it is extraordinarily difficult to remember while bathing.

There is no more delicate and infallible guide to business success than a commercialized conscience.

293

Once a man, whether he is in business or a writer, has so trained his conscience that he has only to ask it what is right to discover what is profitable, he is made. The process is, of course, bad for the man himself, but his prosperity is assured.

Clio is a Muse, and perhaps the most exacting of them; for she requires in her followers not only the gifts of an artist but fidelity to fact. If we cannot believe that the events which an historian describes happened, he is an impostor; if the importance he gives them is false, he is a deceiver; yet unless he interprets facts, his work, however conscientious, can only be a quarry from which some day an artist-historian may build real history. Is Gibbon's account of that vast procession of events which he selected as his subject credible? The realist and the religious man say " No." Gibbon's method of interpretation is one which neither of them can accept. Its conventionality is obvious, but it works. Gibbon pulled together in his mind a mass of facts such as erudition never before, and seldom since, accumulated; and—here is the miracle—his attitude towards all those facts is consistent. If his account is remote from actuality, all its incidents are equidistant from the serene centre of his judgment.

By means of a balanced and ornate style, expressive of self-delighting detachment, he keeps events, and still more the passions behind them, far aloof. The cries of human agony and aspiration never reach to where, like an Epicurean god, he lies upon a cloud, watching the dumb show of a great and ancient civilization passing by. If he stoops to examine more closely one of the human atomies below, some emperor, prophet or general, with his thumb and finger he soon replaces him in that imposing march of circumstance, where he then resumes his proper ant-like stature.

Is this a truth-revealing attitude towards human-nature and history? Some critics have been at pains to prove it is not. Its value, its hold upon the imagination, lies in a congruity between such a method and the emotion which a long backward gaze across centuries naturally inspires, provided the mind makes no effort to recall the past as it was to the living, or to arrange events as a progress, whether under human or divine direction.

Gibbon is unique among the erudite because he could not be dull. As a man he was friendly, faithful, passionless, selfish and benign. His irony and " polished ungodliness " are a perpetual delight to secure and sceptical readers. The French Revolution was the only contemporary event which disturbed his equanimity, for he knew " his was the kind of head revolutionaries cut off."

We cannot be in Johnson's company long, without becoming aware that what draws us to him so closely is that he combined a disillusioned estimate of human nature sufficient to launch twenty little cynics, with a craving for love and sympathy urgent enough to turn a weaker nature into a benign sentimentalist.

JOYCE'S " ULYSSES "

I

IT has been the aim of every story-teller to convince his audience that whatever he narrated
happened thus and thus and not otherwise. His
further end may have been to delight, to excite, to
warn, to teach, to commemorate; but, consciously
or unconsciously, to rouse a willing belief, or to
secure at any rate a " willing suspension of un-
belief," in those he addressed, was necessarily his
first aim. But the kind of facts and the aspects of
things which, when recorded, create such conviction
in others, are different in each age, and probably
often slightly different in each generation. It depends upon the contemporary focus of attention.
In simpler ages bare assertion was sufficient to
create conviction; description—certainly close description—was unnecessary. Here and there in old
novels a few details in some scene may stand out
visible, tangible; but as a rule the name for each
thing was judged sufficient to evoke it in its reality;
the hero came to a wood, a stream, an inn—as the
case might be; if he was afraid, it might be mentioned that the wood was " dark," if he was thirsty
that the stream was " clear and cool," if he was
tired that the inn was " welcome." Moods were
treated in the same laconic fashion; men and
women were described as being angry, hopeful,
despondent, sorrowful, embarrassed, alarmed, relieved, and what they did and said substantiated
and justified those summary adjectives. If the

reader was told what they were thinking, their thoughts were invariably clear and strictly appropriate to the situations in which they found themselves. The anxious lover on his way to his beloved would think of her, or of whatever made their happiness precarious; and no author, except a jester like Sterne, would have dreamt of representing a lover as spending such an interval of time in remembering, say, how the flies used to annoy him as a child by settling on his bread and jam. Later, however, when the focus of contemporary attention grew more inquisitively sensuous (literature and life reacting mutually upon each other), the novelist intensified the actuality of his scenes by making everything in them as visible, audible, tangible and sniffable as possible; and at the same time the humanity of his characters was made to seem, to an increasingly self-conscious audience, more real by analysing their motives and distinguishing between shades of feeling. Except in the hands of a few masters the " story " suffered. Its place was taken by " the slice of life," or the diagram of a human specimen; a gifted writer would rest content with himself as a novelist, if he were confident that he had made his readers see, touch, smell and hear a number of things, experience pleasant and unpleasant emotions, or understand the mechanism of some character from within and above. This form of fiction (it is, of course, no more " obsolete " than direct story-telling, though it is no longer the " latest ") corresponded to the predominance of rational psychology; the " latest " fiction is the offspring of two other influences: the discovery of the importance of the subconscious, and the growth of a general scepticism. This fiction claims to reflect the consciousness of the modern man or woman much more accurately than fiction based on the old descriptive psychology; a consciousness which is more aware of the irrelevance of human emotions, and of the mechanical origin of all thoughts and impulses; and which is littered with scraps and memories of literature that hint at a beauty it has been unable to relate to anything actually experienced. The "latest" fiction also claims to open up opportunities for new aesthetic effects.

The manner in which a general scepticism has contributed to the latest movement in fiction I can now only indicate in a few sentences. If the novelist loses his interest in the way the big, common, conventional world works, and his sense of the value of the prizes which men strive for or miss; if conflicts between right and wrong also appear to him more or less negligible; if, further, he is inclined to think that man is just a bundle of interests and impulses, and that apart from the fact that he must react somehow, there is nothing in the nature of things to make one reaction on his part more relevant than another; then, it is clear, the novelist's subject-matter necessarily becomes limited, externally, either to mere description, to the *picture*, so that all drama inevitably disappears; or to an imaginary stream of irrelevant emotions and thoughts traced through an imaginary brain. A poet can, it is true, still make something of such restricted material, and some "latest" novelists are trying to become poets. With two exceptions they are making a poor job of it.

II

The hubble-bubble of talk round Mr. Joyce's *Ulysses* has now subsided, but the book's influence is likely to be far-reaching. Although copies are destined to find their way into the libraries of those who collect books described in catalogues as " very

298

curious," it is far from being pornographic. *Ulysses* is one of the most obscene books ever written, but not a lascivious one; it is, almost dismally indeed, the opposite of that. A nightmare-congregation of caricatures, parodies, obsessions, verbal clatter, noises, filth, terrors and disgusts, it is at any rate a mass projected with tremendous force and hurled far from its author into the sphere of literature.

Mr. James Joyce has been compared to Rabelais. He has only in common with Rabelais a gust for words and an exuberant command of them: a passion for verbal analogies and assonances, which he often indulges with an avidity reminiscent of that peculiar mental aberration called Echolalia. He yields himself to a torrent of jingles, puns, alliterations, repetitions, which here and there flash into wit, or form an amusing or brilliant collocation of vocables, but more often make an echoing rumble which is not addressed to the intelligence; he flings about a lot of dirty words as well as crashingly learned ones. And here all resemblance stops between the author of the inestimable life of the Great Gargantua and the author of *Ulysses*, though one must add that they are both parodists, the former of general ideas, the latter of literary methods. In spirit, two books could not be wider apart.

Though the most extravagantly fantastical of men, Rabelais was at bottom as sensible as it is possible for an alarmingly solid human-being to be, and of a downright direct simplicity which makes even Montaigne seem a coquettish, cat-and-mouse writer beside him. If you examine what lies behind Rabelais' art as a great story-teller (he excelled there) and as a care-destroying buffoon, what is revealed is the philosophy of common-sense, a gay stoicism. With *Ulysses*, on the other hand, there is a gloomy background to those exuberant verbal torrents, a morose delectation in dirt. In Joyce I touch no intellect below: only nerves and haunted imagination.

> " *Aussi eût-il été bien forissu (sorti) du déifique manoir de la raison si autrement se fût con-stristé ou alteré. Car tous les biens que le ciel couvre et que la terre contient en toutes ses dimen-sions, hauteur, profondité, longitude et latitude, ne sont dignes d'émouvoir nos affections et troubler nos sens et esprit;* "

that is the essence of Pantagruelism. Above all, Rabelais is fearless; he has no more fear of the body, its functions and secretions, than a doctor. The exhilaration he imparts is largely due to the laughing indifference with which he handles what others shrink to touch. Amusement at, not horror of, the body is the infection which the reader catches from his pages. He tells us he wrote his book to cure sick people with laughter; sick or not physically, the imaginations of many are sickly and queasy, and perhaps the most queasy imagination of the first order which has found expression in literature is that of Mr. Joyce himself. *A Portrait of the Artist as a Young Man,* throws light upon *Ulysses.* It enables the reader to measure the depth to which a superstitious horror of the body and sex has been branded into his mind, and explains why passages which appear pointlessly nauseous or exag-geratedly horrible in *Ulysses* came to be written: to us they may seem messes, to the author they represent no doubt the most difficult spiritual victories over private inhibitions. One thing that spoils *Ulysses* as a work of art is that it is far too much a self-administered purge. The author may have freed himself, but he brings no freedom to anyone who is not in his predicament. There is wit in it, but to laughter only an approximation—a croak or a derisive snigger. The quality of its humour may be measured by the fact that in making, according to preposterous plan, each of Bloom's adventures during twenty-four hours correspond, by some far-fetched analogy, to the consecutive subjects treated in the books of the *Odyssey*, Bloom, when the Aeolus episode occurs in Homer, is represented onomatopœically as troubled by wind while looking at a picture of the dying Wolfe Tone in a shop window. Silly? Yes, very.

I do not say that at the base of every good book of this kind must lie a robust and fearless philosophy. Out of hag-ridden horror, and cold hostile curiosity, the adventures of the body can also be written but let us once and for all drop any comparison of Mr. James Joyce to Rabelais.

III

Modern fiction, in so far as it is adventurous, tends to become more and more rhapsodical, episodical, and psychological. The importance of *Ulysses* lies in its carrying these tendencies to the very last limit. It is instructive to see what happens. Of course " the story " disappears (the story has already disappeared from the work of many contemporaries); but, in a very real and significant sense, " characters " have disappeared also. During the latter part of the nineteenth century, and during this one, there has been a continually increasing tendency to go deeper into what is called the " psychology " of characters in fiction, to get behind the motives of which the characters are conscious and to which they would confess if they were asked why they did such and such a thing. Ever since Tolstoy made Anna Karenina think of bathing when she threw herself under the train, the tendency to find irrelevant thoughts and feelings important has increased. Human beings, no doubt, do their thinking and

301

feeling in the interstices of long wool-gathering processes, and at moments even of intense emotion
the mind may fly about in the most erratic fashion.
The older novelists ignored this fact completely;
they did not attend to such phenomena, because
they did not conceive them to be part of rational
human life, the only thing worth writing about.
Nevertheless it was discovered that some suggestion
of this fact helped enormously to give vivid actuality
to emotions described in fiction. Those who wrote
later went farther; and latterly we have had novels
written by authors who are fascinated by this
irrelevant helter-skelter of thoughts, half-thoughts,
and sensations. Now the fact that Anna was incon-
venienced when committing suicide by her little
red bag, and that Vronsky's spiritual misery was
swamped by the toothache, adds nothing to our
grasp of either as " characters "; Kitty and Levine
might have had the same thoughts and sensations
in the same circumstances; we have got to know
Anna and Vronsky through touches of a different
kind. What these incidents illustrate is not " character," but the nature of the human machine itself.
The greater space therefore the novelist devotes to
such facts, and the more exclusively he relies upon
them, the more he tends to destroy his figures as
" characters." His novel, especially if he follows a
system of interpretation like Psycho-Analysis, tends
to become a pseudo-scientific discourse about imaginary cases; utterly worthless, of course, to men
of science, or to anyone in the least scientifically-
minded, and utterly uninteresting to all except
those young readers to whom such partial revelations of possible truths about human nature come as
a startling surprise.

Mr. Joyce has carried this process further than
anyone else. In retailing the thoughts, half-
thoughts, perceptions or inattentions of Bloom and

Mrs. Bloom, he has sunk a shaft down into the welter of nonsense which lies at the bottom of the mind, and pumping up this stuff (it is an astounding hydraulic feat) presented it as a criticism of life.

IV

His work certainly does resemble Rabelais' in the use of the cumulative method and in a passion for verbal patterns, but whereas the infection communicated by Rabelais is a coarse but glorious fearlessness—especially of the body and its functions—*Ulysses* is the product of a frightened enslaved mind. Much of it is cold, nasty, small and over-serious. If ever there was a writer who was afraid of the Devil it is Mr. Joyce. The shadow of that awful sermon, reported in *The Portrait of the Artist as a Young Man*, lies black across his pages. One of Mr. Joyce's critics has said that the climax of *Ulysses* is " only a gigantic *attempt* to attain release," and that where the contrasts in which it deals do not issue in laughter, the result is merely nightmarish. On the whole that is the impression the book made on me. I am inclined to think that the cathartic theory of art, the theory that genuine art springs from the effort of the creator to rid himself of pain and his own weakness, is being overdone. I see no reason to suppose that good works of art may not be produced by those whose conflicts and " efforts towards freedom " are over at the time of writing. The struggles of a fly in a gluepot are not the only objects worth contemplating, though to those in the same sort of glue the spectacle of another's supermuscan efforts may be in a high degree exhilarating and significant. Nietzsche's writings are spoilt for me by being obviously cathartic, so are Mr. Joyce's and Huysmans' novels. Having found remedies for their own desperate predicaments they proceed to thrust them upon everybody else. If you refuse their remedies, that only proves in their eyes that your leprosy is so perfect that you think yourself white and clean. They may be right, but on the other hand they may be wrong. *Ulysses* strikes me as less important as a work of art than as a symptom. For pages and pages it is nearly unreadable, making the reader ache with boredom; but it contains more artistic dynamite than any book published for years. That dynamite is placed under the modern novel. The author of *Ulysses* is a man of prodigious talents, and one by-product of his work is to show what is *not* worth doing in fiction, and he shows that by going one better than the modern novel in the directions in which it is moving. Is the object to put life under a magnifying glass and show its very texture, the stuff it is made of? Mr. Joyce employs a far stronger glass, and writes a vast book about twenty-four hours; one sees the carpet from the point of view of a beetle. Is Mr. X.'s object to catch the patter and interchange of talk? Mr. Joyce has invented a method of record which does it twice as well. Does Mr. Y. work the sex-interest for all it is worth? Mr. Joyce seems to say, "Oh, you rely on lust, do you, to interest people? You are very insipid; I'll give you the real thing." Does Mr. Z. aim at realism, priding himself on shirking nothing which is part of normal experience? Mr. Joyce soon has his hero firmly seated on the water-closet. But, above all, the up-to-date writer flatters himself that he conveys the drift of thoughts and feelings through the heads of his characters, and here Mr. Joyce undercuts him completely. I cannot conceive any modern novelist, who is capable of grasping the merits of this work and at the same time doubts its value, not being utterly discouraged.

V

The reader of the above comments will have perceived that they are those of a critic who resists the recent shift of focus in fiction away from the sphere of will, thought and action. The importance of Mr. Joyce's work lies in its being a tremendous effort to stylize the contents of the Sub-conscious, and to make those contents amenable to literature. In this effort lies the difference between a page of *Ulysses*, or of *Work in Progress*, and automatic writing such as Miss Gertrude Stein's. Both may be unintelligible to you, but the former is deliberately and intricately designed to evoke a particular shade of semi-consciousness. At places in the narrative where previous novelists would have written, " Jumbled fragments of what he had felt and thought that day floated through his mind; presently he was asleep," you will find in Mr. Joyce such a passage as this (it describes Mr. Bloom's short snooze after flirting with Gerty MacDowell). " We two naughty Grace darling she him half past the bed met him pike hoses frillies for Raoul to perfume you wife black hair heave under embon *senorita* young eyes Mulvey plump years dream return tail end Agendath swooney lovely showed me her next year in drawers return next in her next her next." Here each word has a connection in Bloom's mind with the next, which the reader who remembers what has happened to Bloom during the preceding hours can trace—if he takes immense trouble; and in so far as we all, in somnolent states, think in words, sure enough such a passage may suggest a snooze. But it is going the long, dull way to suggest it. And do we think chiefly in words at such moments? I doubt it. If not, are words capable of expressing wordless states of mind? The method is only a convention like the old methods, while the experience in itself is hardly worth recording more elaborately than old conventions permit.

Mr. Joyce never allows for the possibility of his reader being bored. He would doubtless reply that the artist should not, and there is some truth in that. Nevertheless it is up to the artist to address the attentive without boring them. Great writers have done it. I have said that Mr. Joyce has taken to writing, since *Ulysses*, " pitch-dark rig-maroles "; as a general description of *Work in Progress* that is not unfair. Still, the critic must try to understand why he has written thus. It is absolutely certain that Mr. Joyce never writes deliberate nonsense, on the off-chance, as Miss Gertrude Stein writes, that it may contain profound significance and beauty. It is certain that he knows what he is about; his admirers assert, indeed, that he has weighed to a hair the force of every word he invents. Most of *Work in Progress* is obviously humorous, and as in *Ulysses* now and then, a majestic beauty glides ghostlike through our bewilderment.

But are words capable of expressing wordless states of mind? Mr. Joyce is conscious of the difficulty of making them do so. He has therefore invented a language in which he hopes such expression is attainable. Unfortunately it is a language nobody yet knows, and one extremely difficult, if not impossible, to learn; impossible to learn properly because the idiosyncrasies of its inventor, *his* individual knowledge and *his* peculiar experience, which may be unsharable, often determine the precise significance of his new words. Still, ardent and minute study will often reveal an intelligible drift. By means of rhythms (of which he is a master), assonances, puns, discords, and composite invented words—each of which start three or four associations without committing the mind to following any one of them—he is endeavouring to create a language

306

capable of conveying states of consciousness in which objects of thought and feeling (separate and distinct to the rational mind) melt and coalesce under the spell of some predominant mood or vaguely apprehended idea. He is addressing the Sub-conscious in us, in the language of the Sub-conscious; the dreamer in us, in the language of dreams. As we know the language of dreams loses its significance on waking, when we discover we have been talking nonsense. (See page 262.) But Mr. Joyce would persuade us to keep, as it were, our waking-eye open while we are still dreaming, and accept as marvels what is then revealed. His art is an attempt to admit the Sub-conscious as little changed as possible into our normal aesthetic experience. It compels him to a very curious linguistic experiment, and one particularly interesting to modern poets, who are perpetually watching their own processes in the hope of discovering a magic trick.

This new language, with its lawless syntax and its "portmanteau words," constructed out of scraps from a vast linguistic erudition, words often only comprehensible to those who not only know five languages but can recall old music-hall tags and much dead or local slang, is a device for dragging up intact from the Sub-conscious the dream *itself* out of which a poem springs. Dragging up? My metaphor is misleading. It is rather a means of enabling us to descend with him into that region of consciousness whence poetry proceeds, but where the poem is still only " a sound of going " in the poet's head, a running-together of nonsense words and real; where the work of art is still an amorphous feeling, attached by countless delicate filaments to other feelings, and dyed by its propinquity to still deeper dreams and vaguer emotions. Many of those filaments must snap when that feeling or idea is dragged into the light of complete consciousness, and many of its colours must inevitably fade. It is, however, the triumph proper to the poet to preserve in the upper light of man's intelligence some of those trailing clouds of glory and mystery which proceed from the region whence the poem came, and it is his success which produces in us that peculiar excitement which we recognize as *poetic excitement*, easily distinguishable from truth, which is the satisfaction of reason, or from passion which is the excitement of the heart. But this poet instead of bringing the poem to us, in that shorn and limited state of significance, which nevertheless makes it transferable from one mind to another, invites us instead to descend with him to where it lies still undefined in its own dim matrix. When we descend with him, naturally, we do not know where we are, or in what direction our minds are intended to move. He has therefore invented a new language to guide us. If we follow the clue of sound and rhythm, and the associations of his neologisms, he trusts to our feeling something that he has felt, even in a region where ordinary language fails him. His later work is therefore a renunciation of completely intelligible communication, but also an attempt to extend the limits of poetic experience. If the critic concentrates upon that renunciation, Mr. Joyce will appear to him as an artistic failure; if upon his effort to extend the limits of suggestion, as a literary pioneer of the first importance.

To me, when his methods are put at the service ᴏf realism the results seem of small value. Only the surface of the earth is habitable; only his conscious life permanently interesting to man. Except to the curious those nearer approaches to recording more exactly various degrees of somnolence or intoxication which we find in *Ulysses* and *Work in Progress*, are unimportant. They cannot be exact; they too are conventional, and I prefer more summary methods of suggesting them. This estimate of Mr. Joyce as a super-realist I have already expressed in the preceding sections. But compare for instance the passage quoted above from Bloom's snooze with the end of *Anna Livia* which is a part, separately published, of *Work in Progress.* Here, too, sleep is part of the subject; but here sleepiness is used to ends as poetical as those of Verlaine, when out of the sensation of his drunkenness he made such poems as *Un grand sommeil noire tombe sur ma vie,* or *L'espoir luit comme un brin de paille dans l'étable.* And just as we cannot understand the latter sonnet until we grasp that the poet is sitting fuddled and bemused in a wayside cabaret, with a woman in much the same state as himself, watching the wasps buzzing round their empty glasses, while opposite them a stable-door stands open; so this passage cannot be understood until, on re-reading, it becomes clear to us that two old washerwomen are talking at their work beside the Liffy. It is night; and they are tired and sleepy, and about to be fixed in an everlasting dream as a stone and a tree beside the river:

" Can't hear with the waters of. The chittering waters of. Flittering bats, fieldmice bawk talk. Ho! Are you not gone ahome? What Tom Malone? Can't hear with bawk of bats, all the liffeying waters of. Ho, talk save us! My foos won't moos. I feel as old as yonder elm. A tale told of Shaun or Shem? All Livia's daughtersons. Dark hawks hear us. Night! Night! My ho head halls. I feel as heavy as yonder stone. Tell me of John or Shaun? Who were Shem and Shaun the living sons or daughters of? Night now! Tell me, tell me, tell me, elm! Night, night! Tell me tale of stem or stone. Beside the rivering waters of, hitherandthithering waters of. Night! "

Their voices are already blurred with the approach of their transforming endless sleep; their words are distorted by yawns, their ideas confused. "Ho, talk save us! My foos won't moos"; the metamorphosis has already begun. It is the very sensation of change from awareness to permanent unconsciousness, of descending sleep and night, that this passage renders by means of its rhythms and the distortions of its words. Is the method legitimate? All literary methods are legitimate which succeed. But Mr. Joyce's is a particularly dangerous one; it leads to absolutely baffling obscurity. I choose as an example of this obscurity another passage from *Anna Livia*, the life of a river, treated for all I can guess also as part of the River of Life; and I choose it because it has been quoted by one of Mr. Joyce's admirers as a passage of " pool-like lucidity " in contrast to yet others.

> " She was just a young thin pale soft shy slim slip of a thing then, sauntering, by silvamoonlake and he was a heavy trudging lurching lieabroad of a Curraghman, making his hay for whose sun to shine on, as tough as the oaktrees (peats be with them!) used to rustle that time down by the dykes of killing Kildare, for forstfellfoss with a plash across her."

What do you make of it? It is a scheme of words in which female and male take the form of a stream and tree. It is meant to tell us that the Anna Livia began as a slim stream, sauntered into a lake, then came to her *first* cascade (so Mr. Joyce's commentator informs me—I should never have guessed it) through a tree falling across her! The allusions contained in the portmanteau word " silvamoonlake " are not difficult to seize—wood (*silva*), moonlight; but the word " forstfellfoss " gives some measure of the intricacy of the suggestions we

310

are meant to hold in our minds in reading Mr. Joyce. In this case they are, " first," " forest " " fell " and " waterfall "; the foss syllable " coming," says Mr. Robert Sage, " from the Scandinavian word for waterfall." How can anyone master such a language? Another commentator, Mr. Stewart Gilbert, has written a glossary of over a hundred Joycean terms occurring in only three pages of *Work in Progress*. Some are fairly easy to guess at ; " purse-winded " for instance which suggests " pursy " plus " short-winded "—a witty and excellent invention; but how can we be expected to guess that " logan-some " is " lonesome " plus " logan-stone," which is a poised heavy stone at the river's edge, or that " solfanelly " ought to suggest the " tonic solfa " and " solfanelli " (Italian: matches)? How can we ever find our way through such a labyrinth of words, ideas, suggestions? Lured by gleams of beauty, impressed by his astonishing mastery over words whenever he is clear, for a while a few enthusiasts will bring a jemmy and dark lantern to break him open for the sake of meanings which seem all the more precious because they were so hard to come by. And then? He will be dipped into as the most reckless of linguistic experimenters, sometimes " damned good to steal from," and the most pertinacious explorer of blind psychological alleys.